SCIENTIFIC REVOLUTIONARIES
A Biographical Series

Martinus Willem Beijerinck
His Life and Work
By G. van Iterson, Jr., L.E. den Dooren de Jong, and A.J. Kluyver

Alfred Wegener
The Father of Continental Drift
By Martin Schwarzbach

Pasteur and Modern Science
By René Dubos

Robert Koch
A Life in Medicine and Bacteriology
By Thomas D. Brock

Harmony and Unity
The Life of Niels Bohr
By Niels Blaedel

Harmony
and Unity

The Life of
Niels Bohr

Harmony and Unity

The Life of Niels Bohr

By Niels Blaedel

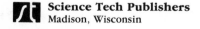
Science Tech Publishers
Madison, Wisconsin

Springer-Verlag
Berlin Heidelberg New York
London Paris Tokyo

Library of Congress Cataloging-in-Publication Data

Blaedel, Niels.
    Harmony and unity.

    (Scientific revolutionaries)
    Translation of: Harmoni og enhed.
    Bibliography: p.
    Includes index.
    1. Bohr, Niels Henrik David, 1885-1962.
2. Physics—History. 3. Physicists—Denmark—Biography.
I. Title. II. Series
QC16.B63B5713 1988   530'092'4 [B]   88-1928
ISBN 0-910239-14-2

Originally published as *Harmoni og Enhed*
© 1985 Carlsbergfondet/Niels Blaedel

Rhodos, Copenhagen

Science Tech, Inc., 701 Ridge Street
Madison, Wisconsin 53705 U.S.A.

Sole distribution rights outside of the USA, Canada, and Mexico granted to
Springer-Verlag Berlin Heidelberg New York London Paris Tokyo

ISBN 0-910239-14-2 Science Tech, Inc. Madison, WI
ISBN 3-540-19334-0 Springer-Verlag Berlin Heidelberg New York

Translation: Geoffrey French
Production supervision: Science Tech Publishers
Editorial supervision: Ruth B. Siegel
Interior design: Thomas D. Brock
Cover design: Katherine M.Brock

Printed in the United States of America
10 9 8 7 6 5 4 3 2 1

Contents

Chronology of
Niels Bohr's Life

1885   Born October 7 in Copenhagen.

1903   Matriculated from Gammelholm School.

             Began studying physics at the University of Copenhagen.

1907   Received the gold medal of the Royal Danish Academy of Sciences and Letters for a prize essay on the determination of the surface tension of water.

1909   Received a master's degree from the University of Copenhagen.

1911   Completed his doctoral dissertation on the electron theory of the metals.

1911–12 Studied in Cambridge with J. J.Thomson.

1912   Studied in Manchester with Ernest Rutherford.

             Married Margrethe Nørlund on August 1.

1913   Published his theory of the structure and spectra of the atom.

             Lecturer at the University of Copenhagen.

1914–16 Lecturer at the University of Manchester.

1916   Professor of theoretical physics at the University of Copenhagen.

1917   Member of the Royal Danish Academy of Sciences and Letters.

1921   Inauguration of the Institute for Theoretical Physics.

             Published theory of the periodic system of the elements.

1922   Received Nobel Prize in physics.

1927   Analysis of the problem of observation in atomic physics (complementarity principle).

1931   Awarded the honorary residence, Old Carlsberg.

1933   Analysis of the problem of measurement in quantum electrody-
            namics (in collaboration with Léon Rosenfeld).

1936   Developed model of the atomic nucleus.

1939   President of the Royal Danish Academy of Sciences and Letters.

            Theory of nuclear fission (in collaboration with John A. Wheeler).

1943   Flight to Sweden.

1943–45   Associated with the Anglo-American atomic energy project.

1945   Returned to Denmark.

1950   Sent "Open Letter" to the United Nations.

1955   Chairman of the Danish Atomic Energy Commission.

1962   Died at Old Carlsberg on November 18.

Preface

This biography of Niels Bohr is primarily intended to present Bohr's life and work to those outside the ranks of physicists. At the same time, I hope that physicists will encounter some aspects of Niels Bohr the man that they have never seen before.

I am very grateful to the many people who contributed to the final form of this book. First, there are the physicists at the Niels Bohr Institute: Hilde Levi, who not only put her technical knowledge at my disposal but also gave me indispensable assistance based on her long friendship with the Bohr family; Erik Rüdinger, whose faithfulness to historical details has been invaluable; and Jørgen Kalckar, whose love for Niels Bohr has been the theme underlying his excellent advice and his constructive criticism. Many others could be mentioned, but I hope that I have given them credit along the way. The following must nevertheless be singled out: Jens Lindhard, Bengt Strömgren, Asger Aaboe, the late Jørgen K. Bøggild, Stefan Rozental, John A. Wheeler, and—outside the ranks of physicists but close to the family—H.H. Koch and Hans Hartvig Seedorff.

I am especially grateful to Margrethe Bohr for her trust in me. She told me much about her life with Niels Bohr and read aloud letters from many years of correspondence. I also received much help from Hans and Erik Bohr—and from Aage Bohr, who opened the doors of the Niels Bohr Institute to me and helped me correct the manuscript. I owe particular thanks to Ernest Bohr for the loan of private pictures. I also profited from conversations with Henrik Bohr of the new generation of Bohrs.

I offer unqualified thanks to the board of directors of the Carlsberg Foundation, who generously supported this project, and additional thanks to the chairman of the Foundation, Kristof Glamann, who gave me advice as an old friend would. Finally, Knud Max Møller of the Carlsberg Foundation's picture archive has been a helpful pathfinder to hidden data, Rolf Berg to useful literature; and Lise Larsen helped me greatly by keeping track of corrections to manuscripts, notes, indexes, and proofs.

Most of the photographs in this book are borrowed from the Niels Bohr Archive of the American Institute of Physics and the Royal Danish Library. *Politikens Pressefoto, Nordisk Pressefoto,* and *Berlingske Tidende* have supplied many photographs as well, and some also came from the picture archive of the former *Dagens Nyheder.* Photographs from private collections have also been used, and photographs of portraits were borrowed from the Museum of National History at Fredricksborg Castle, Copenhagen. The frontispiece photograph of Niels Bohr was taken at the end of the 1920s.

Preface to the
English Edition

The intent of this biography is to portray one of the greatest thinkers of the twentieth century. As a physicist, Niels Bohr revolutionized our understanding of nature, and his profound analysis of the concept of nature led him to the philosophical recognition of an inherent harmony in which he saw a possibility for greater mutual understanding between people and nations. Even before the first atomic bomb was tested—and he himself contributed to this task in the race against Hitler's scientists—he spoke and untiringly struggled for that "Open World" which only now seems dimly visible.

During the years when the new quantum mechanics was being formulated, Niels Bohr was the great inspirer for a large number of scientists. It may seem surprising that he wrote so relatively little. But, like Socrates, he preferred instead to maintain a constant dialogue with his students and colleagues, many of whom have contributed to this biography. While Bohr wrote few books or essays, he did write a great many letters, most of which have been saved for posterity. Among them are the letters he sent home during his many travels abroad. Throughout his life, from the very first period of their engagement to the time of their golden wedding anniversary, he wrote to his wife, Margrethe Bohr. And in these letters, many of them poetically powerful, he expresses his views on the great questions of life. I am especially grateful to Margrethe Bohr for her trust and for allowing me to get a glimpse of their lives through her husband's letters. With these and other sources made available to me, I have attempted to depict the personality of Niels Bohr, the conscientious and deeply responsible humanist. Finally, I want to extend my thanks to the Carlsberg Foundation who invited me to write this book.

Niels Blaedel

Niels Bohr

Introduction

Niels Bohr had lain awake that whole June night in 1921. His own thoughts and the luminescence of the summer night would not let him rest. The bedroom in which he lay was small and narrow, with a high, white ceiling. The house was an old red-plastered peasant cottage which he and his wife Margrethe had rented the year before as a summer house in Tibirke Bakker, a small peaceful area. It belonged to Ernst Kaper, who was the school burgomaster of Copenhagen, and when Kaper picked up the telephone at the city hall that morning to take a call from Tibirke, it was Bohr's voice he heard, anxiously phrasing his timid enquiry in the friendliest way he could: "You see, it's like this, it's so incredibly light at night, and I'm lying in bed with so many thoughts going round in my head, so if it's possible, I'd really be terribly happy if I could be allowed to paint the ceiling in the bedroom dark blue. . . ."

The following year Niels Bohr received the Nobel Prize in Physics for his papers written in 1913, in which he laid the groundwork for his atomic theory; and now in 1921 he was preparing a further step forward that would lead to a better understanding of the periodic system of the elements.

The burgomaster, sensing the seriousness in the deep voice, gave his permission, and from that time on, the ceiling in the bedroom of Kaper's house was preserved as Bohr had painted it.

The three-quarters of a century which have passed since the atomic theory was advanced have altered human existence more than any other era. This book will relate Bohr's part in this scientific revolution. His contribution, like the man himself, became a legend even within his own lifetime. He became a central figure in international physics as well as in his own country.

Why was it so obvious to associate the idea of genius with Bohr? He was frequently likened to Newton and Galileo. What was implied by that? What was the truth about his so-called break with classical physics,

1

and who was really right in the life-long conflict between Einstein and Bohr, a clash in which all contemporary physicists became involved and which still forms a background for new exertions of thought and experiment? And finally is it true, as some have claimed, that Niels Bohr was the father of the atomic bomb? It is to all these questions that we shall try to find answers in the chapters that follow.

A hint of the pace, state, and background of scientific progress at that time is afforded by the fact that in that same summer of 1921 which was the starting point for this introduction, the radium-burned hands of Madame Curie accepted a gram of radium presented to her in the White House in Washington by the President of the United States. It had been obtained with money, corresponding today to two million dollars, collected by American women. During the overwhelming ovation, with her daughters accepting the countless handshakes in order to spare her hands, Madame Curie reflected, tired and despondent, that in France in 1921 there still was not a single hospital making use of radium treatment.

1921 was also the year in which the Niels Bohr Institute was inaugurated in Copenhagen.

1

The Summer House
at Tisvilde

If we pause for a while in Tibirke Bakker, the peaceful area in the
wooded hills of North Zealand, 30 miles north of Copenhagen, it will
assist our sense of perspective to recall the people who once walked
the hills and the appearance the landscape presented. A stone's throw
from Kaper's house occupied by Bohr was the abode of Johannes V.
Jensen, the Danish author and Nobel prize winner. Both dwellings were
thatch-roofed and situated on the easternmost slope with a clear view
toward Ellemosen, the largest expanse of moor in Zealand. Today, it is
overgrown with thick scrub and trees have taken over the formerly
heather-clad hills.

On the other side of the moor dwelt Ludvig Holstein, the Danish
poet and essayist. "The hills are best seen from Ramløse," he wrote.
The art historian Peter Hertz lived up in the hills, and it was here that
he wrote a book on the Danish artist Gerhard Henning, whose sculp-
tures Bohr admired. The hills were the homes of poets and writers. At
the foot of the hills where the heathlands began the poet Hans Hartvig
Seedorff lived in an old and charming farmhouse hedged with roses,
previously the property of Ludvig Holstein. A narrow path through the
heather led to Kaper's house where Bohr was living. One day Niels
Bohr appeared at the open double door of Seedorff's house to call on
him. This was customary in those days when a newcomer moved in,
and Seedorff had just bought his house. Bohr mentioned that he had
considered buying the same house the year before, but "it was a little
beyond my means." The visit became the starting point for a lifelong
friendship, and when Seedorff passed his ninetieth birthday a few years
ago, he said, "In my whole life I have never really met anyone else
with such a direct sense of poetry as Niels—yes, I have, Ludvig Holstein.
Bohr and Holstein had the finest ears for poetry. . . ."

If Bakkerne ("The Hills") belonged to the poets, then Lundene ("The
Groves"), closer to Tisvilde, was the preserve of artists. Here William

Niels Bohr and his three oldest children in front of Kaper's house in Ti-birke, 1921.

Scharff found a house for the Bohr family. Its large grounds adjoined the woods called Tisvilde Hegn, and Bohr purchased it immediately. He felt that the Nobel Prize had given him the means to realize his dream of making his summer home in that part of North Zealand, which appealed so strongly to the artistic mind and the creative spirit. Tibirke Bakker, Lundene, and Tisvilde Hegn with their sunny pathways through the heather, the cool foliage of birches interspersed with spruce and tall pine, surprising the denizens of this rural retreat with unending chiaroscuro interplay. At that time only a winding gravel road, which just permitted two horsedrawn wagons to pass each other, separated Bakkerne from the moor to whose broad fields no hubbub could carry.

In 1922 before the Bohrs moved to Lundene, Margrethe Bohr was expecting her fourth child. Late one evening Niels Bohr went down the path through the heather and knocked on Seedorff's door. "Hans, you have a bicycle: do you mind riding down to Miss Westphal"—the country grocer at Tibirke Bridge—"and ringing Dr. Børge? Say we think it would be so kind if he could come now." That evening Aage was born, the boy who would later make his own career in physics and win the Nobel Prize like his father. It was always said in the family that Aage was born in Kaper's house, but this is not true, the solicitous Dr. Børge arranged for an ambulance to the hospital. The house was too primitive with its minimal kitchen and its bedroom like a pencilcase. Nevertheless, Margrethe Bohr returned to Tibirke with her son immediately after the birth.

Dr. Børge belonged to the circle of summer residents. He was the artists' doctor, both in his capacity as the old family doctor and as a patron of the arts. His year-round house was in Helsinge, a nearby village, and it was filled with art treasures.

The year after Aage's birth the Bohr family moved to "Lynghuset" ("The Heather House") in Lundene, which still stands in a good state of preservation on its large grounds; the move was arranged by exchanging property with William Scharff. Heather grows below a scattering of tall birch trees and in between them stand very tall pine trees of a kind now found in only a few places in North Zealand.

In a letter of reminiscence to Niels Bohr on his seventieth birthday, William Scharff recalled the thrill of the solemn ambience that could imbue their summer walks among the trees. The letter was written in sadness at the thought of everything that had now impinged on the isolation of Lundene and Tisvilde from a changing world. But at the nadir of despondency Scharff breaks off and writes, "But the sky will always shine with the reflections of the sea and Arresø [a nearby lake]. The forest is the same. Generations to come will experience its cathedral-like atmosphere as we have, its drama and its poetry."

Bohr's friendship with William Scharff became lifelong. Julius Paul-

Four portraits of Niels Bohr: top left, Otto Sievert's painting from 1925; top right, William Scharff's, 1955; bottom left, Johannes Nielsen's, 1940; and bottom right, Daniel Hvidt's, 1958.

sen, a famous painter, was already living in Lundene. One of Paulsen's daughters was married to the graphic artist Carl Jensen and the other to the sculptor Hugo Liisberg. And the artists from Lundene and the poets from Bakkerne often met. William Scharff represented a distinct generation gap in relation to Julius Paulsen, but those still alive recall the comradely atmosphere of the gatherings, no matter in whose house they met. Niels Bohr loved the mood of harmony untrammeled by obligation that prevailed during these summer evenings and nights of feasting. Julius Paulsen led the way in conversation and discussion, while Johannes V. Jensen usually sat quietly and listened. In the same letter to Bohr William Scharff tells of Julius Paulsen, his need to have guests and to make the occasion festive for them.

> With him could still be found that atmosphere which was typical of the artist's home in the 1880s. The hospitality was lavish, with serving dishes piled high and a regiment of wine bottles. Even on warm summer evenings the fireplace had to be lit in order to create the proper atmosphere, even though it always smoked horribly. I remember one such evening when you and we were there. The rooms were so smoky that we could not be inside the house at all. We had to move outside, where the table was hastily set, and we ate by the lamplight coming from inside the rooms. Another time you and Ingeborg were at the table together down there, and your conversation turned for a while to the topic of the exceptionally heavy and sweet red wine that was served. Since you were beginning to feel a little giddy, you examined the bottle in front of you a little more closely and discovered that it was a strong port wine that you were drinking with your meal. One had to make allowances for such things with Julius. When the group was gathered at your place, we were always eager to hear from your own lips about all the new things happening in the world of science. Julius Paulsen particularly used to ask you endless questions, which were not always easy to answer.

The importance which the house in Tisvilde was gradually to acquire for Niels Bohr was something he could only have guessed at in those early years, although he felt at once that here he received inspiration, here his mind was in tune with nature. The gatherings in the house and the walks around Tisvilde Hegn also became an unequalled inspiration for a large number of scientists. These were scholars who were already internationally celebrated or who would become so and whom Bohr invited to his Institute in Copenhagen. Many who came as guests to Tisvilde in their young days felt a lifelong yearning to relive the mood of concentration pervading the place where Niels Bohr, with unexpected and surprising ideas and an insatiable urge to penetrate every subject that came under discussion, was always the initiator. The work there was hard too. Bohr was always engaged in dialogues with one or other of his colleagues, hour after hour. And although he had a great need to be surrounded by children, with the arrival of one of five boys it eventually became necessary to retreat to a small pavilion on the grounds. This was originally built by Victor Bendix so that he could compose and play the piano undisturbed. Now it became Niels Bohr's refuge, and he often sat here with a colleague for long days and evenings. A good many research papers attained their final form under the straw roof of the pavilion.

2

Happy Childhood and Youth

Harmony was the key to the life of Niels Bohr. In him it found a superb sounding board, producing spirit and drive to imbue his human existence and high ideals to inspire his never-ending efforts for the cause of science.

By beginning this book with the year 1921 we plunged straight into the midst of great events. Now we must go further back in time to consider Niels Bohr's background, his childhood and youth, in order to gain a deeper understanding of his personality and his mode of thinking and acting.

Niels Bohr succeeded in harmonizing his life and his learning to such a high degree that it seems almost axiomatic for him to have had a happy childhood and a liberal upbringing. It is also difficult to imagine a more rewarding environment than Niels Bohr's childhood home. He was constantly surrounded by a large and tightly knit family. His father (born in 1855) was Professor Christian Bohr, a distinguished physiologist. Christian Bohr knew from boyhood that he wanted to be a scientist. As an adult he was both ardent and progressive, pleading the cause of equality and independence for women. His articles in the University of Copenhagen yearbooks on physiological problems provided the starting point for intense philosophical discussions of the processes of life as they were then understood. Niels Bohr himself believed that this exposure to the central issues of biology underlay his own considerable interest in that science, which manifested itself strongly many years later.

Christian Bohr, supporting the feminist cause so fervently, undertook the teaching of several matriculation classes of adult female pupils. One of the latter was Ellen Adler. Teacher and pupil fell in love, and they were married in 1881.

Ellen Adler came from a Jewish family and was the daughter of a banker, David B. Adler, who established first the Privatbank and later

Christian and Ellen Bohr with their first child, Jenny.

the Handelsbank of Copenhagen. He was elected several times to both Danish houses of parliament, the Folketing and the Landsting, and was the first to protest from the rostrum of the Folketing against the provisional laws of the arch-conservative Estrup; and it was Christian Bohr, Adler's son-in-law, who rejoiced when his own uncle, the conservative

Christian Rimestad, was defeated, his seat being taken by the radical left.

The home in Copenhagen where Niels Henrik David Bohr was born on October 7, 1885 had every advantage to offer, including a solid foundation. In these early days he lived at Ved Stranden 14, an old town house owned at that time by Niels Bohr's maternal grandmother. Later Niels' parents moved to his father's official residence at the Academy of Surgery in Bredgade, Copenhagen, where a wide and constant circle of contemporary intellectuals enjoyed the extensive hospitality.

But the warm disposition of their mother was the source from which Niels, his older sister Jenny, and younger brother Harald, drew special nourishment. There is much identical testimony to the character of this lady, most aptly epitomized in the words spoken by Professor Ole Chievitz of the University of Copenhagen on her death in 1932, when he extolled Christian and Ellen Bohr's home:

> Ellen Bohr's lovable character cast its warming glow over everything, for lovableness was her being: it was so great that I can imagine that people who met her for the first time thinking it must be a pose; but one did not have to be with her very often to discover that this, like everything else about Ellen Bohr, was true, sincere, and strong.

The Adler mansion (with the pillars) in Copenhagen where Niels Bohr was born on October 7, 1885.

The private drawing room of the Adler mansion in 1888. From the left: David Adler, Jenny Adler, Emma Adler (standing), Hanna Adler, and Constance Hannover. The portrait above the sofa is of Jenny Adler's father, the banker John Raphael.

Like Niels' mother, his maternal grandmother Jenny Adler, was also a warm, life-giving, and strong woman. Niels' sister, who died young, was named after her. And some of Niels' and Harald's richest childhood memories were gathered at their grandmother's country house, Nærumgaard, to the north of Copenhagen. Their German-born relative Paula Strelitz, who spent much of her childhood in Denmark and ultimately made her home there, has left this description of Nærumgaard:

> When one thinks far back, trying to recall the world of childhood, what emerge are individual pictures. A child does not have a sense of continuous development. First and foremost for the writer of these lines come pictures from Nærumgaard, where the Bohr family spent summer holidays with grandmother Jenny Adler, whose outstanding, powerful personality, uprightness and goodness quite naturally made her the center and leader of the grand home. She was the beloved ideal of her grandchildren. She sat at the head of the long table in the great dining room—I do not remember any "fine" guests ever being placed at her side. The children sat to the right and left of her, a good distance away from their parents. No danger of "manners" at the table. They were no better behaved than other children, but they were secure and happy and ate properly whatever she gave them. I remember one

Harald, Jenny, and Niels Bohr with their nurse in the dining room at the Academy of Surgery in Bredgade.

time when Niels covered his *rødgrød* (a famous Danish fruit jelly) with an unusually mountainous layer of sugar; it looked very fine. But his father, whose sharp eye had been following the enterprise from a distance, remarked from the other end of the table, "Really, Niels!" But Grandmother intervened at once, quietly but firmly, "Well, perhaps he needs it."

To complete this sketch of the family circle, another lady to whom Niels also became very close must be mentioned. This was his mother's sister Hanna, who founded Hanna Adler's School (Sortedam's Gymnasium) in Copenhagen, where such gifted women as Kirstine Meyer and Thyra Eibe were among the female pioneer figures on the teaching staff. It was at Hanna Adler's School, too, that girls and boys took part in gymnastics together for the first time in Denmark.

In the book published to commemorate the anniversary of Hanna Adler's one-hundredth birthday Niels Bohr wrote:

I have vivid memories from my earliest childhood of her active and affectionate participation in everything to do with her brothers and sisters and their children. Although my brother Harald and I did not directly belong to the school as pupils, we shared in "Aunt Hanna's" educational influence. Whenever she could be spared from her school duties, she would drive us around Copenhagen on Sundays to the natural history and ethnographic col-

The Academy of Surgery in Bredgade, where Christian Bohr occupied the official residence and Niels Bohr grew up.

lections and art galleries; and during the summer holiday at Nærumgaard, when she would come out walking or cycling with us through the woods and fields of the neighborhood, we learned about both nature and human life as she chatted with us in jest or earnest about anything that caught our imaginations.

There were so many positive forces surrounding Niels Bohr. His intellectual inspiration was the constant and seminal solicitude of his father, a solicitude that nevertheless always knew how to leave the initiative to the son himself. The upbringing bestowed by their parents is reflected in the legendary relationship between Niels and his brother Harald. They were inseparable until Harald died at the age of 64.

An expressive but unfortunately damaged (and therefore difficult to reproduce) photograph has survived which was taken of Niels Bohr's class at the Gammelholm School in Copenhagen in 1901. It offers childhood portraits of several men who would later come to the forefront of the Danish nation and also become very important to Niels. But what makes the picture so vivid, and so essential for us to study today, is the face of Niels. Of twenty boys and six teachers, he is the only one who is smiling. He sits with an open and alert face, and his confident smile makes him seem—and this is written quite without hindsight—

Niels' class at the Gammelholm Grammar School in 1901. He is sitting in the front row, third from the left.

to be the unifying center of the class, which of course he was. This is how he is unanimously described by those who have recalled that time.

It was to be characteristic of Niels Bohr that at every stage of his life he formed new and lasting friendships. This began even in his childhood. Professor Ole Chievitz of the University of Copenhagen, who shared a desk at school with Niels for six years, once said, "I remember clearly how impressed we were by him as a person even then. It was so distinctly Bohr's style and personality that stamped the class as a whole." But his schoolmates did not feel it was ambition that drove Niels to his achievement. His brilliance demonstrated itself as a natural and simple thing, without special effort. His mind worked quickly, and even from his schooldays there are accounts of how his thoughts ran faster than his ability to use the eraser when he was standing at the blackboard. He would wipe with both his hands and arms as new ideas rapidly came to him, and neither he nor the blackboard looked too good afterwards. It was not only at the board that he distinguished himself. In those days it was customary in schools for the pupils to recite verse which they had learnt by heart. "For this art Niels had a special talent, and his choice of poetic works was individual and sound."

Around the turn of the century the ordinary schools still showed features borrowed from boarding schools. Each class stuck together with regard to the other classes, and there were boundaries which normally could not be crossed. But Harald Bohr was welcome among older and younger pupils alike. Thinking back on this exceptional circumstance later in life, he attributed it to Niels' position. He also recalled that when he was visiting another class, he did not refrain from relating Niels' achievements.

Vilhelm Slomann, later director of the Museum of Applied Art, who was also one of these childhood friends, thought that Niels' special place in the school was due not only to the impression made by his many-sided interests and intense energy but also to a quite extraordinary thoughtfulness.

If he shone in almost all other subjects, however, he never did receive recognition from his Danish language teacher for the essays he wrote, and the low grades he received gave posterity the impression that Niels was anything but good at Danish composition. Such was also undoubtedly the contemporary belief. But an unprejudiced teacher of Danish today would not have judged so hastily. The subject of one of the essays was: "A walk in the harbor," and the paper read, briefly: "My brother and I went for a walk in the harbor. There we saw ships unloading and loading." Here Bohr has described, as cogently and concisely as possible, the uses for a harbor. He has also incorporated an alliteration

*Harald and Niels Bohr as students
at Nærumgaard in 1904.*

("losse og lade" in Danish) whereby the juxtaposed verbs produce a neat euphony, and Harald related that Niels had been particularly preoccupied with this. But the alliteration certainly escaped the teacher's notice completely. Instead he drummed into the boy the necessity of a proper introduction and conclusion. Niels had the teacher in his sights now, however, so when the next essay came along, on "The use of natural forces at home," his sense of humor asserted itself with the following proposition as introduction: "In our home we do not use natural forces." However, Harald came to his rescue, so reprisals were avoided. The prank went into the wastebasket and was replaced by a more acceptable form.

Although Harald, who was over a year younger, was deemed by many the quicker of the two boys when they were growing up, their father was clear in his own mind very early on that Niels was very specially gifted, with an extraordinarily wide-ranging capacity for thought. He became the first in his class, too, but Harald skipped a year and entered class a year ahead of Niels, likewise taking his doctorate a couple of years before Niels. Nevertheless when Harald was quite young he concurred in his father's feeling, expressed in the words, "Niels is the real one in the family." Harald himself was to attain prominence in the world of international mathematics. Even in his own right he could have brought luster to the name Bohr, yet it was as though he always felt called to support Niels and to place himself behind him.

Left: Niels Bohr in 1917. Right: Harald in 1918.

One day at Tisvilde when Niels' fame had spread far and wide, he was trying to explain a little of quantum physics to Hans Hartvig See-dorff, who said despairingly, "But there is so much mathematics in this that I don't understand how you can even work it out." Niels looked at him seriously and answered, "Well, I'm afraid I can't either, but here comes Harald."

How far this may have been an expression of brotherly affection or whether it contained some truth will very likely be investigated by historians of natural science when all the letters and documents from that time become accessible. The mathematician Richard Courant, who was a friend of both Niels and Harald, has touched on the issue in a reminiscence in which he mentions that the question was often raised why Niels, whose ideas led to such great and profound advances in mathematics, and whose earliest publications exhibit mathematical skill, never himself made much use of mathematical technique. Rather than answer the question himself, Courant preferred to quote Harald, who answered in the same terms as he did when others asked by saying, "Niels possessed a superhuman, intuitive insight into the secrets of nature, and could even comprehend truth without needing to translate it into ordinary language, to which mathematics belongs." Here we may have some part of the truth, although it must not be forgotten that in his mature years Bohr frequently emphasized that every perception of an ambiguous nature must be transmitted through ordinary language.

When Niels Bohr was selected to be a member of the Danish Academy of Sciences in 1917, ten proposers (physicists, chemists, biologists, and mathematicians) based their nomination on the series of pioneering tasks in the field of atomic physics which Bohr had already accomplished, and then they added, "That Professor Bohr commands mathematics as an auxiliary science hardly needs to be mentioned." Mathematics as an "auxiliary science" is perhaps the key phrase. The Dutch physicist Hendrick B. G. Casimir, who played a prominent role in Bohr's circle at the beginning of the thirties, touches on the question in his memoirs, where he writes, "For the theoretical physicist, the reasoning around the model is the essential thing. There have been great scientists who were both mathematicians and physicists . . . but theoretical physicists seldom make outstanding contributions to pure mathematics. It would not occur to me to call Einstein and Bohr mathematicians."

From the years which followed later with the development of quantum mechanics, replete as they were with dramatic episodes, colleagues recall how frequently it occurred that Niels Bohr would break off and say, "Let's go over and hear what Harald has to say." Harald Bohr's mathematical institute was built in 1931 next to Niels' institute, and it also often happened that Harald would turn up of his own accord to take part in the discussions at Niels'.

For Niels, however, Harald was indispensable not only as mathematician and brother, but also as a debater. Niels thought best when he had someone on whom to try out his ideas. He loved to be contradicted in order to get deeper into the subject, but he progressed best when the person with whom he thrashed out the problem had the same attitude as himself, not only in approaching the problem but also in needing to penetrate its depth to the uttermost.

There is an entertaining account from their early youth of the two brothers in discussion. A group of students, followers of the Danish philosopher Harald Høffding, had formed a sort of discussion club where philosophical and scientific questions were debated. The group became known as Ekliptika, and Niels and Harald were invited to join. As well as the Bohr brothers, the archaeologist Poul Nørlund, later director of the National Museum, and his brother, Niels Erik Nørlund, later director of the Geodetic Institute, also took part. The four of them were designated "The Pairs of Brothers," and Niels' acquaintance with the Nørlund brothers was to have a quite vital significance in his life. Other participants in addition to the Nørlunds included the psychologist Edgar Rubin, Peter Skov, later Denmark's ambassador to Moscow (whose daughter, Ann, married Bohr's second son Hans), the philologist Lis Jacobsen and, among still others, the art historian Vilhelm Slomann, to whom, in fact, we are indebted for the account of the Bohr brothers in discussion.

The group assembled a couple of times each week during the winter semester at small cafés, especially one called the à Porta, which, with its Victorian style, warm colors and small rooms, had an intimate charm of which the artists of the time also were fond. The meetings began with an introductory lecture, and after that the discussions went on until well into the night. It is not known whether Niels and Harald ever gave an introductory lecture, but stories are told about their part is discussion. For example, Vilhelm Slomann:

> It often happened that when the discussion was on the point of dying away, one of them would say some generous words about the lecture and continue on those lines in a low voice, at a furious speed and with enormous intensity, but often interrupted by his brother: their thinking seemed coordinated, the one improving the other's or his own mode of expression or defending, at once vehemently and merrily, the best wording. Thoughts shifted color and were honed; what emerged was something new, not a defense of previously held opinions. This reasoning à deux was so dovetailed between the two brothers that no one else could keep up. The chairman put down his pencil and gave them free rein; only when everyone was crowding in closer around them would he utter an ineffectual "Louder, Niels."

If we now turn our attention back to Niels' father, two vital interests remain to be mentioned. The first was philosophy. As Harald Høffding

Left: Christian Bohr at his desk in the Academy of Surgery in 1910. Right: Niels in the same chair, probably on the same day.

put it, Christian Bohr knew his Goethe. Goethe was much discussed in the home, and all through his life Niels could remember and quote long poems by Goethe.

Bohr's father's constant explorations of the problems of life from biological and philosophical approaches brought him into contact with scholars outside his own discipline. Just as there was a group for the young people, so also "the four ph's" met for conversation and lively discussion. These were the philosopher Harald Høffding, the philologist Vilhelm Thomsen, the physicist Christian Christiansen, and the physiologist Christian Bohr. At first they would betake themselves to a café after the meetings at the Academy of Sciences, but gradually they found it more pleasant to go to each other's homes. Niels Bohr often spoke afterwards of the influence it had upon Harald and himself from their earliest youth to sit and listen to the conversation during those evenings when the quartet met at the Bohr home: it was "not so much an influence in the direct sense," Bohr would later say, "but an inspiration to profound understanding of the unity which underlies the entire human search for knowledge, regardless of whether its surface manifestation is via such widely differing human instruments as a biologist, a physicist, a philologist, and a philosopher."

Harald Høffding writes in his recollections of Christian Bohr that as a physiologist he belonged to the school advocating the strict application of physicochemical methods in physiology. Høffding writes of Christian Bohr, "When he expressed himself on practical affairs or on the philosophy of life, it was generally in the form of a paradox and as a rule improvised. The conversation took on new life from his interventions." And Christian Bohr himself has said of his passion for natural science that he was quite certainly already gripped by it in his ninth year, and that the urge was in the same form as that which governed him as an adult. He could only describe it as an instinct.

Finally, Niels and Harald were influenced by their father's marked interest in sports. Christian Bohr was one of the promoters of new ball games and new activities at the Academic Ball Club. Both brothers became soccer players. Legend has it that Niels' prowess was such as to earn him a place on the national team. In the interests of truth, however, it must be said that it was Harald in fact who shared in the winning of a silver medal at the Olympic Games in London in 1908. But Niels was an able player too, and he developed his physical strength playing soccer.

In Bohr's mature years, when the science of genetics was making big strides, he had his doubts over the question whether personal character and intellectual faculties were hereditary. He had greater faith in the influence of environment. But whether Niels Bohr's own success in life was due to heredity or to the influence of his childhood and adolescent environment, a more fortunate upbringing for a scholar can hardly be imagined.

Added to all the other conditions making for a life filled with giving as well as receiving, early on he met Margrethe Nørlund, the lady with whom he was to experience the most enriching human relationship and who would become his indispensable mainstay through all the vicissitudes of life. One day Niels went with Poul and Niels Erik Nørlund to their parents' home in Slagelse, a city 50 miles west of Copenhagen, where their father was a pharmacist. And there he met Margrethe Nørlund. Their meeting was to be one of the happiest occurrences arising from the friendship of the "Pairs of Brothers."

Niels and Margrethe became engaged in 1910 but continued to live in different towns, and later on they were separated for months at a time during his first sojourn in England. This occasioned a copious exchange of letters that helps to fill out our picture of Bohr. In everything he writes home, his outlook on life and attitude to everyone he encounters emerge with an openness to be expected, perhaps, only from a young person brought up under just such favorable conditions as he. To read the letters in the context of the circumstances under which they were written gives a great depth of impression, but even here, and in the next chapter dealing with Bohr's religious views, there

In the Nørlund's garden in Slagelse, 1911. From left to right: Nørlund, Niels Erik Nørlund, his fiancée Agnete Wæver, Poul Nørlund, Margrethe, and Niels Bohr.

are three or four letters in particular that provide an abiding impression of a disposition that is immensely sensitive yet accompanied by a strong personality.

The first letter dates from the time just after Niels and Margrethe had met. He was living in student accommodations in Copenhagen and was sitting alone one evening when suddenly he felt unhappy, even though a few minutes before he had been filled with delight thinking about the feelings which he and Margrethe cherished for each other. But in his happiness he could not bear even the mere thought of any misunderstanding arising between them, and now it had struck him that he would be unable to defend himself if someone, without his knowing it, should take it into his head to speak disparagingly of him to Margrethe.

In his letter he implores her to agree never to have any secrets from one another about such things and adds, "We shall never speak ill of anyone either (unless it is necessary)."

There is nothing very remarkable in the fact that a young man, happily in love, should hit on the idea of writing that one should not speak badly of anyone, but the parenthesis is worth noticing—not because any evidence is known of Niels Bohr's ever having spoken ill of anyone, but because the addition is so characteristic of Bohr's balance between earnestness and jest, and of his need for honesty. The parenthesis contains also an element of the paradoxical similar to that which came to mark his fruitful mode of thought.

Immediately after the parenthesis he writes that Margrethe is to burn the letter "right away." However, perhaps the only secret that ever existed between them was that Margrethe carefully refrained from burning the letter but hid it instead along with all the other letters she received and which she was able, late in life, to bring out in neat bundles, tied with bows of white silk, from the various periods when she and Niels were separated by travels.

Left: Margrethe, the young woman. Right: Margrethe, soon after her marriage.

3

The Young Bohr and
His Religious Outlook

Niels Bohr's actions, letters, statements, and writings all furnish evidence of his outlook on life, his view of religion and philosophy, and his ideas about death.

With his sensitive disposition, Bohr experienced a religious crisis at quite an early age. This came about through the conflict between his gratitude for the great and warm love bestowed on him by his parents and their radical outlook on religion. It has been noted that his father was in the front line of the debate between the biologists of the day. The dispute centered upon the new vitalistic approach and the mechanistic view of the life processes. An entertaining corroboration of the fact that his father was a freethinker was provided by Kristof Glamann in a memorial lecture on Emil Christian Hansen, the fermentation physiologist, who applied for a position with Christian Bohr when Hansen was quite young. The latter wrote to a friend that he wanted to see this "bacteria chap" who had flung himself into a world of fungus and beer. "As far as I can judge he is really an erudite man with wide interests and an impartial outlook. He is very hard working too. I was very happy that he was a definite freethinker. Furthermore he was obviously pleased to see me with S. Demokraten (the "Social Democrat" newspaper) in my pocket (it is vulgar enough, God knows)."

But Niels emerged from his crisis by his own efforts and without telling his father, who on the other hand had at no time attempted to influence the boy. Evidence of all this is furnished in a letter sent by Niels to Margrethe from Cambridge in 1911, just before he went home to celebrate Christmas. In its simple charming intimacy, the letter reveals the same spontaneously affectionate traits that recur over and over again in the many letters he wrote later.

He begins his letter by asking Margrethe to imagine that he has already arrived for Christmas. But first of all he wants to be quite alone with her, before any of the others see him. The two of them, invisible, will

The engaged couple in Slagelse in 1911.

enjoy visiting her father and mother, and then his family. "Let us first just see how they are," he writes, "how happy they are for you, both your father and your mother and Poul and your old grandmother; and then we shall go into your little room where we sat last Christmas Eve. . . ." No, he breaks off, first they must look in at the other places where "I have promised to come this evening. Look, there are three people sitting in a room; let us see what they are thinking about. Very quietly, ever so quietly, let us be with them a while."

And then he comes to what he has been leading up to with this intimate introductory scene. He writes:

> Look into my soul: look. See the little fellow walking to church with his father through the snow-covered streets. This is the only time in the year his father goes to church. And why? I think so that the little boy would not notice that it was any different for him than for other small boys. Because in his father's view there was neither faith nor doubt over such matters. My own little beloved, you have never met so brilliant a man. I think he sat and thought about this world and perhaps about his own childhood (look at him). The father never said a word to his little boy about anything to do with faith and doubt, and when the little boy became bigger and after his own quite lonely battles came one day and said to his father that he could not imagine anything as frightful and terrible as this (as what he had believed with all his little soul), his father still did not say anything, but only smiled at his ardor. That smile, little one, has taught the little boy a great deal. And look; look at the little boy, who has sat with open mouth and looked at all the lights, and been so moved in his little soul, look at him hurrying home with his father, and his brother and sister, and look at his mother receiving them. And now the impressions become so many and so bright and so varied that the little boy would find it hard to express them in words, but when he has become bigger they center themselves around his father's loving earnestness and his mother's indescribable goodness of heart. . . .

In this letter, intended only for his fiancée, there are quite original features of language not exhibited in his academic writings but which recall Seedorff's words about Bohr's marked sense of poetry. No one else would have expressed himself in quite the same way, and only a few would have evoked a common experience with such affection.

The letter also reveals a poetic vigor unmistakably belonging to the land of Hans Christian Andersen. In its intimacy that is the very reverse of self-centeredness, it relates in the fewest possible words the battle of a young spirit with life's first great challenges.

A little further on in the letter, Niels asks Margrethe to imagine that together they are flying high toward the north, "the home of Christmas," and to "the world's loveliest fairyland," where they come to a great illuminated house in the middle of the snow between the "fantastic shapes" of the fir trees. "See the raftered hall with the huge fire and the gigantic Christmas tree, and all the happy people . . . and the

little boy has grown big and is talking philosophy with an old gentleman.''

From the faith and doubt of religion Niels has reached philosophy.
We recall how he and Harald listened to the "four ph's" during their
gatherings at home, and in a letter to Harald in the spring of 1909 we
hear of one of their first encounters as adults with philosophy. It was
written at the parsonage of Vissenbjerg on Funen in Denmark, where
his father had persuaded Niels to go in order to find quiet so that he
could concentrate on his examination for his master's degree. From
here he sends Kierkegaard's *Stages on Life's Way* to Harald, who had
gone to Göttingen to study. Niels wrote in the accompanying letter,
"This is the only thing I have to send; nevertheless I do not believe
that I could find anything better. At all events I have had enormous
pleasure from reading it; I feel quite simply that it is one of the finest
(books) I have ever read.''

On first encountering Kierkegaard's linguistic powers and some of
his ethical ideas Niels was carried away, but he soon shook off his
excitement, and neither at that time nor later did he adopt Kierkegaard's
religious outlook. In his next letter to Harald he writes, "When you
have read the *Stages* once, which you definitely must not hurry with,
you will hear a little from me; the fact is I have written some observations on it (disagreeing with Kierkegaard); but I have no intention
of being so banal as to try to spoil the impact of such a fine book with
my feeble twaddle.''

The next time we hear about Kierkegaard is three years later, in a
letter from Cambridge in 1912 to Margrethe, who has just written that
she has begun to read Kierkegaard: "I was so pleased with what you
wrote about Kierkegaard's book, but I am afraid it may be much too
heavy. . . .'' He suggests that they "will either read it together sometime
or, if I have time, then I will read it again very soon and really talk to
you about it; I am sure I have told you how strongly I was affected by
it, for it is so wonderfully fine, and so earnest, so crushingly earnest.''

In a letter immediately before this, Margrethe had written that her
parents had talked with her about religion, and she asked Niels if he
was unhappy about the way she answered her parents. He assures her
that in fact she has answered very sensibly, and then he relates that he
has received "the most sweet and loving letter'' from her mother on
the same question, "and right away I wrote a long letter to her and
tried to explain my standpoint. But you know how stupid and incapable
I am, and I am afraid I have done it so badly; but it is not so easy to
write about religion either, because it cannot be done in a few words,
being almost as long as life itself. But look how time has passed, and
I can only send you a few lines despite the fact that I only came to the

Niels Bohr in Cambridge in 1912.

laboratory today after lunch (now what do you say to that)." And he continues, not "stupidly and incapably" but vigorously and clearly,

> I feel that I believe in so much (I believe that I believe in rather more than your father and mother do), for I believe in happiness and the meaning of life. But I cannot and will not believe in what is not true, and to me what is not true is anything that would deprive life of meaning, and that applies equally from the greatest to the smallest thing; therefore, and only therefore, it is not true that 2 and 2 make 3, and therefore it is not true that a person must beg from and bargain with fancied powers infinitely stronger than himself.

He concludes his letter: "I believe in you more steadfastly than in anything else in the world. . . . I believe in so inexpressibly much, and so much that is inexpressibly wonderful."

Margrethe Bohr on a visit to Cambridge in 1912.

A few days later he writes to Margrethe about the future:

Does it not shine marvellously all in bright colors, yet at the same time—
and this is the great thing about it—it is so earnest. This grave aspect of all
things, which perhaps is to be sensed most strongly about the future, this
terrible but wonderful earnestness, means, you see, that life is only a One,
a single Oneness, be our dreams never so many.

Although Kierkegaard with his crushing earnestness never became Bohr's
chosen guide on the cognitive road, Bohr did allow himself to be inspired to a much higher degree by Poul Martin Møller, whose insight
into human nature led Bohr to refer to him not only as a poet, but also
as a philosopher. His mode of thought and his humor captivated Bohr,
who even in his youth was preoccupied by problems of the ambiguity
of language. In Poul Martin Møller's description of the human psyche

Bohr in 1921. This photograph stood on Margrethe Bohr's desk.

Bohr found elements paralleling those with which, leaping mightily from poets to atoms, he was later to contribute to the harmonization of classical physics with the new perception of the conceptual world of the atom.

4

Scientific Beginnings

Niels Bohr's first scientific work existing in written form is the paper he wrote for an essay prize offered by the Danish Academy of Sciences in 1905, for which he was awarded the gold medal. The paper was entirely experimental. As a basis for investigating the oscillations of rays in different liquids, he employed a theory which had been advanced by Lord Rayleigh, an English physicist. Bohr began, as was later to be characteristic of him, by subjecting the existing theoretical basis, which was assumed to be satisfactorily finalized, to careful revision. This led Bohr, who was then just 20 years old, to improve Rayleigh's theory, supporting his arguments with meticulous and ingenious research using apparatus which he constructed himself in his father's laboratory. The paper was later published in the *Philosophical Transactions of the Royal Society of London*.

In his next work, the written paper for his master's degree examination at the University of Copenhagen in 1909, Bohr turned to the physical properties of metals and thermoelectrical phenomena, all in the light of the electron theory as developed by the Dutchman H. A. Lorentz, the German Paul Drude, and two Englishmen, James Jeans and, most notably, J. J. Thomson at Cambridge. Just as Bohr had revised the draft for the prize essay so now he began by scrutinizing in detail the work on which the electron theory was based. He also demonstrated defects in Thomson's calculations, although Thomson, more than anyone else, stood as the discoverer of the electron and the true father of the electron theory. As we shall see, Bohr was to have a somewhat ambivalent relationship with Thomson.

Immediately after his master's degree examination, Bohr began his doctoral dissertation. Again the subject was the electron theory of metals. He carried out various mathematical calculations with a view to finding agreement among the properties of metals which the electron theory could explain. And again we get something of an insight into

The discoverer of the electron, J. J. Thomson, Cambridge.

Niels Bohr's relationship to mathematics. The evaluation of his dissertation notes that he made excellent use of mathematical formalism. But was this as more than an auxiliary science. The evaluation further states that he identifies the critical questions very shrewdly, establishing in conclusion that the properties of metals cannot be explained within the framework of the contemporary electron theory.

The young Niels Bohr was already attracting, by the force of his personality, the attention both of students and teachers at the University of Copenhagen. On the day appointed for his defense of his dissertation, the auditorium was overflowing, with some people standing far down the corridor. There was hardly any opposition of which to speak. Professor Christiansen, acting as sole examiner, said flatly that there was probably no one in Denmark knowledgeable enough on the subject to be capable of judging the dissertation.

Niels Bohr did not say very much. It was all there in the dissertation, and there were no objections and hardly any questions. A newspaper report described the candidate as "a pale and modest young man." The fact that he was pale could not have surprised those who knew his methods of working. After handing in the dissertation he had worked on without stopping, all the time trying to penetrate more deeply into the subject. He had not allowed himself any rest before the defense, and what was now being so sweepingly praised for its breadth and thoroughness was already, we can almost say, past history for Bohr himself. As late as the night before the defense he had advanced a step further. He had a large number of major and minor corrections in the draft and was only longing to include them in the printed version of the dissertation.

Professor Christiansen regretted in his conclusion that the dissertation had not been published in a foreign language, and this was just what Bohr wanted. The final improvements would be incorporated in the translation he had already started. His next objective was to travel to Cambridge in order to meet J. J. Thomson himself and to discuss with Thomson his criticisms of the defects in Thomson's theory of the electron which Bohr had demonstrated in his dissertation. Bohr's open nature, his urge to seek the full truth and his belief that this must be the ideal for which every scientist strove, inspired him with the hope that Thomson would not only read the dissertation and discuss it but even help him to get it published in England.

Thus Bohr wanted to be off to England, and the sooner the better. He applied to the Carlsberg Foundation, which gave him a grant—the first of many subsequent awards—for the trip to England, which was to be of incalculable significance both for Bohr himself and for atomic physics.

He was already writing his first letter home to Margrethe while on the ferry boat on the way to England. At the very beginning of the letter is a sentence that says much both about the mood in which he began the journey and about his opinion of himself: "I am setting off in all my ignorance and reckless courage. . . ."

In truth, the next two years would show that he had courage. But none of the many letters he sent home contain a single arrogant phrase. If he was "pale and modest" during the defense of his dissertation, then letter after letter gives expression to that very quality of modesty which was to be so much remarked upon subsequently. It revealed itself later in so many ways that inevitably, as his stature became obvious and his fame grew, the question eventually arose: was this modesty feigned? Could it possibly be genuine? This manifest trait of character was often interpreted as bashfulness, to which many situations attested, especially in the earlier years. But the letters do not require any profound analysis in order to establish that the modesty expressed by Bohr was a true reflection of his mind.

Once he arrived at Cambridge, his first letters home show with what openness and expectation he met Thomson, whom he sought out at once. He writes to Margrethe, "He was enormously kind, and we talked together a little, and he said that it would interest him to see my thesis. You can believe I was happy when I left him, I was so pleased to be getting the formulas written in quickly, for of course it is exciting, what he will say about it all and the many criticisms."

The letter ends with these lines: "I found myself exulting inside this morning as I stood outside a shop and chanced to read the address Cambridge over the door."

He told Harald a few days later:

Oh Harald! It is going so splendidly for me. I have just spoken with J. J. Thomson and explained to him as best I could my ideas about radiation, magnetism, etc. You have no idea how it feels for me to speak with such a man. He was enormously kind to me, we talked about so much, and I do believe he thought there was some sense in what I said. He is now going to read my dissertation, and he invited me to dinner with him at Trinity College on Sunday; so he will talk to me about it. . . .

Another letter to Margrethe a week later says, "You can imagine that I

King's College and King's Chapel in Cambridge, which are often mentioned in Bohr's letters.

am excited about what Thomson will say tomorrow evening. He is a very, very great man . . . and I am already very fond of him, but now I shall find out whether all my silly talk may nevertheless have made him cross."

The letter continues, "Now I am going to read a little more about electrons, and afterwards if there is time I shall read a little of *David Copperfield*. . . ." It was not just for relaxation that Bohr went to *David Copperfield*. He did this whenever there was an opportunity for improving his English, and he has himself related that he looked up every single word which he did not know in his dictionary—which later went with him on all his travels.

But let us now pause for a moment, while Niels Bohr is waiting for Thomson to read his dissertation, in order to see how far the physicists of that time had come in their understanding of the structure of the atom.

5

The Dawn of the Atomic Age

Toward the end of the nineteenth century, when the Frenchman Antoine Henri Becquerel discovered that certain minerals emit invisible rays, and when Marie and Pierre Curie found radium to be the most powerful of the radioactive materials, physicists were divided into two camps, one which refused to believe in the idea of the atom and another which considered atomic concepts to form a good working hypothesis. The smallest particles of the elements were called atoms and chemical combinations of atoms were called molecules. This hypothesis explained the fact that a given chemical combination always appeared to contain its elements in a completely fixed weight relationship. From this it was concluded that all the atoms of a given element have the same weight, while at the same time these weights are different for different elements. For chemists the concept of the atom had great utility. But the concept also afforded a deeper understanding of physical phenomena. The computed number of atoms in a given quantity of matter could be obtained and, with that, a determination of the size and weight of the atoms. The figures for sizes of atom were staggeringly tiny, while those for their numbers were colossally big. However, the devotees of atomic theory believed that with this the interpretation of our knowledge of the physical world was complete. The smallest building blocks of matter had been reached. The circle to Democritus, who gave the name atom to the smallest unit, was closed. The transition to the twentieth century, however, coincided with the birth of modern physics, with new discoveries giving certain proof of the existence of atoms, while at the same time showing that atoms are not indivisible, but can be split into parts so small that almost only the most daring imagination can picture them.

After the Curies, Ernest Rutherford enters the scene as the great figure of the dawning atomic age. In Manchester in 1902 he proposed the hypothesis that in radioactivity one is dealing with the transmutation of an element.

37

Shortly before the turn of the century it was discovered that, just as molecules are the particles of chemical combinations and atoms are the smallest units of the elements, electrons are the smallest units of electricity.

Even before Bohr came to England, Rutherford had carried out in Manchester the first experiment with the direct object of penetrating the world of the atom and bringing back new knowledge. It was now accepted by physicists that an atom must contain electrons with negative charge and a positive element as well, but how was the atom organized? Rutherford's epoch-making experiment consisted of sending "spies" into the world of the atom. For the first time the unknown land of the atom would be scouted by a tale-bearing traveler.

It was known that radioactive matter emitted so-called alpha particles, which are electrically charged. If such alpha particles were now sent into an atom, they must be influenced by the atom's charge. And the influence must reveal itself to be greater or less with the more or the fewer alpha particles deflected on their way through the atom. Those which encountered no hindrances at all must go through by straight paths.

The experimental arrangement was extremely simple. Rutherford made a narrow stream of alpha particles hit a metal foil so thin that the particles could pass through. Immediately behind the foil he placed a zinc sulphide shield. He knew that the alpha particles would emit a

Ernest Rutherford, after whom Bohr's youngest son was named. A big enlargement of the drawing hung (and is still hanging) in Bohr's work room at the Bohr Institute.

green flash when they hit the shield. Rutherford's assistant then sat in front of the zinc screen with a magnifier and observed the green flashes. The flashes disclosed that the great majority of the particles went through the metal foil without being deflected very much, but the interesting thing was that a few of the particles were deflected by up to 180 degrees. To all intents and purposes they were thrown back the way they had come.

Rutherford reasoned that if the positive charge on the atom and the electrons were uniformly distributed, it would be impossible to understand this result. Therefore the positive charge of the atom and its mass, apart from the electrons, must be concentrated in a very small area which was struck by these particles. He called this the "nucleus" of the atom, and the name has stuck. Moreover, he visualized that the electrons, being light in weight, circled like a swarm around the nucleus at such distances that the heavy alpha particles could find a way through the swarm without hindrance. Only those which came too close to the nucleus were drastically deflected. And Rutherford managed to go even further. From the frequency with which the major deflections took place, he calculated the charge of the nucleus of the atom. It sounds quite simple, but Rutherford's strength lay not only in the ingenious experiment but also in his sophisticated mathematical calculations, so that from the distribution of the alpha particles dispersed in various directions he was able not only to determine the charge of the atomic nucleus, but also to conclude that its size is exceedingly small in relation to the dimensions of the atom as a whole. He made not just one but many experiments with different materials, with concurrent results. Thereafter it had to be accepted that Rutherford's model of the atom applied to all atomic elements, built up in the same way as a miniature solar system with the nucleus as the sun and the electrons as the planets around it.

At this point we return to Cambridge. Had Thomson got round to reading Bohr's dissertation? Anxious but still patient, Bohr waited. Week after week passed, however, without any apparent reaction from Thomson. After two months, Bohr writes to a friend: "Thomson has so little time, I gave him the dissertation when I came, but he still has not read it, I have only spoken with him for a few moments on some simple points, and I still do not know whether he will agree with me or not." But he always writes to Margrethe with optimism: "It is going so well for me, not actually better with Thomson, but for me myself, I am in such good spirits and have so many plans. . . ."

The next term begins; Thomson has still not read the dissertation, and Niels writes to Margrethe: "I shall not go to the laboratory this term but only listen to lectures and read, read, read (and perhaps also calculate a little and think). . . ." And a little later: "Sometimes, e.g.

today at the big lectures (by Jeans and Larmor), I feel that there is so much, entire worlds, that one is permitted to peep into, and that I am so small and incompetent, more incompetent than you and others suspect. . . ."

Nevertheless disappointment over the unread dissertation did not prevent Niels from telling Harald enthusiastically about a lecture delivered by Thomson on the motion of the golf ball: "You cannot imagine how entertaining and illuminating it was, and what splendid experiments he demonstrated, and then the flashing, sparkling humor with which he spoke. It was just right for me, having as you know a bit of a mania for such things myself. . . ."

Eventually Thomson sent the dissertation, unread, to the *Cambridge Philosophical Magazine*, whose editor felt, however, that it was much too long to be printed, yet when all the hopes he had placed in Thomson are thus extinguished, Niels nonetheless writes to Margrethe, "J. J. Thomson is an extremely great man, I have learned an incredible amount from his lectures, and I am so fond of him."

Niels did indeed keep his word given in the letter written to his newly betrothed from Copenhagen that lonely evening, when he referred to never speaking badly of anyone—even now, when some sharp little remark might almost have been felt unavoidable.

But did Niels Bohr resign himself to the flagging of Thomson's interest? One factor was that he did not want to write anything critical of Thomson, whom he admired in spite of everything—and Thomson, the discoverer of the electron, was not just anyone. But it was not Bohr's nature to give up, and in his eyes there was not the slightest doubt that his criticism was justified. Thomson's electron theory, and with it his model of the atom, rested on the basis of classical physics, and Niels Bohr's calculations proved it to be impossible to explain the properties of metals on that basis.

It has been suggested as a reason for Thomson's not reading through Bohr's dissertation that, as head of the celebrated Cavendish laboratory in Cambridge, he had to undertake many time-consuming tasks. But that was hardly the sole reason. It may have been directly contrary to his taste to devote time to the young Dane's abstract visions. It would also have taken a lot of time to read Bohr's English, as Thomson had discovered during their conversations. Much later Bohr himself joked about his inadequate linguistic ability of those days. There were certain sections where Thomson, if he read that far, may simply have not understood what Bohr was getting at. Bohr used the word "load" or "loading" to mean the charge of the electron ("ladning" in Danish), whereas Thomson and everyone else would use "charge" in that context. But realization of this came to Bohr only later; and the Russian-born physicist George Gamow related in his account of the story of quantum theory that there was a series of exchanges of opinion between Thomson and Bohr. Bohr could be trenchant in oral discussion. And from quite an early age he had had a gift for driving an argument home. However all that may be, when it came down to the crunch the Thomson/Bohr combination was not promising. But the sojourn in Cambridge was to be of absolutely crucial importance nonetheless. It was a tradition that the annual Cavendish banquet also brought together leading scientists from other centers, and it was here that Bohr received his first impression of Ernest Rutherford of Manchester. A mutual friend of Rutherford and of Niels' father arranged for them to meet, and after two terms in Cambridge the impatient Bohr was invited to go to Manchester. Now his work would begin at last.

6

Rutherford and Bohr

The tall, powerfully built, pipe-smoking Rutherford with his colonel's moustache was thoroughly English in appearance and also, in a way, with his jovial and seemingly lighthearted attitude to life, in his disposition; but there was a deep seriousness behind all this, and the young physicists who came to his laboratory from many countries looked up to him as a father figure. He could have been taken for a native Englishman, but he was born in New Zealand, and he came to Manchester via Canada.

Every manifestation of humor, including the more subtle, was in Bohr's nature, and with the years they reflected more and more of the wisdom of life. Rutherford and Bohr understood each other's sense of humor. In their attitudes they also had common traits, but in temperament and appearance they were widely different. If Bohr had stood perfectly straight, he might perhaps have approached Rutherford's height. Out walking on one occasion at Tisvilde, when a ditch had to be crossed by jumping it, friends accompanying him were astounded to see him straighten up on the other side of the ditch after completing the jump. He was surprisingly tall for a brief moment. But however active and athletic he remained over the years, his thickset form seemed heavy—and heavier year by year, stooping forward, with the powerful and heavy seeming head slightly bowed. The voice harmonized well with the deep-thinking figure Bohr presented. Always engaged with some problem, and trying to make sure of bringing out the sense and the significance that were essential, he was continually seeking for words. But in his eagerness his thinking often ran ahead, and anyone who was listening missed those sentences which Bohr had only hastily conceived. Since his shifts of emphasis caused him one moment to whisper, another to give weight to his words with a searching voice dragged laboriously up from the depths, keeping up with him was as a rule a matter involving no little exertion. Bohr's English was, as al-

Rutherford in his garden in Cambridge. He and Bohr both smoked pipes.

Niels and Margrethe Bohr with Rutherford and the wife of M. L. E. Oliphant in 1930.

ready noted, not the best at first either, but even during their early conversations Rutherford, who for his own part expressed himself simply and clearly, sensed that Bohr was an exceptional person.

If Thomson sacrificed none of his time to the young Dane's abstract visions, Rutherford gave Bohr all the attention he hungered for. It says much for Rutherford's human understanding and scientific intuition that he saw Bohr's qualities immediately, the more so since Rutherford was emphatically an experimental physicist. From the start of their collaboration he was absorbed by Bohr's ideas, although he could not always follow his line of thought and actually did not take much interest in the more abstract kinds of theorizing. On the other hand Bohr had a considerable flair for experimental research. True, he was a theoretician, but from the beginning of his scientific career he attached crucial significance to experimentation. His own first scientific work was experimental, and while still a student he had assisted his father with much successful research. Now he was to breathe the life-giving atmosphere of the Manchester laboratory. He gave himself to his conversations with Rutherford with almost filial affection. And his colleagues, now as later, soon learned to recognize the shifting play of shade in Bohr's blue eyes: they could appear dim and dark under the thick eyebrows when he sat bent forward, pondering, but quite light when he leaned his head back and "disappeared" into his thoughts.

Niels Bohr's openness, his surprising humor, his strong charisma and his propulsive ideas and conversation often created close and lasting friendships. But the Rutherford/Bohr partnership, as the prelude to the next epoch-making years in atomic physics, was by far the happiest constellation and the background for Bohr's lifelong sense of fraternity with English scientists. His encounter with many of the young physicists in Manchester was to have permanent and, in certain areas, undreamt of significance.

The words which famous men like to use are often quoted. During his collaboration with Bohr, it was not long before Rutherford, on being asked a theoretical question by another colleague, replied, "Ask Bohr." And soon everyone was saying in the laboratory: "Ask Bohr."

When Rutherford was asked one day why his attitude to Bohr was so different from his attitude to theoreticians in general, he is said to have answered with a roguish smile, "Bohr is different, he's a soccer player."

7

Bohr's Atomic Model

The atomic age began with Rutherford's entry into the world of the atom. A kindhearted scientist, full of humor, with a lust for life, a hearty optimism and a sparkling intelligence, in his mature years he had sown the seeds which Niels Bohr would bring to flower. And Niels Bohr arrived in Rutherford's laboratory with no less optimism and a stupendous energy. For Bohr there was something about Rutherford's model of the atom which seemed deeply disturbing. Up to Planck and Einstein, the laws of classical physics had never failed for a correctly conducted experiment in physics, but the same laws proved wanting in terms of the model of the atom. However, the explanation and the solution soon provided by Niels Bohr were to lead—as George Gamow later expressed it—to earth-shaking developments and great progress.

According to Rutherford's model, with the nucleus as the positive charge surrounded by the electrons with a corresponding negative charge, the electrons should, figuratively speaking, orbit around the nucleus like planets around the sun. And according to Rutherford's experiments this was probable, yet nevertheless the model was at variance with the foundation on which physics had hitherto rested. The planets can keep on revolving around the sun because they do not noticeably lose energy in the form of radiation.

But right away the objection presents itself to Rutherford's model that such an atom could not exist at all for more than a fraction of a second, for the electrons are electrically charged and must therefore radiate electromagnetic waves while changing velocity and direction, which involves a release of energy. The electrons, therefore, following the loss of energy, must travel in smaller and smaller orbits until at last they collapse into the nucleus of the atom. However, the elements have been stable for millions of years, but according to the laws of classical physics Rutherford's atom would be quite different. In an infinitesimally short instant, they would shrink virtually to nucleus size, with catastrophic results for all matter and all life.

Facsimile of Niels Bohr's first (and extremely brief) application to the Carlsberg Foundation. The traveling scholarship was granted and enabled Bohr to go to Cambridge and Manchester. The application reads: Copenhagen—20 June, 1911. The undersigned has the honor to apply for a travel stipend of 2,500 kroner for a one-year period of study in residence at foreign universities.   Sincerely, Niels Bohr, Ph.D.

Rutherford's atomic model did not at first rouse any great interest among the Manchester physicists themselves, and this may well have been due to its inconsistency with the classical laws. A wait-and-see attitude was adopted. Rutherford himself was very guarded about drawing any conclusions, and when Bohr advanced his first theoretical considerations, the experimental physicist cautioned him. The foundation was too flimsy to build theories on, Rutherford felt.

If Rutherford and his colleagues were hesitant, Bohr was not and things began to move quickly. Toward the end of May 1912 he was still disappointed at not finding greater interest in the fundamental problems and ends a letter to Harald, "I have absolutely no one here who really takes an interest in such things. . . ." But by May 26 something was taking shape. He had been to a performance of *Othello* the evening before, and he writes to Margrethe, "It was really lovely (perhaps not as well acted as one might want! But perhaps not so badly either!) and so many, many thoughts were running through my head; but in the midst of all my wandering thoughts and wild dreams I felt that all the time there was something that I thought I could sense growing in my mind, something which you most of all have helped to create. . . ."

In the letter of the following day we soon find what kind of conceptions are taking shape, but it is still exciting to discover toward the end of this letter the extent to which the fact that he was approaching a breakthrough was influencing his mood and finding poetic expression. The formulation is so wholly his own, so spontaneous and immediately experienced with such a strong impression that he has to pass it on. He relates that the same morning he had gone for a long walk in the city, out to the meadows by the river: "It was so beautiful and peaceful." And then he inserts this long parenthesis:

> Tell me, may I have leave to walk on sunlit footpaths lined with hedges in bloom, breathing the scents of spring flowers; may I, in a silly little letter written when I came home, send you these buttercups picked from the grassy border by the hedge; may I stand and watch the leeches swimming against the current, and the bumblebees flying across the river to the clover on the other side; may I stand and follow the eddies that glide with the stream and sometimes pull the surface deep down into their little holes. . . . ?

He asks if he may do these things but he doesn't wait for Margrethe's answer, he does them spontaneously. He draws her into the moment, into the midst of the experience. The pressed buttercups remain in the letter to this day, their color intact.

The next day, in another letter to Margrethe, he writes, "It may be very silly and there may be nothing at all in it, as usual; but I do believe that perhaps I have solved a tiny something." (Here he inserts a "Ssh!", as he does in many other letters when he feels he has made progress but is still not sure enough to want to tell anyone else but Margrethe and Harald.) And he continues, "What I can do with it, and what can come out of it, I don't know at all." He then asks, "Are you tired of my being so silly that I can get a fever in my blood for so little, and of my longing so inexpressibly for the time when you will keep account of my thoughts and make them flourish for me, if I possess anything that is capable of flourishing?"

On June 4 he sends a short letter; he is busy. "I am expecting company this evening (for the first time in Manchester), only one person, to be sure, a young and very capable mathematician called C. G. Darwin (grandson of the original Darwin), who is a sort of docent (reader) in mathematical physics here, but it may get a bit hot, for I am not sure that we agree (Ssh!). . . ." He writes to Harald a few days later:

> Things are not going too badly for me at the moment, I had a little idea a couple of days ago with regard to the understanding of absorption of α rays— the way this happened was that a young mathematician here, C. G. Darwin, has just published a theory on this question, and I felt not only that it was not entirely correct in its mathematics (this aspect did not amount to all that much) but that it was somewhat unsatisfactory in the basic concept, and I have worked out a little theory about it, which even if it is very little perhaps can still shed a little light on certain things with regard to the structure of the atom. I am thinking of publishing a little paper about it very soon.

And the letter closes on an elevated note quite different from that of two weeks earlier: "It is nice to be here, I can tell you, there are so many people to talk to (my laments last time applied to more general theoretical questions). . . ."

These optimistic but still somewhat cryptic reports cloaked an almost historic event: Bohr's investigations of the capacity of radiation to penetrate matter had given him an important key to the structure of the atom. He writes to Margrethe on June 16: "What kind of trail it is that I am following, and where it can lead me, if it will, I cannot tell yet. But if I am not completely wrong, then it has led me past some small clearings, to which I will perhaps be able to turn back when the trail itself will not lead any further. This is only a very hasty little greeting, after a Sunday of calculations. . . ." Three days later, and only 14 days after beginning to write his paper on the structure of the atom, he writes to Harald: "It could be that perhaps I have solved a little something . . . which perhaps is . . . a small piece of reality." The beginning of a new view of nature could not be expressed more modestly yet hopefully. And he added, "It has all grown out of a little piece of information I got from the absorption of radiation."

It is neither the first nor the last time that he surprised himself by

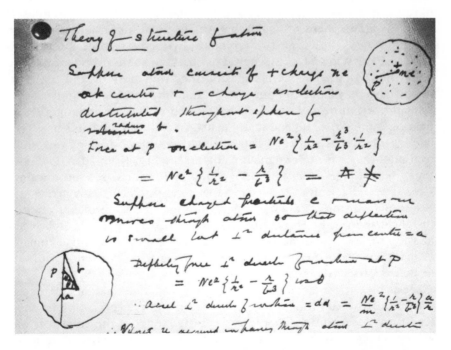

Facsimile reproduction of Rutherford's notes, made on the manuscript sheet, on the theory of his model of the atom.

achieving some vital step forward through correcting someone else's misapprehensions.

Bohr was now in full swing with the model of the atom. In the course of two summer months during which, as he wrote home, he was working day and night, he came a long way with his thinking on the structure of the atom. His colleagues testified to the enormous intensity with which Bohr was able to work and keep on working, when others would long since have been exhausted. They said of him in this period that he only emerged when it was necessary to come up for air.

And there he was working alone. There is no doubt that Bohr had a basic knowledge of mathematics. He alluded to this himself much later on, although he would readily give Harald all the glory. It was in the spring of 1939, during a visit to Princeton, his son Erik was with him, and it is he who has related the episode. During their visit the biologist Dorothy Wrench, who worked at the Carlsberg Laboratory with Kaj Linderstrøm-Lang, arrived from Denmark. She gave a lecture on the structure of molecules which Bohr attended, always having been greatly interested in biology. However, during the discussion period after the lecture she came under heavy attack, and Bohr began to defend her. He found in her arguments a new possibility for interpreting the effect of resonance. Then Bohr was attacked as well and had to defend himself also. The atmosphere was such that Erik felt that his father was on thin ice. Afterwards, however, two eminent physicists (George Placzek and Eugene Paul Wigner) could not resist making some calculations. The more they calculated, the more astonished they became and after two hectic days they came to Bohr, totally dumbfounded, and admitted that he had been quite correct. Erik later asked his father how, merely by hearing the lecture, he had really managed to foresee what Princeton's leading physicists had then had to spend two days working out. Bohr replied that it was not remarkable at all. "If you had any idea," he said, "how hard I worked in my early years, how I calculated and recalculated, then you would understand that later one can easily arrive at a result by intuition." Harald's understanding of Niels' intuition, and the insight displayed by the colleagues who in recommending Bohr's admission to the Danish Academy of Sciences emphasized his command of mathematics as an auxiliary science, seem here to form a synthesis in Bohr's own utterance.

Let us go back to Manchester. He calculated and recalculated, and it was in this two-month period that he launched the revolution in physics. It was clear to Bohr that it was not the model of the atom that was wrong. The situation was as simple to him as it was shattering to many physicists: the classical laws did not apply to phenomena inside the atom.

Now let's return in our thoughts, as Bohr did, to the beginning of the century.

In the year 1900 Max Planck had discovered that the radiation from warm bodies is not emitted continuously but in "packets" of minimum energy, a quanta as they later came to be called. Added to this there was Einstein's interpretation of the so-called "photoelectric effect," whereby when a metal surface is irradiated with light of a given color, electrons are emitted with velocities which depend upon the color. Einstein showed that this behavior was unintelligible in terms of the classical conception of light as a spatially extended wave; but it could be simply explained if one interpreted Planck's discovery to mean that light itself is composed of separate "quanta," now called photons, each of which has a definite energy depending on the color of the light.

The amount of energy carried in the smallest "packets," the quanta, is exceedingly small. All phenomena in our daily world are composed of an immense number of quanta, and here there is full agreement with the laws of classical physics. But as far as the smallest units are concerned, the dual nature of light—as waveform and as energy particle—presents a paradox. Light, which had previously only been understood as a wave phenomenon, was now revealed to have a new property in the quantum aspect of its nature. The numerical value which was arrived at for the minimum amount of energy was given the name "Planck's constant" or the "quantum effect." As Robert Oppenheimer emphasized much later, this is the heraldic symbol over the portal to the new world.

Bohr stuck to Rutherford's model of the atom, in which the atoms ran wholly counter to classical physics by remaining stable, and he was occupied day and night in trying to explain this disagreement. Since Newton and Maxwell it had been possible in all physics research to proceed step by step verifying every advance by experiments without abandoning strict causality. But as firm as this foundation was, it was now necessary to think afresh. The progress already made by Planck and Einstein with the interaction between radiation and matter had early convinced Bohr of the limitation of the classical theories. As there was no question of a logical continuity along known paths to attack the problem of the stability of the Rutherford atom, it can rightly be said that Bohr now took the first step. It was thanks to his creative power of intuition, which perhaps applies to all great scientific advances and which would in time to come also make him the central figure of international atomic physics. He broke with the past and thought in new ways.

With his new view, Bohr introduced Planck's quantum of action as the stabilizing element. He made use of a hypothesis which was inspired by earlier application of the quantum of action to the thermal properties

Facsimile reproduction of Niels Bohr's earliest sketch of the atom with an orbiting electron, from the note to Rutherford, July 1912.

of matter. In June and July of 1912 he worked out his thoughts on the structure of atoms and molecules in the so-called ground state, using the hydrogen atom as the simplest atom with one electron. "Ssh, ssh!" he writes to Margrethe and Harald, "perhaps this is a small piece of reality." There was still a gap which he could not fill, but he wrote down his ideas for Rutherford, and these are historic documents, the majority of which still exist. They are preserved as carefully as such unique, handwritten documents merit. After Bohr had handed them over to Rutherford, however, he had to break off his work—for another reality. He and Margrethe had arranged for their wedding to take place in Copenhagen on August 1, 1912.

The honeymoon should actually have taken place in Norway, in whose scenery Niels Bohr often found repose in later days. But on account of all his new thoughts he was behind schedule with the short paper on alpha radiation which he had just started, so instead the newlyweds traveled to Cambridge, where the paper was completed. The couple went on to Manchester, where the paper was delivered to Rutherford, and the new term was due to begin. During this term Bohr would make considerably more progress in clarifying the role of the quantum of action in the constitution of atoms. Margrethe Bohr helped him, as she so often did later, when he needed to get his thoughts written down. He was uneasy about the gap in the theory which he could not fill, however. Rutherford tried to reassure him: there did not seem to be any others engaged on the same problems.

The first week of February, 1913 had just ended. Bohr could not sleep for thinking. Then all at once lightning struck. Bohr's fellow student and future colleague, the spectroscopist H. M. Hansen, reminded him of the formula of the Swiss physicist J. J. Balmer who had shown—thirty years earlier—simple regularities in the optical spectrum of the hydrogen atom.

"As soon as I remembered Balmer's formula, the whole thing became quite clear to me," said Bohr later—and how clear is evident from the time it took for Bohr to chart the new territory he had won. He introduced Balmer's formula into his calculations after February 7, and on March 6 he sent Rutherford the paper for which he would go down in history even if he had accomplished nothing else in his life.

The Belgian physicist and scientific historian Léon Rosenfeld has traced the progress of events in Bohr's letters. Rosenfeld picks out these two dates, February 7 and March 6, as evidence of a quite incredible creative process in which all the knowledge Bohr had acquired previously and all the ideas he had formed on the structure of the atom now fall into place. Then, with the placement of the last piece of the puzzle, Bohr reached the overall view that made it possible for him to compose in less than a month, the celebrated first part of the paper on the structure of the atom. Here, the agreement with the optical spectrum has become a cornerstone of the edifice.

The fact that every element has its own characteristic pattern forms the foundation of spectral analysis, which makes it possible to determine what element or elements an unknown material contains by examination of its spectrum.

In these spectra, differing for each element, the various wavelengths appear as sharp bright lines of different colors, which are called spectral lines. And it was observed very early on that the spectral lines were organized more or less regularly by the hand of nature. In some spectra the lines occurred in series, and in 1885—the year Niels Bohr was born—Balmer succeeded in finding a numerical relationship between the wavelengths of the various lines in the hydrogen spectrum. He expressed the frequencies of the lines by a simple formula. A few years later, the Swedish physicist Janne Rydberg showed that the spectra of many other elements could also be represented by a similar formula with exactly the same numerical constant as Balmer's formula. This seems to indicate a certain uniformity in the structure of the different atoms, and this constant came to be called the Rydberg constant.

8

Stationary States

When Bohr set to work on Rutherford's model of the atom, it was only reluctantly that he used the picture of the electrons traveling around the nucleus of the atom like planets around the sun. He did it in order to illustrate the constitution of the atom with the language and concepts then available. He took as his starting point the paradox that the electron does not lose energy by its motion and disappear into the nucleus, precipitating the death of everything. But instead of rejecting the paradox, for which at that time there was no resolution, he raised it to a postulate. He introduced the concept of *stationary states*, in which electrons orbit at fixed distances around the nucleus without giving off energy by radiation. Further, the concept of the ground state of the atom is introduced, in which the atom is absolutely stable if there are no external disturbances.

Starting out from the hydrogen atom with a single electron, Bohr realized that the electron in the hydrogen atom must necessarily be in one of a series of states with definite energy values corresponding to the numerical relationship between the frequencies expressed in Balmer's formula. According to classical electrodynamics, an electron which orbits around a nucleus should continually emit light, with a color which is determined by the time (the period of revolution) taken by the electron to travel once around the nucleus. But Bohr postulated that the light observed during experiments results from the electron's jumping (under the influence of heat and light, to which it is incessantly subject) from one stationary state to another; and he postulated that the emission of radiation occasioned by this jump took place in quanta of energy, just as was found by Planck with heat radiation. He formulated it thus: the radiation emitted or absorbed by an atom in its movement from one stationary state to another has a frequency which is determined by the fact that Planck's constant multiplied by the frequency is equal to the difference in the energy of the atom in the two stationary states in question. The radiation, or light, in other words, is not determined by the period of revolution of the electrons. The lowest in the series of stationary energy states is called the *ground state* or normal state. From here the electrons can be "struck" by electrical discharges or by high temperatures so that the electron is brought out of the stationary state it is in, falling back shortly afterwards to a lower state or else down to the ground state, accompanied by emission of a quantum of light. Emission of light ceases when the electron has reached the normal state, and the atom remains stable. Now in the case of the hydrogen atom on which Bohr built his theory in the first instance, when it lingers in one or more stationary orbits on its way back to the normal state, it will not emit energy corresponding to all the spectral lines of hydrogen. The fact that in experiments with a discharge tube with hydrogen, the entire hydrogen spectrum can nevertheless be observed is ascribed to the fact that such an enormous number of atoms are struck in different states that all possible movements between the various states are experienced at the same time.

Thanks to the Rydberg constant, it was now possible to carry over the concept of stationary states from the hydrogen spectrum with its single electron to the atoms of all the other elements with their increasing numbers of electrons.

When Bohr set to work on the Balmer formula and the Rydberg constant together, with the surprising results noted, he was asked whether he thought it strange that no one had previously hit upon the idea that this formula and this constant, so different from anything otherwise known in physics, might reveal fundamental regularities. He answered, "They were perceived in the same way as the beautiful patterns on the wings of summer birds, whose beauty one can marvel at, but which no one presumes will display fundamental biological regularities."

The ideas, or postulates, as they became termed, of Bohr's atomic theory mark the decisive break with classical physics. Firstly, the existence of "stationary states" is completely excluded according to clas-

The Niels Bohr medal of the Danish Association of Engineers, executed by H. Salomon.

sical electrodynamics. Secondly, classical physics requires a link between the color which the light emits and the period of revolution itself. But such a link is impossible in Bohr's theory, where the light is emitted when the electron jumps from one orbit with one period of revolution to another orbit with a different period of revolution. That the color of the light should not match exactly the period of revolution of the electron seemed quite unthinkable to contemporary physicists, and Bohr's theory met with not a little opposition at the beginning. Opponents could, for example, refer to earlier research which had confirmed convincingly the classical theory's claim for a link between color and period of revolution. How could the new theory possibly be united with the knowledge derived from earlier experiments? However, Bohr was in a position to answer this question as well. For if one reaches larger and larger orbits, thus approaching the conditions under which classical physics should apply, the periods of revolution of two neighboring orbits will come closer and closer toward each other, toward a common value. And if one now calculates the color of the light which according to Bohr's theory is emitted when a jump occurs between two such orbits, it appears that the color approaches more and more closely the color which, in the classical theory, would be calculated based on the common period of revolution. Although the mechanism is quite different from that of the classical theory, the results arrived at approach nearer and nearer to the classical the closer one gets to the conditions under which the latter are valid. In other words, Bohr's theory can be said to contain the results of the classical theory within itself as it were, to be a generalization of or to correspond with the classical theory. By thus introducing the *correspondence principle* into atomic theory, Bohr expanded the classical theory. With the word "correspondence" he linked the new physics with the classical physics. In the beginning there were those who sarcastically called the correspondence principle a magic wand, and they added, "Only effective in Copenhagen!"—but that was only for a while. The key to the principle's formulation is the quantum effect whose finite magnitude is characteristic of the new features in atomic physics. Where the effects are great in comparison with the quantum effect, then the classical laws of Newton and Maxwell will apply.

From two such neighboring orbits, which have to be in dimensions large enough to be "tangible," since the number of revolutions corresponds to the frequency of the light emitted, Bohr was able, by making the number of revolutions equal to the wave number found in the postulate, to establish an equation which permitted the Rydberg constant to be calculated exclusively with the aid of the known value for Planck's constant and for the charge and mass of the electron. This

Left, the two Danish stamps issued in 1964. Right, the graphic artist Birgit Forchhammer's preliminary design for a stamp marking the centennial of Niels Bohr's birth.

calculation gave a value in close agreement with the value for the Rydberg constant found by spectroscope measurement.

The circle was closed with this first triumph for Bohr's theory. It took him less than four weeks to think out a unity as splendid as this. The correspondence argument formed the cardinal feature of the paper that resulted—"this marvelous dissertation, which has few counterparts in the history of physics," as Léon Rosenfeld later put it. And Bohr was to develop the correspondence principle further in the years that followed, so that at last it became the key to quantum mechanics itself.

In the letter which Niels Bohr sent to Rutherford along with the paper, he could barely conceal his happiness and pride at having found "the most beautiful analogy between the old electrodynamics and the considerations which are applied in my dissertation. . . ." But Rutherford's answer was disappointing. It was clear that he had not fully understood Bohr. The paper was too long, he wrote. Here Bohr was being faced with the same problem as when Thomson had sent his thesis to the Cambridge Philosophical Society. The editor insisted that it should be cut down to a half, if it were to be accepted. Bohr gave up, and the thesis was not printed in English in the very years when there was such a great need for the theory of the electron to be further developed. It can be imagined, therefore, what an effect it had on Bohr when Rutherford emphasized in his letter no fewer than three times that the paper must be reduced in length. Moreover, he wrote in a postscript, "I presume that you do not have anything against my using my own judgment in cutting out whatever I feel is superfluous in your paper. Please let me know."

Bohr, who was in Copenhagen at the time and in fact had sent on some further additions to the paper just before Rutherford's letter arrived, did not waste time replying. Instead of writing, he traveled to Manchester forthwith in order "to fight matters out."

In the meeting which now took place, Rutherford experienced all Bohr's vigor and capacity for insisting, intensely yet amiably, on every *single* word as significant for understanding. How many times the paper was rewritten in those four weeks is not known, but draft after draft had steadily made the ideas and calculations clearer and clearer. Now Rutherford—indeed he last of all—must not stop him.

Rutherford never forgot Bohr's visit, which involved hours of discussion. Many years afterwards he related, "I could see that he had considered every single word in it, and it impressed me how energetically he stuck by every sentence, every expression, every quotation; everything had an absolutely fixed reason, and although I felt at first that one could easily eliminate many sentences, when he explained to me how the whole hung together, it then appeared that it was impossible to alter anything."

The first part of Bohr's theory of the structure of atoms and molecules was published in the July number of the *Philosophical Magazine*, and by then the manuscripts for parts Two and Three were already prepared in final form for printing. In addition to the main points as stated, these also contained a first attempt at a detailed account of the periodic system of the elements, which was to be Bohr's next major contribution.

To explain Bohr's atomic theory, with its formulas and calculations, would require much more space than we have here. The theory bears on many areas and throws light on the most diverse facts, giving endless new ideas to other scientists for the development of their own thinking. But one main proposition of the theory that merits mention is the proposition that almost all physical and chemical properties of the elements have their origin in the outer electron system of the atoms.

The electrical and magnetic properties of the elements and their propensity to enter into chemical combinations are conditioned by the number and distribution of electrons in the atom. The same applies to the optical properties of the elements. Only the weight and radioactivity of the atom are attributable to the atomic nucleus, independently of the electron system. And it goes without saying that it was not only physicists who were able to profit by Bohr's theory but also chemists, to whom it became clear that it is the nucleus which determines by its electrical charge the number of electrons in the system. Here also is the reason why one element cannot be changed to another simply by removing one of the outer electrons. The nucleus will immediately attempt to capture a new electron and reconstitute the original atom. This is its stable nature. Only by a change in the charge of the nucleus will a change in the number of electrons automatically occur, and only now will a new element be formed. Rutherford had already suggested that radioactivity can involve transmutation of elements, and from Bohr's theory it appeared that the charged particles emitted by the radioactive elements come from the nuclei of the atoms, whose charge is altered, so that transmutation of elements occurs.

Just as chemists were able to turn Bohr's atomic theory to account, so also were wide perspectives opened for astronomers and astrophysicists. By systematically examining and tabulating the characteristic spectral lines for all possible elements—these spectra are like a sort of identity card for the elements concerned—it is possible to infer the composition of elements of the sun and other stars through an analysis of the spectral lines in the light which we receive from them. But the strength of the spectral lines does not depend only on the chemical composition but also on the physical conditions, such as temperature and pressure, and here also Bohr's theory led to decisive advances.

9

Early Reactions to
Bohr's Theory

Bohr's contribution of 1913 ushered in "the heroic years," as Robert Oppenheimer later called the epoch during which a succession of leading physicists from various European countries, constantly exchanging results and inspired by the central figure of Niels Bohr, gained an insight into the energy states of the atom and the forces which hold the atom together. Put in another way, Bohr's theory of the structure of the atom led step by step to an understanding of quantum mechanics as well.

But actually it was not everywhere that Bohr's theory was regarded as the base from which to conquer a new age. Although in some quarters it was received as a grand inspiration, many physicists had their doubts. The University of Göttingen had one of Europe's most distinguished mathematical and scientific faculties, and the reaction there was more than chilly. Harald Bohr was a big name on the faculty at that particular time, and although he eagerly assured them, "When Niels says it and considers it to be important, it must be a great advance in physics," the Göttingen physicists were completely unresponsive.

Just when the first paper came out in the *Philosophical Magazine* the physicists' society was assembled for a meeting in Göttingen, and Harald reported home on the reaction. Many years later—in fact the year before he died—Niels Bohr recorded a tape in Tisvilde containing recollections from those first stirring days after the publication of the atomic theory. He tells of the reaction of the German physicists. Listening to the tape one is in no doubt that now, after so many years, Bohr found it amusing to talk about it. There had been complete agreement in Göttingen "that the whole thing was some awful nonsense, bordering on fraud." Bohr can be heard chuckling.

At the Göttingen meeting the German spectroscopist Carl Runge further added:

What is all the more lamentable is that so many years' work has been done on these regularities in the hope that the information one had might be of crucial importance in discovering the mechanisms of the atom. For that reason it was regrettable in the highest degree that the literature should be contaminated by such wretched information, betraying so much ignorance of our knowledge of the spectrum.

Harald also reported that after this attack, Runge had expounded his conception of the spectrum. As soon as Niels heard this exposition he wrote back to Harald, "I am terribly pleased to hear of this, because someone has seized on a point which can be determined by experiments." And later when these experiments were performed, Runge had to admit his error.

Einstein was discouraging as well. He wrote to George de Hevesy that if the theory should really prove to be right, physics would be at an end—it would not be possible to do physics. But, Bohr added, Einstein did not act as consistently as that.

Bohr's theory was better received in Munich, where the theoretical physicist Arnold Sommerfeld had established a school. Bohr tells also of his first meeting with Sommerfeld—one which was to take developments a surprising step further. It was the year after the harsh reaction in Göttingen. Niels and Harald were on a walking tour in the Tyrol,

Arnold Sommerfeld and Bohr. Sommerfeld was the first German physicist to visit Copenhagen after World War I. This picture was taken in Lund, Sweden, in September 1919.

and Bohr was invited to give a lecture at Sommerfeld's institute. But before the lecture they had lunch "in the loveliest park. I remember so clearly we had such a fine Rhenish wine, but I was not accustomed to drinking wine, so I was dreadfully worried about how I would do at the lecture, which was to start shortly after lunch. But Harald said, 'It will probably help.' " Bohr's hearty laughter can be heard again on the tape, and with a slight but unmistakable note of pride he related, "And actually it went tremendously well. I spoke fluent German and knocked it properly into shape, and I like to believe that it was on that occasion that Sommerfeld fully grasped that it was real fact, as far as anything can be at the primitive level."

It was true that Sommerfeld had written a comment on a postcard to Bohr that he, Sommerfeld, "was sceptical about atomic models as a whole." But he added that although this was his view, "in the calculation of Rydberg's constant there is undeniably a great achievement."

In spite of his scepticism, Sommerfeld was in fact also still much intrigued by Bohr's paper. We learn this from the French physicist L. Brillouin, who related that he came in through the door just as Sommerfeld had read the issue of the *Philosophical Magazine* which included the paper, and Sommerfeld exclaimed, "There is an extremely important paper here by N. Bohr which will be a milestone in theoretical physics."

In England, too, the older physicists were noncommital over Bohr's theory, and one or two wrote opposing it, but the paper was an event at the meeting of the British Association for the Advancement of Science. This was held in September, just after publication of the second part. Bohr was invited as a special guest, and the theory already was discussed in Sir Oliver Lodge's keynote address. Rutherford made a contribution as well, and Bohr's paper was introduced in detail by Sir James Jeans, whose lectures had so absorbed Bohr at Cambridge. Jeans said, "Bohr has arrived at an especially ingenious and thought-provoking and—I believe I may add—convincing explanation of the laws for the spectral series." On the postulates he commented as follows, "The only justification which can be offered for the moment with regard to these hypotheses is the very important one that they work in practice." But one person who avoided committing himself on the issues raised was Lord Rayleigh, whose theory Bohr had elaborated on in his very first paper, the prize essay for the Danish Academy of Sciences. Rayleigh confined himself to a humorous remark to the effect that even if he no longer stood by the opinion he had held when younger—that a man over the age of sixty ought not to take part in a debate on current problems—he nevertheless adhered sufficiently to it not to participate in the present deliberations.

The discussion over Bohr's interpretation of Rutherford's atomic model

Niels and Margrethe Bohr with George de Hevesy in Manchester in 1913.

was affected for a short time by a confusing circumstance which was soon, however, to reveal itself as an important argument in favor of Bohr's perception. Bohr began of course with the hydrogen atom with its single electron around the nucleus. But if one of helium's two electrons is removed, helium and hydrogen resemble each other so much that at that time it could have been difficult to say which spectral lines stemmed from hydrogen and not from helium. And then there were some lines which hitherto had been attributed to hydrogen but which could not be fitted into Bohr's interpretation. If there really was such a discrepancy (which though small was still real), Bohr's entire theory would fall down. But Bohr pointed out that the spectra in question agreed precisely with his formula for the frequencies of light emitted from helium from which one electron had been removed (e.g., by a collision). And E. J. Evans, one of England's most prominent experimental physicists, took up the challenge at once, even though at that time it was immensely difficult to procure pure helium. Evans' experiment was followed with the greatest excitement, and it turned out to be entirely in agreement with Bohr. Evans produced the spectral lines in question from extremely pure helium without a trace of hydrogen lines.

The distinguished English expert in spectroscopy, Ralph Fowler, was still not convinced and contended that the wavelengths of the lines did not agree exactly with Bohr's formula for an atom with a nuclear charge corresponding to helium. Bohr clarified this contradiction as well. For if account is taken of the fact that the nucleus travels around the common center of gravity, agreement is complete—and with that Fowler was convinced. This more exact calculation also permitted Bohr to predict helium lines which had not yet been observed and which Evans found the following year precisely where Bohr had calculated they ought to be.

The prediction had been worth the entire discussion. During a congress in Vienna in the same month as Evans found the predicted helium lines, George de Hevesy spoke to Einstein and mentioned the result of Evans' experiments. Hevesy then asked Einstein for his view of Bohr's theory. The answer was surprising. Einstein said that he had entertained many similar ideas even earlier, but that he had not had the courage to develop them. When Hevesy now said that it had been established with certainty that the Fowler spectrum pertained to helium, Einstein was quite disconcerted.

In a letter to Rutherford, Hevesy describes the episode in these words: "Einstein's big eyes appeared even bigger, and he said, then this is one of the greatest discoveries." Hevesy also wrote to Bohr and reported that Einstein had gone on to say, "So the frequency of light does not depend on the frequency of the electron at all." This was exactly Bohr's postulate, in which he broke decisively with the classical conception, asserting that the light emitted does not depend on the period of revolution of the electron but on the difference in energy between two states. Einstein agreed and added, "This is a tremendous achievement—Bohr's theory must be right."

Among the group of young scientists working with Rutherford, Hevesy was the one with whom Bohr formed a lasting friendship. Hevesy became an early colleague at Bohr's Institute in Copenhagen, and he made a historic contribution in many fields. Now he closed his letter to Bohr with the words: "I can hardly tell you how happy I have been . . . almost nothing else could give me such pleasure as this spontaneous opinion of Einstein's, who had now realized that it was still possible to work at physics."

10

The Prelude to
Quantum Mechanics

Evans was not the only one who followed in Bohr's footsteps. Naturally, the immediate enthusiasm was greatest in Manchester. There and also in Oxford, H. G. J. Mosely carried out measurements of the wavelengths of spectral lines from the so-called characteristic X-radiation lying outside the visible range, and he saw that the lines moved regularly from element to element. There must be a fixed quantity changing by one unit from element to element, and this could only be the nuclear charge or the number of electrons in the atom in question which is of course equal to the nuclear charge. This supported Bohr's conceptions most handsomely and was all the more welcome because Bohr's original theory had nothing to do with X-ray spectra: it was devised for optical spectra, whose wavelengths are thousands of times bigger than those of X-radiation. The correspondence showed that Bohr's general principles for the emission of light from atoms also apply to states completely within the atom. Moseley's proof was interpreted in the following year by the German physicist W. Kossel, who assumed that the characteristic X-ray lines appear when an electron is removed from one of the inner orbits and an electron from one of the outer orbits jumps into its place during emission of the radiation demonstrated by Bohr.

The discovery by the German physicist Johannes Stark in the same autumn that one spectral line is split up into several when the atoms are placed in an electric field was no less crucial. This corresponded completely to the so-called Zeeman effect, which dated back to before the turn of the century, when the Dutch physicist P. H. Zeeman made the important spectroscopic discovery that certain spectral lines split up into three sharply differentiated lines when he placed a light source between the poles of a powerful electromagnet. The distance between these lines increased as the strength of the magnet increased. The Dutch physicist H. A. Lorentz subjected the experiment to theoretical analysis and showed that the light emission was due to oscillations of the electrons in the atoms.

When Stark now made his discovery, Rutherford wrote to Bohr immediately and reminded him of the Zeeman effect. Sommerfeld had already asked in the postcard which he sent to Bohr after the publication of Part One of the paper, "Will you also apply your atomic model to the Zeeman effect? I want to tackle this." Rutherford's letter came in December, and Bohr started immediately. Part Three of Bohr's paper had just been published. At the same time, other physicists besides Bohr began to apply Bohr's theory to the Stark effect. Soon things were moving fast.

In the March number of the *Philosophical Magazine* Bohr published his investigations of the Zeeman and Stark effects with a still more refined analysis of the theory's postulates. Sommerfeld came to play a decisive role in the further investigation of these problems, and with that the prelude to the great work on quantum mechanics had begun in earnest. But let us look first at the conditions under which Bohr was working and the prospects for the future that he had at that time.

11

The Birth of the Institute

It is hard today to understand how Niels Bohr managed to cope both financially and professionally in the early years. While his ideas flourished and inspired more and more investigators in the celebrated centers of physics, he must have felt more or less out on a limb personally. By the spring of 1912 his Carlsberg Foundation scholarship had already been used up in Cambridge and Manchester, and a plan which was floated after his dissertation defense for the creation of a professorship for him at the University of Copenhagen was again abandoned. He was given a readership, concerning which he wrote to his Swedish friend Carl W. Oseen in the spring of 1914,

> I only have the duty of instructing the medical students in physics, and I thus have no possibility of getting pupils or assistance. . . . I am therefore working for the establishment of a teaching post in theoretical physics (you may recall that there was talk of it after my doctoral thesis), but there does not appear to be much hope that this will succeed, as the faculty still does not want the creation of such a position.

The readership did not include access to a laboratory either!

With Bohr in this precarious situation, Rutherford was not slow to recruit him again. A readership in Manchester became vacant after C. G. Darwin left, and Bohr obtained a leave of absence from his position in Copenhagen to enable him to start in Manchester in the academic year 1914–1915. But because of the war he had his work cut out to reach England. Before setting off he went hiking with Harald in the Alps, where the two old soccer players showed that they were still in good form. Niels especially had kept up his training with tennis. They walked up to 35 kilometers a day and did not intend to return home until sometime in August. But the outbreak of World War I caused them to hurry homeward, and they left Germany just before the frontiers were closed. Even so, normal shipping links with England were broken off. Should Niels give up his plan to go to Manchester? An exchange of

Niels Bohr at age 35 in 1920.

telegrams followed between Copenhagen and Manchester. Rutherford kept urging him, and finally in October Bohr and Margrethe succeeded in getting on a ship which sailed round the north of Scotland to England.

In Manchester events in the physics field were gathering momentum, and with the war dragging on Bohr decided, even before the end of his first year, to extend his leave of absence.

In the meantime in Copenhagen the strings were slowly being pulled for a teaching post for Bohr. There was no lack of recommendations from abroad, and the university was now beginning to fear that Niels Bohr would be lost to Danish research. The government rejected an application for a professorship, however. Further appeals were made, and in May 1916, at long last, the appointment was approved. A letter of congratulations is still extant from Bohr's old teacher at the university, Christian Christiansen—one of the quartet to whom Bohr had listened during his formative years. Christiansen wrote, "I have known you since you were young; I have never met anyone like you for probing everything to the bottom, having the energy to carry it through, and as well as that for having such a manysided interest in life as a whole. . . ."

Although the government had approved the professorship for Bohr the arrangements for it were badly handled. The readership from which Bohr had taken leave was to be abolished, but the teaching of medical students would continue along with the professorship. Everyone at the university could see what a patent absurdity this was, and Bohr received backing for an arrangement whereby the lecturer who had taught the medical students during his absence would continue to do so although being paid from sources outside the university! Only when his substitute had had to teach the final term without any pay at all did the government agree in 1918 to reestablish the abolished readership.

It is interesting as well as amusing, incidentally, that Bohr's generous substitute was H. M. Hansen, of whom we have already heard, and who was much later to serve for a record number of years as the rector of the University of Copenhagen. During his rectorship Hansen was to play a major role in implementing a plan of Bohr's for the betterment of Danish science as a whole.

At the same time that Bohr at last began his work as professor in the autumn term of 1916, giving lectures on mechanics, elasticity theory, thermodynamics, electron theory, and atomic theory, and holding seminars with students, he went on with his own scientific work. For this he had a room measuring fifteen square meters. Moreover he had to share it with his first assistant. The room was on one side of the library of the Technical College of the University of Copenhagen and Bohr had no space at all in which to conduct experiments.

In 1917 he applied to the Faculty of Natural Science for funds to establish an institute. Bohr had dreamed of getting a site in the Botanical

Gardens *gratis*, but when that had to be abandoned and the value of money was falling rapidly, an old friend and former schoolmate, Aage Berlème, launched a private fundraising scheme to collect 80,000 kroner to purchase the site which was chosen on Blegdamsvej in Copenhagen.

The amount does not sound very impressive today, but the adversities of World War I were even reaching neutral Denmark with the onset of inflation. It is difficult to say how things would have gone if Berlème had not thrown himself into his talk with such enthusiasm. He himself made the first donation, but no fewer than 40 private donors and 20 large firms had to contribute before the target was reached. The large number of donors is evidence that Bohr's growing international fame was becoming widely known in Denmark. The manner of some of the refusals, too, was a reflection of who he was. One potential donor refused simply because "Bohr supports the Radicals." Another would gladly contribute 1,000 kroner if he himself could also have 1,000 kroner for his art collection, and a third would only participate if Bohr's work would be useful to agriculture, which Berlème did not dare to promise. He had no inkling of the implications of atomic structure for agricultural research in the future.

Although Berlème's fundraising campaign reached its target at the end of 1917, negotiations between government and city over the designated site on Blegdamsvej dragged out for so long that the purchase was not implemented until a year afterward. And just when the Ministry of Education finally gave the green light for construction to begin, World War I ended with all its catastrophic consequences for the world economy. Social clashes accompanied prolonged wage disputes and strikes, and the amount set aside for the building did not cover the entire or even half the cost, although Bohr's estimate had been thorough and realistic. Supplementary applications had to be prepared, only to be rapidly upset by new costs. One sign of the times that was almost comical was an unexpected rise in costs occasioned by a sudden shortage of bricks in Copenhagen. Bricks had to be brought by ship all the way from northern Jutland, a distance of about 100 miles.

The actual building costs, previously calculated at 120,000 kroner, little by little reached 389,000 kroner, and only now could the battle begin for the Institute's equipment, most of which would have to be imported. Where to begin or end, now that the value of the Danish krone had fallen to half compared with the time when the budget had been drawn up, and when prices all over the world were rising with inflation? New applications were drafted, and slowly the appropriations rose from the original estimate of 60,000 kroner to 175,000 kroner, but private contributions which did not stop with the fund raised by Berlème, were equally important, a generous gesture being made by

Torben Meyer, a stockbroker, in the form of foreign currency made available at prewar rates of exchange.

The largest donation, however, came from the Carlsberg Foundation, to which Bohr had applied for funds for the Institute's first large item of equipment, a lattice spectrograph. Both Rutherford and Sommerfeld were among those who submitted recommendations when Bohr applied to the Carlsberg Foundation, Sommerfeld concluding his letter with these prophetic words: "It may be that in future, just as formerly at the radium institute in Vienna, scientists from every land will meet in Copenhagen for special studies, pursuing their common cultural ideals at the Bohr Institute for Atomic Physics."

Sommerfeld's hopes were fulfilled, and the Carlsberg Foundation later made numerous other grants to the Bohr Institute—119 of them by the time of Bohr's death.

Equipment for the Institute arrived item by item, but when inauguration was delayed, Bohr impatiently began inviting foreign physicists to come for collaborative work anyway. However, visitors had to live in temporary accommodations in the Technical College, where Betty Schultz, a secretary who was to become the Institute's factotum, had also joined Bohr and his assistant in their diminutive waiting room.

After two years of delay, it was decided that the Institute could be inaugurated in 1920. Bohr ventured to invite Rutherford to the ceremony, but when Rutherford arrived there were bricklayers, carpenters, electricians, plumbers, and painters everywhere. The inauguration had to be postponed once again, but Rutherford's visit was still an event. An honorary doctorate was conferred on him by the University of Copenhagen, and he returned the compliment with three lectures and a report of the first artificially produced nuclear reaction. In Manchester he had bombarded nitrogen atoms with alpha particles and produced hydrogen nuclei, so that the nitrogen had been transformed to oxygen. Rutherford's triumph made a great stir. It was the first time in human history that one element had been transmuted to another by human action—though in infinitesimally small quantities.

At long last things were looking up for the Institute. On January 21, 1921 Bohr was able to write the first letter from his new office: it was hardly a coincidence that it was to Rutherford. The inauguration ceremony was finally and definitely set for March 3. Over one hundred guests were present, and the Minister of Education, Jacob Appel, introduced the succession of speakers, whereupon Niels Bohr outlined his conception of the physics discipline:

> By physics is understood, as you know, the study of natural phenomena or, more narrowly, the study of the general laws which apply to inorganic nature. Now various procedures have proved fruitful in physical investigations: firstly, it has often been possible to consult nature directly by making physical

POLITIKEN

tredivte Aargang Nr. 61.   Kjøbenhavn. Torsdag den 3. Marts 1921.   Tolv Si

Torsdag.

Torsdag Kongt og blæssende.

orrede har i Gaar i London i lange
stket Tyskernes Modforslag (S. 1).

skr.g hersker voldsom Ophidelse
igrne karakteriseres som en Ud-
(S. 1).

claud imødeser man Resultatet af
cen ved fuldkommen Ro. (S. 1).

center et Ultimatum med Krav om
:e Pariserbeslutningerne. Svaret
Nej (S. 1).

ledende Artikler handler om den
de Hovedperborhøgelse og om de
d'orslag paa London-Konferencen.

r Grundskylddebat i Folketinget.

ingen afsiet Grundskrylddeforsla-
3).

r bebudedes der Lock-out i Tran-
a og overfor Murerfaget i Provin-
6).

omandens Forseg paa at mægle
lovedorganisatiounerne i Gaar blev
et (Cd. 6).

... gares et sidste Forseg paa at
oo tal i Overmorgen varslede
er. (S. 6).

er Overbye anklager nu en Kace-
-eder Svendsen, for Meddelagtig-
rhrydel erne (S. 4).

'a gamle Formidro maatte i Gaar
endes Sag. (S. 4).

;ljc Atom-Institut indvies i Dag

-Qetteroe indenfor Portmanet

.errben af Bil-Tekisterne vil omte

Universitetets Atom-Institut, der indvies i Dag

Instituteta store Laboratorium og Medlemmer af Staben.

Ved en Højtidelighed indvies i Eftermiddag Universitetets Institut for teoretisk Fysik, populært kaldet Atom-Institutet, hvis Grundlægger og Leder er den kun 35 Aar gamle, allerede verdensberømte Videnskabsmand, Professor Niels Bohr.

Paa det store Billede ses detBum, hvor de videnskabelige Forsøg med Atomerne foretages efter den af Professor Franck opfundne Metode.

I Hjørnet ser vi enkelte af Institutets Medarbejdere. I øverste Række fra venstre til højre: Unga-
reren, Professor Hevesy, Docent H. M. Hansen og Professor Niels Bohr. Nederst Tyskeren, Professor Franck og Hollænderen, Dr. Kramers.

Telegrammer om Verdenssitu

sidste Henstilling, vil hele Sagen
blive overgivet i Marskal Fochs
Haand.

Pen.

I Tyskland imødeses Resul-
tatet med fuldkommen Ro.

**Man venter et Ultimatum,
som kræver Vedtagelse af
Pariserbeslutningerne. —
Tyskland vil svare Nej!**

Berlin, Onsdag.
Privat for Politiken.

Det mest bemærkelsesværdige
ved den kritiske Situation, der er
opstaaet som Følge af de Allieredes
Afvisning af de tyske Tilbud, er
den fuldkomne Ro, hvormed den
tyske Presse og Offentligheden
modtager de truende Meddelelser
fra London og Paris.

Der hersker absolut Enighed
om, at de tyske Forslag betegner
den yderste Grænse, Tyskland kan
gaa til, og at de Allierede, hvis de
ikke engang saaligt vil drøfte For-
slaget, selv kan komme og hente
Skadeserstatningen.

Sanktionerne staar ikke længere
som en Trusel, hvis Udførelse for
enhver Pris maa undgaas.

Der er ingen som helst Udsigt
til, at Udenrigsminister Simons vil
gøre Indrømmelser af Betydning.
Han har ikke Fuldmagt til at træffe
Afgørelser, der afsiger meget for
det tyske Tilbud. En saadan Be-
slutning skal Kabinettet i Berlin

De tyske Sagky
at for at kunne
riserkravene m
Tyskland forlæt
tilintetgøre en
landsk Konk

B
Den sagkyndige K
morandum angaaend
ningerne betoner, a
med Anuiteter paa 6
mark vilde raume d
aiing med 100 Guldma
pirsmark pr. Hoved t

Den tyske Handels
seloverskud for 11
mindst 2½ Milliard G
nu ugunstigere er den
balance. Totalsumme
Aarsydelser, eskkl. Er
ne, snslaas variirt til 1
ledes at det tyske Foll
ornde mindst i Milli
til Udligning af Pass
landel.

Ved at indskrænte
Tyskland ngson rumm
de neutrale Lande me
indskrænke Indførsle
ler er umuligt af Het
skende Ernaringskisa
For at udligne t v
a Milliarder tuil b ...

world of the atom was demonstrated for the first time to an invited group at the University. At the end of his speech Bohr spoke, as he often also did later in life, of the hopes he placed in the new generation.

> It is inherent in scientific work, of course, that no one dare make definite promises for the future; we must be prepared for the fact that on the road which at this moment we think we see lying open before us, obstacles may arise which completely block our path or require entirely new ideas for their surmounting. Therefore it is of the greatest importance not to be dependent merely on the abilities and powers available within a limited circle of scientists; the task of guiding a constantly renewed body of young people through the methods and results of science contributes in the highest degree to the continual debating of issues from new angles, and not least, of course, new blood and new ideas are brought to the work through the young people's own efforts.

The celebrated philologist Otto Jespersen, who was then rector, was at last able to declare the University of Copenhagen Institute of Theoretical Physics to be open. This was the official name until it was changed in 1965 to commemorate what would have been Bohr's eightieth birthday. Since then the sign on the facade of the main building

The initial staff members of the Institute. From left, standing: J. C. Jacobsen, Svein Rosseland, George de Hevesy, H. M. Hansen, and Bohr. Sitting: James Franck, Hans Kramers, and Betty Schultz.

simply agrees with what everyone over the years has always called it anyway: The Niels Bohr Institute.

Up to that time, when the term "theoretical physics" was used, it corresponded to what we understand today as "fundamental physics." Thus "theoretical physics" also implied experimental research, by which Niels Bohr set such great store, and for which laboratories were also furnished. Gradually, as later extensions were added, the space for experimental work was correspondingly enlarged in accordance with the original plans.

When Niels Bohr and his family moved out to the Institute and into a private apartment on the first floor (it was common practice at that time for directors to live at their institutes) it was still a long way from any neighbors. Nevertheless the location was ideal, because the Technical College was fairly close by. At the same time the Institute's surroundings on Blegdamsvej were as peaceful as could be desired.

A few years before, the area consisted of open fields and a few small ponds. Here the laundry men had their wooden huts where they washed and hung out their linen for bleaching by sun and wind. This was the origin of the name of the street (*blegdam* in Danish means a bleaching ground at a pond), and when the Institute was first erected there was still a view to Trianglen, a square several kilometers away. Now the

The Institute as it appeared in the 1920s.

first trees had been planted and paths and playing fields had been laid out, but the view was still open on all sides. A municipal streetcar, one of the oldest in town, the Number 3, ran along Blegdamsvej, and because of the vibrations it produced, a deep well was dug in the Institute for the lattice spectrograph, which needed to be shielded from vibration. It was this expensive apparatus that was able to deflect light of different wavelengths and so separate the light emitted from an atom and measure wavelengths.

The well was seven meters deep, but even so the vibrations from the streetcars still affected the sensitive instrument. The well therefore had to be abandoned for this purpose, and the instrument was moved to a position further back in the building where the Institute's spectroscopic laboratory, with its numerous other apparatuses, was also located, in the vicinity of a workshop building.

However, the Institute did make use of the well later. When Niels Bohr turned fifty in 1935, a group of friends presented him with a gift of 0.6 grams of radium, which when mixed with beryllium, became a source of neutrons for many forthcoming experiments. The well was selected as the best place to store it.

Incidentally, there was one quite different way in which the well acquired special significance for it very quickly became traditional to

Niels Bohr, James Franck, and H. M. Hansen at the Institute in 1921.

hold the annual Christmas celebration in the well room, and the Christmas tree used to stand on the cover of the well. All the staff would assemble for sausages and beer, and Bohr would give a talk on the achievements of the past year. The tradition continued as long as the staff was not too large for the room to accommodate. When the isotope venture began, the well immediately acquired a growing significance, not merely as a depository for the radioactive sources, but also as the most secure place for conducting experiments with them.

12

The Periodic System

Going back to the Manchester days of 1914–1915, we find Niels Bohr eagerly engaged in the further refinement of his atomic theory while waiting for news from the University of Copenhagen. He produced a number of papers at this time, and in one of them he introduced a correction to his formula for the hydrogen spectrum, applying the theory of relativity to the circular orbits of electrons in the hydrogen spectrum. At the same time in Munich Sommerfeld had demonstrated that the hydrogen lines could display a dual character, and he had suggested that if the theory of relativity is applied to the elliptical orbits found in the hydrogen atom simultaneously with the circular electron orbits, then the result will be that the ellipse will make a turning movement so that the electron describes a series of "loops" around the nucleus. This could be the reason for the dual character of the hydrogen lines. This was to turn out to be the beginning of the next great advance in physics.

Sommerfeld had followed Bohr's original ideas, and by applying the theory of relativity to the elliptical orbits he added a new feature to Bohr's theory. Bohr had only dealt with electron movements which were periodic, i.e., movements which repeat themselves after one revolution, but once Sommerfeld had deployed his theory, it became possible to also deal with many nonperiodic movements, and he was able to give a complete account of the double line spectra. When Bohr read Sommerfeld's papers, Bohr wrote: "I don't believe I have ever enjoyed the reading of anything more than I enjoyed the study of these."

We have now reached March 1916. Bohr had just received the proofs of a paper which later, in revised form, was to become famous. It was on the quantum theory for the line spectra, but he immediately began to revise the proofs in accordance with Sommerfeld's theory. The close collaboration between physicists of the time was growing in abundant measure. New papers constantly led Bohr to new reflections and revisions, so that it was two years before he completed a totally new paper.

Bohr returned to Copenhagen in the meantime, and during his further work on the revision of the paper he hired his first assistant, a young Dutch physicist named Hendrik Antony Kramers. It was a happy choice, or more correctly, an extraordinarily fortunate one. At the age of 21 Kramers arrived in Copenhagen. He had been studying with the great physicist Paul Ehrenfest in Leiden, but this was during World War I, and Kramers wanted to study in a neutral country. He came without a penny in his pockets, but he was so eager to become Bohr's assistant that Bohr—after consulting Harald—gave him the chance; Bohr also requested, and was granted, a stipend for Kramers from the Carlsberg Foundation. Kramers remained not just for one term but stayed on as an invaluable colleague for over ten years. His great strength was in mathematical methods, and this, coupled with Bohr's intuition, led to unforeseen results.

Kramers' familiarity with the mathematical formulation of classical mechanics became of particular significance when Bohr was preparing the paper on the quantum theory for line spectra, of which the "correspondence principle" forms the central feature.

The gist of the correspondence principle was a merging of the concept of the quantum with the classical modes of theoretical description in atomic theory, at the margin where Planck's quantum effect is very small in relation to the effects to be described. For many complicated electron motions it was possible to arrive at a mathematical "solution" of the motion in partial movements. Every displacement from one stationary state to another now "corresponds" to one of these partial movements.

The point was that Bohr could infer back from the classical solution to the probability of the displacement of an electron into the inner stationary states, where one was remote from the classical conditions.

In order to speed up the publication of his paper on "The Quantum Theory for the Line Spectra," Bohr decided to issue it in parts as he had done with his atomic theory. Parts One and Two appeared in the *Publications of the Danish Academy of Sciences* in April and December, 1918, while Part Three had to wait until 1922.

Quantum mechanics was still only fragmentary and did not yet form a rounded whole as did classical physics. A decisive breakthrough was still to come. But in the meantime much else was happening for Bohr. In 1922, at the time when the further development of the atomic theory was engaging so much of his thinking, and when the Institute was just getting its stride, Bohr succeeded in clarifying the periodic system of the elements.

In the previous century the Russian chemist Dmitri Mendeleev and the German scientist Lothar Meyer had found that the 92 elements which chemists had detected could be arranged in a series according to increasing atomic weight. They also found that fixed chemical and physical properties recur with certain periods. There were certain gaps in the series which must correspond to elements which were still undiscovered, and Mendeleev was able to predict from the vacant places the properties of the missing elements.

But this index of the elements in a sense did no more than state the facts. The laws underlying the periodic system were only successfully formulated with the development of Bohr's atomic theory; in this the X-ray spectroscope was helpful with Henry Moseley's law of displacement in explaining the X-ray spectra of the elements.

After Bohr's theory of X-ray spectra, it became possible to determine directly the charge of an atomic nucleus and therefore the atomic number if the frequencies of the X-ray line was known. This kind of systematic reading of all X-ray spectra gave information not only about which elements were still missing but also about the elements' true numbers. At this point it was clear to Bohr that the nuclear charge is equal to the atomic number of the element, and that the elements must be arranged in ascending order of nuclear charges to enable the regular change of properties to be seen in the periodic system. Previously, of course, the elements had been arranged in ascending order of weight, but in fairness it should be mentioned that with few exceptions the two procedures gave the same order.

Now the deciphering of the relationship of the elements is closely linked with the grouping of the electrons in the different atoms. And it was through a series of comparative observations of spectra of all the elements that Bohr succeeded in deducing, from the series of element periods, that the electrons in each atom are arranged in certain groups or *shells*, each in turn containing a fixed number of electrons, which within each group interchange with the next element in the series. And Bohr showed that the division of the elements into fixed periods results from the fact that the various electron groups in an atom can contain only a limited number of electrons.

Bohr's interpretation of the periodic system of the elements is one of his most epoch-making contributions to physics. And as a sequel to it, the Austrian physicist Wolfgang Pauli, whose collaboration with Bohr in these years became a vital factor in the quantum theory, succeeded in giving us a deeper understanding of why the various periods contain only a limited number of electrons at intervals according to a fixed pattern. He formulated a rule, which became known as the Pauli exclusion principle, limiting the possible number of electrons in each group. Many years later this rule would also contribute to the understanding of the structure of the atomic nucleus. •

As a footnote to Bohr's theory of the properties of elements we may draw attention to the discovery of the element hafnium. It was understood that an unknown element—number 72—was missing, and it was believed to belong to the rare earths group. If this was correct, it was understandable that it had not been discovered, because rare earths are very similar to each other. Now, however, according to Bohr's theory, it had to be concluded that the subgroup of these rare earths ended with number 71, and that the unknown element number 72 had certain similarities with its opposite neighbor, zirconium. Therefore it may be found in nature along with zirconium.

The Dutch physicist Dirk Coster and George de Hevesy looked for element 72 by analyzing zircon minerals by X-ray spectroscopic methods, and they found in one of them the spectral lines that would be expected for element number 72. Here was the unknown element, and since the analysis had been carried out in Copenhagen, the name hafnium was given to it, after *Hafnia*, the Latin name for Copenhagen. The discovery confirmed Bohr's theory of the elements as elegantly as anyone could wish.

13

Bohr's Working Method

All the physicists who collaborated with Bohr quickly got to know his working method. It was so special that they could later only characterize it as "Bohrian." These colleagues also soon experienced the pleasure of the paradox, that form of surprise leap of thought which was part of Bohr's nature.

In oral discussions with physicists, Bohr could be sharp and strongly critical on rare occasions, especially when trying to get to the bottom of the current problem. He could express himself in conversation in picturesque language and with great power, whether in admiration or criticism, and his lectures often gave the greatest pleasure to his listeners when he spoke without notes.

When expressing himself in writing, on the other hand, he put enormous effort into his choice of words. He could tirelessly twist and turn a sentence in his mind in order to bring out a point more clearly. Time was of no concern. Hours and days could pass before the meaning of a sentence had been fully refined. The whole succession of Bohr's collaborators, who gradually—one by one—became self-activating triggers for Bohr in the elaborating and clarifying of ideas, experienced this. Besides helping with the scientific papers themselves, Bohr's collaborators took turns helping him draft letters and lectures.

Bohr had many lonely hours, when he had to argue with himself, and when he had his visions. This was especially true at night. But he was happiest when he was up against a talented opponent. As Rosenfeld has described it, Bohr had to have someone with him with whom he could feel free to think out loud, and on whom he could literally try out the formulation of his thinking

to verify its appropriateness for fulfilling its one crucial function: to effect unambiguous communication. From time to time he would dictate a few sentences to pin down the thrust of the argument. These were intended mostly as a help for his colleague, since Bohr's incredible memory made such notes superfluous for himself. When it came to the point he would hardly ever look at the notes; instead, he would redraft the sentences from the beginning, over and over again and with inexhaustible patience, slowly getting closer to the meticulously balanced form he would at last consider fit for publication.

When a dialogue first began, it was a special delight for Bohr when he found his colleagues sharing the pleasure of overcoming the difficulties. In the written form he was impeded, as he expressed it to the physicist Jørgen Kalckar, by the complementary relationship between the one-sidedness of the convincing expression and the many reservations and nuances of the truth. He was conscious of the difficulty of communicating both the thought itself and its limitation in one breath. Jørgen Kalckar, one of his much younger collaborators who knew how to listen to Bohr and to get his thinking started, has given a lively description of an afternoon that alternated between dictation and exchanges of ideas. Bohr used to make the apparently curious demand that all sections of a dissertation should be of equal length. Therefore much time was spent shifting the dividing lines, moving sentences, and switching words around. One day Kalckar could not resist bursting out, "But this really is not verse that we are writing."

"But perhaps," answered Bohr, "what we are doing is really only superficially different from writing verse."

Kalckar objected, "You may remember that Georg Brandes [a Danish writer and philosopher] warned Ibsen that whatever one can express in prose one should not try to put into verse."

Bohr replied, "Brandes was an extremely wise man. I certainly do not want to make myself out to be half as wise as he."

Then there developed a lengthy conversation about Brandes during which they drifted away from the starting point, until Bohr broke off,

> Where were we? Oh, yes, you must not believe that I am such a fool as to think that it makes any real difference if one section is a little shorter or longer than another. What matters is finding some point or other which can be taken as a challenge to ask yourself: "Could all this not be said better?" The significance of the verse form lies in the difficulties it presents, which compel the poet to use the greatest precision of formulation.

And Bohr then began to analyze poems of Bjørnson, Goethe, and Wildenvey as evidence for his assertion. "Do you agree? He would never have found a way of saying this so strikingly if he had not had to search for a rhyme for *Tor* and at the same time consider the meter." The afternoon hours passed by, and Bohr broke off again: "Oh dear, is it so late? We must get on: can you stay a little longer? Would it bore you to read the chapter again from the beginning? Perhaps we could make it a little better. . . ."

When Bohr became animated at the blackboard he used both hands and arms for erasing so there would be enough room for the symbols expressing the further development of his ideas.

Rosenfeld gives an account of a subsequent occasion when Bohr's method of working produced results in a critical situation. This happened in 1935, when Einstein, together with B. Podolsky and N. Rosen, advanced what they considered to be a vital defect in the quantum theory. In fact it came as a bolt from the blue, but although Bohr was deeply engaged in other speculations, he pushed everything to one side. The misunderstanding had to be cleared up immediately.

At first Bohr wanted to reply by using the same examples which Einstein had used, and with great excitement he began to dictate a rough draft, but he soon hesitated. "No, this will not do. We must try again from the beginning . . . we must make it completely clear." This went on for some time. Earlier, during the Solvay Congress in 1927, Einstein had tried to refute Bohr's arguments for the limitations of the modes of description in classical physics. Now he was saying it again in a different way. After trying for some time to find the formulation he wanted, Bohr broke off with a remark which many would have recognized: "We must sleep on it." Next morning he took up his dictation again, and now a change had come about in the tone of the sentences; the sharp expressions had been dropped. When Rosenfeld remarked on this, Bohr said, "It is just a sign that we are beginning to understand the problem." And then the real work began. Day after day, week after week, the entire argument was patiently scrutinized with the aid of simpler and more transparent examples. Einstein's problem was restated and its solution reformulated with such precision and clarity that the weakness in the reasoning of the critics became self-evident and the entire argumentation fell to pieces. "They do it smartly," was Bohr's comment, "but the important thing is to do it right."

The young Danish experimental physicist J. K. Bøggild, who constructed the first cloud chamber at the Bohr Institute and who also worked as one of Bohr's assistants for a time, described the work procedure one day when a grant application had to be written.

The scene opens with Bohr wandering around in his office and his colleague sitting at the typewriter taking dictation:

> For page after page it goes steadily on, carried forward by immense concentration and therefore independent of the rumbling of the streetcars and the hammering of the workmen (there have almost always been workmen somewhere or other in the Institute). When someone suggested going out to stop the banging, Bohr refused: "Noise that is not directed at me I do not hear at all." When he was called away to the telephone, he resumed dictating at the next word of the letter as soon as he came back through the door, in between giving the typist instructions for correcting a word or a sentence many pages back. When the letter was finished, it was back to the beginning again adding new sections and improvements. After perhaps the tenth version it could happen that Bohr would come happily in through the door one morning and say, "I have had an excellent idea—we shall start the whole thing over again." After the fifteenth or the eighteenth version the application is almost ready; there are just a few individual words to be corrected and the placing of some commas to be discussed. And then Bohr himself would delete some misplaced letters with a sharp knife and carefully write in the correct ones with a pencil ("so that Mrs. Schultz will not need to type the pages again").
>
> Then when a pen had been found, and Bohr had made sure that it worked, the signature was applied, and all those standing around breathed a sigh of relief.

Bohr was asked one day if it was still necessary for applications to be so long and detailed, to which he replied that he was certain that if they had been so often successful with applications and received the desired grant, it was precisely because of the painstaking project descriptions.

Stefan Rozental, who also became a valued colleague, has given a vivid account of Bohr's working method during Bohr's preparation of the foreword to the work called *The Culture of Denmark in the Year 1940*. Rozental was Bohr's assistant during the writing, and he describes the toilsome "yet fascinating time as the thoughts gradually built up, often in peculiar ways, with the starting point in some little observation or idea." It was here more than at any other time that Bohr imposed on himself the formal restraint that the individual sections should be of equal length, and that each should deal with a self-contained thought.

The preparation of the nine-page article took almost two months, and Rozental was in the habit of arriving at Carlsberg in the morning and leaving there late in the evening.

> The content and form of the article were like a living being that could be followed from its frail beginning, when one hardly knew which way it would develop; which grew and grew and changed character and all the time drew nourishment from the most varied sources. Often a single word, or the significance of this expression or that, would be discussed at length and in this way the meaning achieved complete clarity. It was Denmark's position as a small country with old traditions, but open to all currents from outside, which became the leitmotif of the article.

The publishers of the book pressed for the manuscript many times,

> but it did not leave the Institute until it had been gone through in the smallest details. Harald Bohr or various friends were often called on for their opinions during the various stages of development of the text. When the manuscript eventually went to the printer, it still took seven proofs before it saw the light of day—in a completely altered form.

Bohr was rarely still when he was thinking—even when he was formulating his arguments during a dialogue. All of his colleagues had to accustom themselves to the way he would often wander incessantly around the table at which they were sitting. Whether in his workroom at the Institute or at home at Carlsberg, he got up time after time in order to walk about. The more the thoughts were pressing, the faster he walked. Now and then he would go to the cupboard in the corner to get a piece of chocolate. In between times he would light his pipe, which he always forgot to keep going. He used to relight it repeatedly, and it was a recurrent good humored prank on his birthday for the staff of the Institute to present him with a stack of huge boxes of matches. Without exception, everyone who has ever spent any time with him has experienced the incessant relighting of his pipe. On the tape containing the informal recollections recorded shortly before his death, his voice breaks off time and time again as a match is heard being struck, followed by repeated deep sucking to get the pipe to draw.

It is known of course that nicotine increases the supply of blood sugar to the brain. And with Bohr's perpetual mental activity it is not so strange that he should always need to have his pipe lit—but it is not strange either that as the pipe was always going out because he forgot to smoke while he was thinking, he was often forced to make for the chocolate, whose sugar content has the same effect. "Potential energy," he called it. Oskar Klein relates that in the early years the unending

Bohr in front of the pavilion, his workplace, at Tisvilde in 1960.

flow of dictation, corrections, and discussion were interrupted now and then by brief running expeditions to the store for tobacco and chocolate.

And we can cast our minds back to the occasion at Nærumgaard when the young Niels sprinkled a mountain of sugar on his rødgrød and his grandmother said understandingly, "Well, perhaps he needs it." Later, when they lived in Carlsberg, Margrethe Bohr saw to it that the corner cupboard was always supplied with chocolate. But his sons also knew what was in the corner cupboard, and for that reason Bohr had another hiding place which only one person knew about. This was his secretary, Sophie Hellman: On one Christmas Eve when she was invited to the Bohr's house she gave Bohr a box of home-made quince candy. He thought the candy was just the thing. Bohr was so delighted with it that he hid the box from his sons, but Mrs. Hellman discovered the hiding place and when the box was empty, she quietly filled it again, whereupon Bohr continued to enjoy the contents. But in this "quince alliance," neither Bohr nor Mrs. Hellman gave any sign of knowing about the other's actions. Bohr gradually came to expect that the box would be full when he opened the lid, and Mrs. Hellman received her own enjoyment from performing the ritual without a word about it being exchanged between them. This continued until the winter, and then a new box came the following Christmas. Bohr's omission of thanks each time the box was filled was undoubtedly due to the boyish fun he derived from the secret game, and Mrs. Hellman relished this to the utmost.

Bohr took the greatest pains in all sorts of matters, as his assistant Hendrik Casimir could testify from the days when he worked with Bohr at all hours of the day and night. He was put severely to the test as secretary early in 1930, when Oskar Klein sought a vacant professorship in Stockholm. Bohr was appointed to sit on the judging committee, and although Bohr believed from the beginning that Klein was the obvious choice, there were two particular competitors who had special competence. But the closer of these was younger than Klein and therefore had time to wait. However, Bohr was much too conscientious to let it go at that. "First he carefully went through all the work produced by the four candidates. We certainly did not read every word and did not really check every single formula, but Bohr did analyze them carefully and he explained to me many of the finer points." When the report was to be written, Bohr rendered full justice toward each of the four candidates. Every sentence, indeed every word, was carefully weighed. But when the report on the professorship was finally typed out, it became evident that this was only the first version, and Bohr started the whole thing over again. Casimir began to wonder by the third version whether the document was now gaining anything vital from the alterations, but his objection was brushed aside with the plea: "Don't leave me in the lurch now." And so Casimir went on listening and writing and correcting and cutting and pasting together. Finally it was version number nine that was sent off.

Bohr used to like to finish a paper on a Saturday. "Then it travels on Sunday, and we gain a day." That particular Saturday was March 1, and Casimir has among his books a Danish edition of *The Icelandic Sagas* with a greeting from Bohr dated March 1, 1930: "In memory of joint drudgery and with thanks for faithful help."

If Bohr spent a lot of time on a positive recommendation like Klein's, he was no less painstaking in the case of a rejection. Bengt Strömgren was once involved in framing the written assessment of a doctoral thesis which without the slightest doubt would have to be rejected. But Bohr took up every point for consideration; and when much time had passed in formulating the argumentation against it, Bohr broke off suddenly and looked gravely at Strömgren: "Now we must be careful that we don't get into trouble." By that he meant that the rejection must not unnecessarily wound the feelings of the unsuccessful candidate.

Now the fact that a colleague understood how to listen did not always mean that a dialogue would begin; but the fact of his presence could be of significance in assisting Bohr's thoughts. The young theoretician Jens Lindhard, now president of the Danish Academy of Sciences, experienced this when he was working with Bohr in the late 1940s on a paper dealing with the passage of charged particles through matter—a continuation of Bohr's earlier paper, already mentioned, dating right back to 1912.

Every morning Lindhard presented himself at Bohr's house, where a blackboard was hung, and where they would often sit with few interruptions until twelve o'clock at night. In another room beyond, Mrs. Hellman sat in readiness at her typewriter. It had happened once that Bohr had inadvertently picked up Lindhard's pipe—something which other colleagues had also experienced—and for that reason the day used to begin with Bohr and Lindhard both laying all their pipes out on the table and sorting out which belonged to whom before lighting up and sitting in silence for a while as they smoked. There was a day when the silence continued. They carried on smoking. Bohr was concentrating with a distant look in his eyes. Still nothing was said. The pipes were refilled and lit up again, and after a while Bohr said, "Now I have it, we shall simply begin the sentence with 'notwithstanding'." This was considered a little, and written down, whereupon they sat a while longer, smoking quietly, and then suddenly Bohr said, "I am so pleased at how well our work is progressing." After which the silence continued.

The paper, which came out in 1954 and is still widely read, bears the names of both Bohr and Lindhard. It only happened a few times over the years that the contribution of a colleague was sufficiently original for his name to figure alongside Bohr's when the final paper was published. The introduction to this paper written in collaboration with Lindhard uses the word "notwithstanding" quite often, and Jens Linhard, who of course has been asked what the word actually signifies, has answered, "This is an old English word which sometimes can mean 'in spite of,' and it also has a juridical meaning—almost all legal documents in England begin with 'notwithstanding'—but I can say that 'in spite of' is probably one of the meanings of the word. Actually, Niels Bohr had his own style of English in a way. In time he became very good at English, but the language he wrote was a special Bohr-English. This does not mean that it was bad, but it was special."

Just as Bohr had his own methods in the preparation of a paper, he also had his own Bohrian mode of driving a car. It may be mentioned here because Jens Lindhard was an unwilling victim of the method when he used to accompany Bohr to and from his home in Old Carlsberg during the time when their paper was being written. It is true that they often cycled, but occasionally Bohr might take the car and sit behind the steering wheel himself. He also had a theory about traffic lights. "When he saw a green light ahead, he had foresight: he knew that it would soon change to red, and therefore he must slow down. On the other hand, he knew it would change to green whenever he saw a red light ahead, so then he speeded up." But if the correspondence principle did not operate, then Bohr would drive through the red light. Perhaps he was misled by his thoughts of the longer time it took for the light to change when he was on his bicycle.

As far as Bohr's working method was concerned, he felt strongly that every collaboration had to be borne up by a common enthusiasm; only in a condition of complete harmony could he find the right inspiration. For that reason, Jørgen Kalckar relates, Bohr could become uncertain and depressed if during a joint task he noticed a decline in the enthusiasm of his collaborators. Sometimes when working out a difficult point in a paper, they might be unable to reach unanimity on the final formulation but in order to get on would accept Bohr's suggestion without really assenting to it in their hearts; then Bohr would stop his wandering around the table, regard someone gravely and say, "Now you must not get fed up with this. Do not think that I have become a complete idiot, but. . . ." And then he would go through the disputed argument from all aspects, unravel the threads and explain the finely modulated nuances, until he sensed that he had won over the sympathies of his young pupils. When we later read through what had been written, his face would light up in a big smile every time we reached the passages in question and he felt that they were now approved of in earnest. "There, you see," he would say, "I knew you would be happy with that."

For most people, collaborating with Bohr had the character of a teacher-pupil relationship, but of a unique type. Jørgen Kalckar was one of the young people who felt privileged at being part of Bohr's magic circle. He wrote: ". . . Bohr did not simply become the earnest teacher and father friend, but also, and in spite of the enormous superiority of his ability, position and experience, he became a playmate and co-conspirator, always ready to participate wholeheartedly in all joys and sorrows and to lead the way on mysterious expeditions rich in adventure." Kalcker relates how an unbroken series of lighthearted working days was dominated by the blackboard with its drawings and calculations, the chocolate box, the pile of drafts, outlines, and unanswered letters. The happy atmosphere of Tisvilde lends further elements to enrich the picture.

> Arranging the wood properly in the tiled stove of the little summerhouse was an art which had to be learned first, and the walks in the woods were adventures from which one returned rich in experiences. I wonder if anyone who has not known Bohr can appreciate the utter delight of picking and eating ripe black currants in the pouring rain? For me the word "summer" is always associated with the scent of wet leaves, the taste of black currants and the image of Bohr half-hidden in a bush in the middle of analyzing a difficult argument or getting toward the point of a complicated anecdote.

Piet Hein, who was connected with the Bohr Institute in his early youth, assisted with putting the finishing touches to some papers during another summer at Tisvilde. He described his role as that of a ping-pong partner during conversations in which Niels Bohr cleared his mind and polished his thoughts. The task was carried out in Bohr's still oil-lit little "work pavilion," and in the following account Piet Hein recalled one of Bohr's famous digressions in the midst of their labors:

> One evening, when it had gotten late, and the darkness outside had turned the windowpanes black, there was a pause after some observations on the need to use complementary but mutually exclusive wave- and particle-descriptions in order to account for the properties of light; then Niels Bohr returned from an interval of deep pensiveness with the words: "It is sort of . . . have you *ever* thought of . . . what . . . what it is that makes a ghost sinister?" The answer came after a long pause, in which both the darkness of the night and the light from the oil lamp seemed to grow, in a voice which, though Bohr's sounded oddly disembodied as through projected from a large room: "What is sinister . . . with a ghost . . . is that . . . one does *not* believe in it.
>
> "If we simply *did* believe in the ghost—well then it would only be *dangerous*, like a burglar or a wild animal can be. But the fact that at the same time we do *not* believe in it—that is what changes it from dangerous to *sinister*. It is these two complementary irreconcilable attitudes, existing simultaneously, that create the highly real phenomenon of eeriness."

Bohr's method of working has provided material for numerous anecdotes contributing to the creation of the Bohr legend, as has his capacity for work. Many of his collaborators, worn out by the strain of twisting and turning every sentence, then rewriting the final proofs into new works, never got over their astonishment at his appetite for work. The many similar stories testify to an intellectual and physical strength whose counterpart is difficult to find. The results of Bohr's unusual method of working were especially happy when inspiration accelerated the play with words and thoughts. But only a few outside the Institute knew of the periods of fatigue which Bohr had to suffer when wearisome planning and administrative duties weighed him down while at the same time new ideas were crowding into his consciousness. Then writing a paper or a lecture became a painful process for him, and he was distressed at being unable to write as much as he really wanted to. There are many who regret that he did not leave more writings for posterity, although they knew how much he was troubled by what was left undone. However, he kept most of his troubles to himself and only sought strength from Margrethe Bohr, who gave him all the support at her command.

14

The Institute Expands

From his earliest time in England, Bohr had looked forward to international cooperation in the world of science. He was not thinking of atomic physics alone, but of a richer interchange between the various sciences and across national boundaries—not only for the sake of research, but also with the aim of paving the way for greater international understanding. To that end he also dreamed of making his own institute an international center. But that required space. Just as monasteries have their monks' cells, so must theoreticians have their rooms for meditation. As well as rows of new small rooms there was a need for accommodation of experiments with ever-larger and more complicated instruments. So the Institute needed to expand almost before it was finished.

While Bohr was engrossed with these plans, one splendid offer after another came from abroad. Rutherford had already tried in 1918 to get him firmly attached to research in England so that together they could really "make physics boom." Now Rutherford had become Thomson's successor at the Cavendish Laboratory in Cambridge, and he tried yet again to get Bohr to join him. The approach came from the secretary of the Royal Society in London, James Jeans, who in 1923 forwarded an offer to Bohr of a professorship at Cambridge. This probably constituted the greatest temptation as far as Bohr was concerned, although Planck had already offered him membership of the Berlin Academy in 1920, a professorship with free research facilities and the same terms as Einstein had.

The offer from the Royal Society was followed up by a letter from Rutherford, who pressed Bohr earnestly to let himself be persuaded this time. Figures were put on the table too. He would more than double his annual income compared with what the University of Copenhagen could offer him, and he would be free of all the trouble of administering an institute and battling with government authorities over every little grant.

Bohr in the 1920s.

An interlude not unknown in Denmark now occurred. On the same day that Bohr received Jeans' offer, he also had received a "no" from the minister of education to an application, strongly supported by the faculty, for two lectureships, one of them for Kramers, who had been living on grants from Carlsberg, and who had already played a prominent role in Bohr's research. It was not Bohr himself who whispered a word or two into the minister's ear about the offer from England, but whoever it was, the minister suddenly retracted his refusal and decided to establish the two new posts, using the sort of words one uses when not wanting to lose face: ". . . so that the teaching can be carried out in a proper manner. . . ."

In his choice between Cambridge and Copenhagen there was now no doubt in Bohr's mind. He could not spurn the contributions made not only by the public sector but also from private sources in order to give the Institute a roof; and at the same time he emphasized that he felt himself inseparably linked to Danish culture.

Immediately after this Bohr was invited to give lectures at a large number of universities in the United States, and he was received everywhere with enthusiasm. There were many who expressed the view that American physicists felt themselves to be lagging behind Europe in the field of theoretical physics. Several new and tempting offers which followed in the wake of the tour showed that these were not empty words. A professorship would be established in Chicago if Bohr would only suggest what salary could tempt him. And from the Franklin Institute in Philadelphia came an offer of a professorship with a salary four times more than Bohr's current salary in Copenhagen, and they were also ready to appoint George de Hevesy as a colleague for him. Bohr declined with thanks and referred again to the trust placed in him at home.

Back in Denmark, the number of visiting physicists increased. Five came in the first year and ten in 1923, the year Bohr visited the United States. The next year 15 visitors were competing for space with the Institute's first staff of colleagues—Hevesy, Kramers, Frank, H. M. Hansen, J. C. Jacobsen, Svein Rosseland—and also Bohr, who was soon near to being banished from his apartment on the first floor, while Betty Schultz and Holder Olsen, the legendary chief technician, did everything they could to help all of them.

After the young American Erik Jette had spent half a year with Bohr, he wrote on his return to the United States: "In spite of our 'oh so famous' masses of money and our equipment second to none, very little research is done here to compare to what is going on in Europe." From its vast resources could the United States spare a little something for European research in return for the inspiration coming from Europe? The question had already become topical the year before Bohr traveled to the United States. When in New York H. M. Hansen had met Christen Lundsgaard, a Danish physician affiliated with the Hospital of the Rockefeller Institute for Medical Research, and told him of efforts to interest the Rockefeller Foundation in supporting international research. After a rapid exchange of letters with Bohr, Lundsgaard made an application on Bohr's behalf to Dr. Wickliffe Rose, president of the International Education Board (IEB), which John D. Rockefeller, Jr. had set up "for the advancement of education all over the world."

Aage Berlème, who also happened to be in New York just then, played a role once again on behalf of the Bohr Institute. Bohr sent an outline for an application to Lundsgaard and thought that he might ask for $20,000, but Berlème suggested leaving the space for the amount blank for Lundsgaard to decide. And Lundsgaard, more realistically, wrote in $40,000.

Since Bohr would soon be coming to the United States, Wickliffe Rose invited him for a talk. This took place on November 5, 1923, and on November 21 the International Education Board announced that $40,000 (250,000 Danish kroner at that time) had been granted for the expansion of the Bohr Institute. This was the first of many Rockefeller grants to Danish scientific research. A contact of enormous significance had been made.

The grant was made on the condition that the Danish government would assume all other expenses in connection with the expansion. First of all Bohr consulted his father's old friend Harald Høffding, the occupant of the Carlsberg honorary residence, who wasted no time before discussing the expansion with Jens Jensen, the mayor of Copenhagen. Jensen accepted an invitation for a cup of tea at the Bohr Institute, remarking afterwards, "This will probably be an expensive cup of tea for the city." Shortly afterwards the city donated 1400 square meters of land for the expansion, doubling the Institute's area.

In his early plans Bohr had considered enlarging the building by ten rooms. But before the IEB grant and the land offer had been confirmed, the pressure from outside was so great that at last the architect proposed erecting two entirely new buildings—a laboratory annex and a house for the Bohr family—whose former apartment could then be taken over for laboratories.

As word of all these exciting new developments got out, the Institute became population with the public at large. When a nonscientific assistant was needed to look after the large complex of buildings, boilers, and gardens, there were no fewer than 227 applicants, ranging in age from twenty to sixty and from widely varying occupations. One was a dairyman and another an organ builder. The one selected was an am-

Bohr is breaking ground for the 1935 expansion of the Institute. Fourth from the left in the first row is Bohr's aunt, Hanna Adler.

ateur actor, which meant he nourished a certain degree of egoism. However, he was also an outstanding carpenter, and therefore the fact that he was also a considerable tyrant toward those whom he found himself able to lean on tended to be ignored. Bohr's sons suffered from this particularly, although Bohr was glad that they got a practical grounding in the workshop, just as he himself had received in his father's laboratory.

Also in these early years there came a stream of letters from non-physicists with good ideas for Bohr's understanding of atoms or with requests for explanations of this or that point of atomic theory. As a rule Bohr answered letters pleasantly with a reference to a popular book which Kramers had written in collaboration with Helge Holst, the librarian of the Technical University. This book was called *The Atom and the Bohr Theory of its Structure*. The book achieved rapid success and was translated into various languages—with a foreward by Rutherford in the English edition. Undoubtedly the extensive discussion in the press of Bohr's Nobel Prize, and more recently the large grant from the United States, were what lay behind this popularity.

The International Education Board grant to Bohr was the first given to any scientific institution and before the International Education Board was abolished and merged with the Rockefeller Foundation in 1938, these two bodies together had granted large sums of money to a total of seven Danish scientific institutions. The biggest combined grant of 1.8 million kroner was given to August Krogh, the zoophysiologist and Nobel Prize winner, for the large institute-complex built for the Zoophysiological Laboratory and Medical-Physiological Laboratory in Copenhagen. August Krogh had started his scientific career with Christian Bohr, and the Zoophysiological Laboratory was the scene of his later collaboration with Niels Bohr in the field of radioactive isotopes.

Apart from the money for the Bohr Institute, the International Education Board also granted stipends for the exchange of physicists between the USA and Europe. In the Institute's first ten years, no fewer than 15 guests came on IEB stipends alone. Others were financed by the newly-established Rask-Ørsted Foundation and the Carlsberg Foundation, which also made a grant to the experimental physicist J. C. Jacobsen, until the Ministry assented to his permanent appointment in conjunction with the expansion program.

What kind of relationship did Bohr have with his students? We may recall the weight which he attached at the inauguration of the Institute to the task of initiating younger people into the discoveries of science and the significance he saw in the new ideas emanating from the young. There is testimony to so many other aspects of Bohr's achievement, but few—if any—accounts are to be found of his spending time with his students. However, Bengt Strömgren remembers the very earliest days

Hevesy and Bohr by the high voltage apparatus of the Institute in 1936.

of the Institute. Bohr did not give many lectures. He had many good intentions at the beginning of term, but time never sufficed. Nevertheless Strömgren has a clear recollection of the brilliant delivery of the lectures Bohr did give. One is inclined to forget that Bohr was also a university teacher, but Strömgren, who is one of the very few left today who experienced him in this role, recalls that his lectures were clear and pedagogically well suited, so they inevitably had an inspiring effect. Strömgren remembers especially the student seminars held by Kramers, H. M. Hansen, and Bohr, who gave detailed commentaries which did much to interest the young people. Bohr also followed each individual student all the way through his studies. When Strömgren was about to take his master's degree examination, with written and oral tests in physics, he was called in beforehand to Bohr, who spent half an hour explaining the most important points in preparing for it—only to end up by drifting away into distant thoughts. "Finally he said, 'The most important,' and put his hands over his face in order to concentrate properly—but nothing else came . . . and I didn't ask."

While the expansion of the Institute was going on and quantum mechanics was demanding his major attention and inspiration, Niels Bohr also undertook other important cultural tasks between his travels. The Danish National Museum had always inspired him, and from Margrethe's brother, Poul Nørlund, who later became the museum's director, he had some idea of the awful conditions in which the museum's collections were housed. Bohr saw the absurdity of the fact that the accommodation problem was hindering the museum in its great task of educating the Danish people about their country's past. So in 1925 he joined a committee to raise the funds required for a new museum by public subscription. A sum of two and one-half million kroner was collected from more than 200,000 contributors, and the government supplemented this with the necessary means for the restoration and adaptation of Prinsens Palæ ("the Prince's Palace"), the Museum's premises in Copenhagen, and for the construction of a new three-story building behind the Palace which was finally fully equipped and ready for inauguration in 1938. Bohr sat on the committee along with Harald Høffding, Knud Rasmussen, Vilhelm Thomsen, and H. N. Andersen, and it was by no means always an easy job. There was much disagreement over where the museum should be located. This occasioned fierce debate, but Bohr was the intermediary and the spokesman for its remaining at its old location.

Bohr's friendship with Ole Chievitz also led him on to the board of directors of the Danish Radium Foundation, and when the Finsen Institute, celebrated in the field of cancer treatment, was short of money for exploiting the new possibilities of treatment with radium, Bohr intervened as president of the Danish National Association for the Fight Against Cancer. This was not merely an honorary post: on the contrary, it involved many weighty duties. Bohr participated in the administration, and there is much testimony to the ingenuity with which he contributed to the National Association's early success.

15

The Nobel Prize

In 1917, the year after Bohr became a professor at the University of Copenhagen, he was elected to The Royal Danish Academy of Sciences. Ten proposers based the nomination on his series of pioneering works "which are of quite fundamental significance for the further development of both physics and chemistry." Bohr's admission took place during the presidency of the great Danish philologist Vilhelm Thomsen and only four years after Bohr's presentation of the theory of the atom. If the faculty of the University of Copenhagen had been hesitant, (see Chapter 11), the Academy of Sciences was quick to make up its mind. It was also to publish many of Bohr's later papers and a good many others written by both Danish and foreign colleagues at the Institute.

From this time on, honors followed swiftly. In 1922, the year after the inauguration of the Institute, Niels Bohr, then aged thirty-seven, was awarded the Nobel Prize in Physics. This was the fifth Nobel Prize awarded to a Dane and the first to a Danish physicist. He received the medal from the King of Sweden on December 10, 1922, who said simply: "For your work in studying the structure of the atom and the radiation originating from it."

At the ceremony, Svante Arrhenius of the Nobel Committee described the significance of Bohr's work, and during the banquet that followed, in a brief speech Bohr underlined the importance of international scientific cooperation, saying,

> It is especially natural for me to call to mind the emphasis on the international character of science on which Alfred Nobel's great foundation is based. This is very obvious to me, because the small contribution that I have had the good fortune to make to the development of physical science, has consisted in joining together contributions to our knowledge of nature which we owe to investigators of various nations, who have built on widely different scientific traditions.

He added, "That it has been my undeserved good fortune to be a connecting link at a stage of this development is only one piece of evidence among many of the fruitfulness, in the world of science, of the closest possible intercommunication of research work developing under different human conditions.''

Students at Cambridge celebrated Bohr's Nobel Prize that same evening by proposing a happy-go-lucky toast to ''the electron, which cannot be of any use at all.''

Einstein too received his Nobel Prize at the same time as Bohr. Not that they shared it, but the prize in physics had not been awarded in 1921, which was why two prizes coincided in time. This afforded Bohr the occasion for sending Einstein a letter in which he declared that it was the greatest joy and honor for him to receive the prize simultaneously with Einstein, but at the same time he emphasized the relief he felt that Einstein had been awarded the prize before him. Einstein thanked Bohr for his letter and wrote that he could say without exaggeration that the letter had pleased him as much as the prize itself. ''I find especially charming your fear that you might have received the prize before me—this is truly Bohrian.''

More underlies these letters than is immediately revealed. In Bohr's view it was self-evident that Einstein should have had the Nobel Prize for the theory of relativity long since, but Einstein's theory was still regarded as heresy in certain philosophical circles, and this was why the Nobel committee carefully avoided specifying the theory among

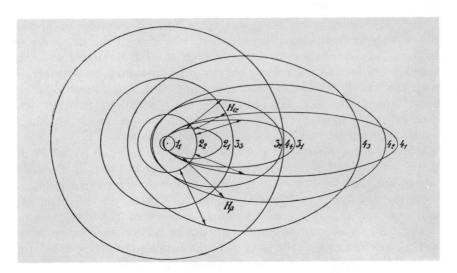

One of the elegant figures with which Bohr illustrated motion in the stationary states in his Nobel lecture. The figure indicates relative sizes and shapes of electron orbits.

the reasons for the eventual award, which mention only Einstein's demonstration of the photoelectric effect and his general work in theoretical physics.

Einstein did not take part in the ceremony in Stockholm, but during a world tour the same year he lectured in Gothenburg and then traveled to Copenhagen. Bohr met him at the railway station, and together they took the streetcar to go to the home of Bohr's mother, where he was staying while his quarters at the new Institute were being finished. On the tape recorded at Tisvilde in 1962, Bohr himself has related how he forgot that they were to get off at the stop in Bredgade, so that they rode all the way to the terminus in Hellerup. On the way back, they again forgot to get off at Bredgade. "Einstein was not any more practical than I was." Still engrossed in the problems of the theory of cognition, they continued the discussion going back and forth for many hours. "What people thought about us, I do not know." The same thing happened again on the Number 3 streetcar, when Einstein came to visit the Institute.

George de Hevesy comes into the picture again during the events surrounding the Nobel Prize. His and Coster's discovery of the element hafnium was not only an elegant confirmation of Bohr's theory of the elements, but has also stood ever since as a great achievement both in physics and chemistry, and it now became the first scene of a drama.

For almost every scientist who makes a discovery great or small, it is vital to establish that he or she did so first. More than vanity is involved, for it is also a question of one's reputation in the scientific world. The history of science offers many examples both of competition and of bitter disagreement over precedence. In the case of the discovery of hafnium, both aspects came into the picture, and the drama was triggered, in as arresting a manner as could be imagined, in connection with the festivities attending the award of Bohr's Nobel Prize in Stockholm. Two Frenchmen, George Urbain and Alexandre Dauvillier, had claimed earlier to have found this element among the rare earths, which would have meant that Bohr was mistaken. What now?

A little before Bohr went to Stockholm to receive the Nobel Prize, Hevesy and Coster were very close to the result of the crucial experiment, but they were not quite finished. However, on the evening of the same day that Bohr received the medal, Coster was able at last to telephone and report the certain proof that element 72 had been found in the mineral zirconium. And while Coster was on the line to Bohr, Hevesy was jumping on the train in Copenhagen in the hope of getting to Stockholm in time for Bohr's Nobel lecture which was to be given the next day. He managed it, and when Bohr made the announcement about number 72, Hevesy was truly moved. Everyone present knew about the claim of the two Frenchmen. The hall was buzzing, and the news spread quickly. Matters were not improved when Alexander Scott, a leading English chemist, also alleged that it was really he who had come first. Sometime earlier he had found an unknown substance in black sand from New Zealand, which he now—after he heard the announcement from Stockholm—interpreted as the same substance demonstrated by Hevesy and Coster, so that he considered the honor should belong to him.

The priority battle was conducted in the scientific periodicals and was also brought to the attention of the public through an article in the London *Times*. That newspaper wrote: "Science is and should undoubtedly be international, but it is gratifying that this chemical achievement, the most important since Sir William Ramsay isolated helium in 1895, turned out to have been carried out by a British chemist in a laboratory in London." Rutherford sent the article to Bohr with the comment: "We need pay no attention to such irresponsible utterances," and later on Rutherford summed matters up this way: "To continue the discussion is almost as meaningless as flogging a dead horse."

However, after Scott read Hevesy and Coster's paper, he quickly withdrew his claim, whereas the Frenchmen stubbornly stood by their assertions and demanded that the name hafnium be deleted from scientific literature. Their unrelenting stand was undoubtedly the reason why the Nobel committee hesitated to award a Nobel Prize to Hevesy and Coster even though a clear recommendation existed. This was the only lasting concern that Hevesy felt about the whole affair. The name hafnium has become permanent and provides the definitive answer to the question of who found element number 72 first. But even when Hevesy received the Nobel Prize twenty years later for his method of using radioactive isotopes in living organisms, it remained a disappointment to him that he was passed over on the earlier occasion.

After he had received the Nobel Prize, Bohr was asked if he would accept the appointment of Knight of the Danish Order of Dannebrog. It had always been difficult for him to say no, but now he was of two minds about it. He did not aspire to distinctions, but he realized that the requirements which had to be met to enable the Institute to keep pace with developments in the rest of the world called for every possible kind of support including visible symbols of honor. As usual, however, he had to consult someone. He went to his old friend Karsten Meyer, who was not only wise but also practical and had considerable insight into the norms of society. Meyer told Bohr that one cannot receive great awards without beginning with small ones, and he advised Bohr to say yes. And as it happened in 1947 that Bohr became the only civilian who held the Danish Order of the Elephant, although this too was one of the paradoxes of his life. This award is normally only given to members of royal families and presidents of foreign states. To appear decked out with decorations, ribbons, and stars was not a role which he enjoyed. But he carried it through, and the government's grants toward the steady furtherance of his research, and the weight attached to his words, confirmed Karsten Meyer's judgment. Later it also became Bohr's silent hope that the position that he attained in his homeland could help to advance those ideas of an open world for which he worked at every opportunity, when heads of state paid visits or other events brought him into contact with new and influential figures, whether they belonged in the wings or on the great political stage.

16

Heisenberg and Pauli

The 1920s were perhaps the happiest period for Niels Bohr, who saw everything blossoming around him. The resistance which his atomic theory had encountered in the early years had been overcome long ago, and Copenhagen became a Mecca for physicists from all over the world.

One of the future great men who became connected with the Institute during this period was Werner Heisenberg, who was to contribute quite decisively to the breakthrough in quantum mechanics; and the way in which their collaboration began says much about Bohr. Their first meeting took place in the summer of 1922 at the University of Göttingen, where Bohr was invited by the faculty of mathematics and natural sciences to give a series of lectures. Here, where the atomic theory had been received in 1913 just about as negatively as was possible, Bohr was now listened to as *the* great man. These lectures became so renowned that they were afterwards commonly known as the Bohr Festival. And there were so many celebrated figures from the world of physics among the listeners that Oskar Klein, in a subsequent discussion of "Die Bohr-Festspiele," had to refrain from naming the individuals concerned because "it would almost become the crew list of an Homeric ship." During the discussion after one of the lectures a twenty-year-old student ventured to put forward an objection, which Bohr thought could be refuted, but which appeared to touch on a point requiring further elucidation. The student was Werner Heisenberg, a pupil of Sommerfeld, and Sommerfeld had brought him to Göttingen because he had noticed Heisenberg's great interest in Bohr's theory.

After the discussion Bohr went over to Heisenberg and suggested that they should "go for a walk together" on the heaths of Hainberg outside Göttingen. "Going for a walk" with Bohr is an experience which many people, young and old, have found to be an inspiration for the rest of their life. Heisenberg has related how their conversation led them the length and breadth of Hainberg's forest-covered ridges. Toward the end of the conversation Bohr invited him to come to Copenhagen and Heisenberg agreed.

Thus in 1923 Heisenberg arrived in Copenhagen for his first visit, and in the beginning he was "thrown into a condition of deep depression." He could not express himself in any of the languages which the others spoke. It appeared to him that they were all far more familiar with the atomic theory than he was, and he felt that they were superior to him in their familiarity with the culture and poetry of many countries. They all "played various musical instruments with consummate skill." But Heisenberg now revealed himself to be an excellent pianist. Bohr too was fond of music, but in his own way: one thinks so well to Bach, he said, and while Heisenberg had typically slender pianist's hands, Bohr's were very powerful. Bohr shone only in his ability to beat time, which in fact was the only thing his teacher at school had permitted him to do during singing lessons.

Among the colleagues whom Heisenberg met were H. C. Urey from the United States, Svein Rosseland from Norway, Hevesy from Hungary, Kramers from Holland, and Wolfgang Pauli from Austria. Heisenberg and Pauli had known each other well beforehand, but everybody quickly made Heisenberg feel welcome, and like most of the others he too

A family outing with Heisenberg during his first visit to Copenhagen in 1923.

would learn excellent Danish. Bohr appreciated this skill in his colleagues because it was very helpful for teaching the Danish students.

Pauli was already Bohr's colleague at this time, and he made his mark on the Institute. No form of approval, wrote Rosenfeld, was appreciated more highly by the physicists, Bohr included, than Pauli's kindly nod, and Pauli himself was almost as devotedly attached to Bohr as a son to a father. Pauli acknowledged that he could not plumb as deeply as Bohr into the problem of complementarity, but he perceived the broad perspectives and the deeper harmony. It was probably he who understood the complementarity principle best.

Léon Rosenfeld, who also showed an early understanding of the complementarity concept and thereby entered upon a fruitful collaboration with Bohr, has given this comparison between Heisenberg and Pauli: "A marvelous combination of profound intuition and formal virtuosity inspired Heisenberg to brilliant, dazzling ideas. Pauli did not dazzle. Rather like Bohr, he placed the emphasis (sometimes heavily) on the logical side of problems, and his contribution was the fruit of thorough criticism rather than of imagination." Bohr for his part had the greatest respect for Pauli's criticism. He was amused by his wily and often sarcastic expressions. On one occasion a visitor to the Institute pronounced himself to be perhaps a little unimpressed. He justified himself by declaring loudly that it was as if disrespect was part of the spirit of the Bohr Institute; and Bohr replied with mild irony, "Yes, and we don't even take disrespect too seriously."

But although Bohr did not take Pauli's sallies seriously, he attached great weight to the ideas behind the jesting. A letter from Pauli was an event. Bohr would take it with him wherever the duties of the day called him, and he missed no opportunity of looking at it or showing it to anyone who was interested in the problem under debate. On the plea of preparing a draft of a reply he could keep an imaginary dialogue going for days, as though Pauli were actually sitting there in front of him and listening with his mischievous smile. Casimir relates that one day, however, a letter arrived from Pauli with some ideas about which Bohr could not immediately decide his position. So he asked Margrethe to write a nice letter to Pauli and say that "Niels will write on Monday." Three or four weeks later a further letter came from Pauli, this time addressed to Margrethe. It was very wise of Mrs. Bohr, wrote Pauli, that she had not said on *which* Monday Bohr would be writing. "Er soll sich aber keineswegs an Montag gebunden fühlen. Ein Brief an irgendeinen anderen Tagen geschrieben wäre mir genau so lieb." ("But he should not feel in any way committed to Monday. A letter written on any other day at all would be just as welcome to me.")

Bohr for his part was not always content merely to be amused by Pauli's playful attacks. He could retaliate, also in letter form, and then

Wolfgang Pauli whom Bohr called "the conscience of physics." (Courtesy of the Center for History of Physics, American Institute of Physics.)

his language became so light and free that it would hardly be recognized from the style of the much more compact dissertations. A letter of December 22, 1924 reveals the character of the friendship, although the contents are somewhat cryptic for us today:

> Dear Pauli,
> I cannot easily describe how welcome your paper was. We are all enthusiastic about the many new elegancies which you have brought to light. I do not need to put forward any general criticism, of course, since you yourself do it better than anyone else could when you characterize the whole thing in your letter as sheer lunacy. Neither do I believe, on the other hand, that with your customary impulse-comments you can lay more stress on the lunacy than we have done in discussions here even before we knew your final results. Although we are not blind to the possibility that the Lamor theorem's limited validity in the classical theory perhaps occupies a central place in the whole humbug, Heisenberg's conscience, whatever it might find difficult to endure, has not been made materially worse by your remarks on this point. Taken by and large the two varieties of lunacy stand in far too close a relation to the truth to be subject to criticism on isolated points. . . .

The special tone between them appears again in a letter from Pauli in August, 1928. He writes impatiently after coming to Copenhagen in order to discuss his latest paper: "Be so kind as to write where I can be from August 15 to 24, and also when you will be leaving your abominable country place." He emphasizes that he will not be annoyed if his visit will not be possible, "but I shall be annoyed if you do not write at all."

Pauli was a typical city and night-person, and Bohr did not take his reference to the Tisvilde house seriously, but wrote:

> Dear Pauli,
> I hope you have got the letter I wrote the other day, but after receiving the cards from Zurich testifying to your holiday spirit, I nevertheless hasten to reiterate that I am looking forward so much to your visit to Copenhagen. I am longing to chat with you about everything possible and hope to learn a lot. You are welcome to stay at the Institute as soon as it suits you. At present we are living in the despised Tisvilde but will go in to Copenhagen in a week's time. I would rather wait with the physics until you come. You will still find everything written from me to be "false" although I would rather say "one-sided."
>
> Your complementarily devoted
> Niels Bohr

17

The Clarification of
Quantum Mechanics

During Bohr and Heisenberg's very first conversations at Hainberg, Bohr had explained how he himself viewed the atomic theory. Ever since 1913 it had been crucial for Bohr to use everyday language to convey the clearest possible pictures of the structure of the atom in terms of the simple concept that the electrons revolve in orbits around the nucleus. But even Bohr doubted whether these conceptions could be sustained in the future when atomic theory would be described by a mathematical formalism—a formalism which, being based on Planck's quantum, would acquire the name of quantum mechanics. During the walk at Hainberg, Heisenberg was surprised by Bohr's doubts, which were in contrast to Sommerfeld's faith in the conception of orbits. The question for Bohr, however, was when the time would be ripe, when the physical concepts would be sufficiently well founded for the next step. When stationary states came into the picture, electrons were still in orbits.

This was certainly interesting to the astonished Heisenberg, who—with the abandonment of the orbital conception—was to bring mathematics to Bohr's theory. In 1925 he and Kramers worked closely together on laying mathematical foundations, and they were in constant discussion with Bohr, who continued trying for a physical interpretation. Here are Heisenberg's own words describing the framing of the problem:

> The central point in our discussions at that time was dispersion theory; i.e. the theory of the scattering of light on atoms. Kramers had just published a very important paper on this subject. Kramers' considerations should be extended to include the so called Raman-effect (scattering accompanied by a change of color of the light). Here it was obviously a question of guessing the correct mathematical formulae on the basis of analogies, for one could not derive them; at that time one had no basis for such calculations. It was very instructive for me to see how Bohr continued to try to advance through the physical interpretation of the formulae and thus to reach a decision,

while it was much more natural for me to use a formal mathematical view which in some sense was an aesthetic judgment. Fortunately, both methods led to the same result in the long run, and I tried to convince Bohr that this had to be so if the theory was to be simple and clear. But I noticed that mathematical clarity had in itself no virtue for Bohr. He feared that the formal mathematical structure would obscure the physical core of the problem, and in any case, he was convinced that a complete physical explanation should absolutely precede the mathematical formulation. I was perhaps, already at that point, more prepared than Bohr to leave the models and take the step over to mathematical abstraction. At any rate, I found in the formulae, which were the result of my collaboration with Kramers, a mathematics which in a certain sense worked automatically independently of all physical models. This mathematical scheme had for me a magical attraction, and I was fascinated by the thought that perhaps here could be seen the first threads of an enormous net of deep-set relations.

I was just as happy about the result of a discussion with Bohr and Kramers on the question of the polarization of fluorescent light. Bohr had written a draft to a short note on this question in connection with some experiments at Franck's institute, while, disregarding all pictures and models, I used my more formal viewpoint on Bohr's problem and reached quantitative results that went somewhat further than Bohr's work. I succeeded in convincing Bohr and Kramers of the correctness of my formulae, but when I again returned to Bohr's office after lunch, Bohr and Kramers had agreed that my formulae were wrong and tried to explain their viewpoint to me. This developed into a long and heated discussion, during which, as I recall, the necessity for detachment from the intuitive models was for the first time stated emphatically and declared to be the guiding principle in all future work. Bohr's way of thinking, which in history is perhaps most clearly represented by such figures as Faraday and Gibbs, enabled him to expose the core of the problem with inimitable clarity, but he hesitated to take the step into mathematical abstraction, though he did not speak against it. We finally concluded that the formulae were correct, and I felt that we had come a good bit closer to the atomic theory of the future.

After months of intensive work at the Institute, Heisenberg again gave lectures at Göttingen and from there went on a brief sick leave to the island of Helgoland in the North Sea. Here in the summer of 1925 he worked out the first outline of the theory of quantum mechanics. It represented for him the mathematical formulation of Bohr's correspondence principle and the quintessence of the conversations in Copenhagen. "I hoped that, by means of a mathematical method which for me was still new and very strange, I had found a way to the remarkable relations, which had already been glimpsed from time to time during discussions with Bohr and Kramers," he wrote modestly. Later on it became clear to others that his formulation represented a breakthrough with very few parallels in the history of physics. His new method became part of that history under the name of matrix mechanics.

For Bohr there was no doubt that Heisenberg's matrix mechanics was the decisive breakthrough toward the realization of a coherent quantum mechanics. He wrote to Rutherford on January 27, 1926: "In fact, due to the last work of Heisenberg prospects have with a stroke been realized, which although only vaguely grasped, have for a long time been the center of our wishes."

Together with Max Born and Pascual Jordan, Heisenberg continued to work on his mathematical formulation while he was lecturing again at Göttingen. Born and Jordan had already made vital progress in the mathematical analysis of the new mechanics, and independently of them, Paul A. M. Dirac had reached the same result at Cambridge. "In this way," Heisenberg wrote, "during the whole winter term we were fully occupied in opening the road to the newly claimed mathematical land and making it passable." Soon thereafter H. A. Kramers was appointed to a professorship in Holland, and Heisenberg took over his position in Copenhagen. Beginning in 1926 he became a co-worker at the Institute, "where, just as earlier, the daily conversations with Bohr formed the most important part of my scientific life."

At this time the Austrian physicist Erwin Schrödinger had further developed the wave and particle concept of wave mechanics, and he had been able to prove that it had the same mathematical validity as the newly developed theory of quantum mechanics. Bohr was enthusiastic about this development because it strengthened his confidence in the new mathematical formalism which could now be called quantum mechanics just as well as wave mechanics. According to the historian of science Thomas S. Kuhn, Bohr was now ready to consider the particle concept and the wave concept as two equally essential stones in the foundation of quantum theory.

In the late summer of 1926, Schrödinger was invited to give a lecture in Munich on his new wave theory. At first, his audience was very enthusiastic, until he suddenly began to interpret wave mechanics in a way that obviously conflicted with virtually all previous results. Schrödinger attempted to interpret "electron waves" heavy handedly as "actual" material waves and stationary states in the atom as "standing waves of electron shock" corresponding to standing air or sound waves in an organ pipe.

Heisenberg, who was present, put forward a number of objections, but without success. At this point Wilhelm Wien, the head of the Institute for Experimental Physics at the University of Munich, became critical of Heisenberg. Wien probably thought that Heisenberg was upset about Schrödinger's lecture and that all was now over for quantum mechanics. The difficulties that Heisenberg was raising with his objections would be disposed of by Schrödinger in short order.

When Bohr heard what Schrödinger had said, he reacted immediately, as he always did when a vital new problem arose. The episode must be described, because it shows once again Bohr's enormous power of persistence when he himself felt sure about something. As soon as Heisenberg had reported to Bohr about the meeting in Munich, Bohr invited Schrödinger to come to Copenhagen, and Heisenberg, who is our witness to the drama, attended their discussions. The showdown between Bohr and Schrödinger even started at the Copenhagen railway station, and it continued for several days from early morning until late at night.

> The discussions left me with a very strong impression of Bohr's personality. For though Bohr was an unusually considerate and obliging person, he was able in such a discussion, which concerned epistemological problems which he considered to be of vital importance, to insist fanatically and with almost terrifying relentlessness of complete clarity of all arguments. He would not give up, even after hours of struggling, before Schrödinger had admitted that this interpretation was insufficient, and could not even explain Planck's law. Every attempt from Schrödinger's side to get round this bitter result was slowly refuted point by point in infinitely laborious discussions.

Heisenberg goes on to relate that Schrödinger became ill, presumably from overexertion, and had to stay in bed as a guest in Bohr's home. While Margrethe Bohr was nursing him as best she could, Bohr himself scarcely left his bedside, and the sentence, "But Schrödinger, you must still admit, that. . . ." was constantly heard until at last Schrödinger exclaimed desperately, "If we still have to go on with this confounded quantum leaping, then I am sorry I ever had anything to do with atomic theory," to which Bohr replied, "But the rest of us are so thankful that you did, because you brought the theory a vital step further."

Despondently, Schrödinger left Copenhagen. His wave equation, which was able to explain the existence of stationary states in the atomic theory, remained as a brilliant contribution to physics, while his interpretation of the quantum theory, advanced too rashly using the classical theory as a model, was refuted.

But how did relations between Schrödinger and Bohr develop after such a rough passage of arms? Would they be able to work together again? It was not long before Schrödinger wrote Bohr several letters in which he thanked Bohr movingly for his cordial hospitality and also expressed gratitude for their unforgettable discussions. Bohr likewise endeavored, equally characteristically, to smooth things over later in a memorial lecture he gave for Rutherford. He included in his recollections of the events of those years an account of his conversations with Schrödinger that was formulated as a tribute to Schrödinger. It was issues that the battle was about, not personalities. Yet in one way there was also good reason for Bohr to take a generous stance, because the debate with Schrödinger did contribute further to clarifying Bohr's and Heisenberg's thoughts and paved the way for the uncertainty re-

Erwin Schrödinger and Paul A. M. Dirac.

lationships and the principle of complementarity, which brings us close to the completion of the entire edifice.

After Schrödinger had left, the paradox of wave and particle concepts was immediately tackled again in Copenhagen. Heisenberg continued to view quantum mechanics from a mathematical viewpoint. He demonstrated the uncertainty relationship between the quantities which determine the position of the electron in space and time and those which characterize its dynamic properties. This again gave Bohr the key to a precise analysis of the complementarity relationship, which would finally complete the efforts of the 1920s.

In order to understand Heisenberg's uncertainty principle and Bohr's interpretation of it, we must first consider in terms of classical physics how waves behave when they are forced to pass through a narrow aperture whose dimensions are not much larger than the wavelength itself. Light waves which fall at right angles on a plate with a small aperture will normally form a sharply defined spot the size of the aperture on a screen placed behind it. But this applies only when the aperture is large in relation to the wavelength of the light. If the aperture is now made smaller and smaller, down to a small fraction of a millimeter, the spot will gradually grow in size. The smaller the aperture becomes, the more strongly the light is deflected by the edges of the aperture. The same thing will happen with electrons, which because of their wave-like properties, will be deflected like light waves around the edges of a tiny aperture through which they are sent; a photographic plate placed behind it will be darkened by a spot that grows bigger as the aperture is made smaller.

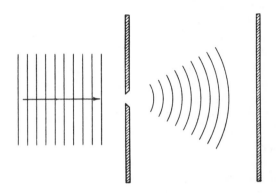

If we imagine an experiment in which we reduce the number of electrons so that we can follow what happens to each individual electron passing through the aperture, we shall find that, within the deflection patch, an electron falls now on one spot, now on another. Our "experiment" will show that we cannot say in advance where the electrons will strike other than that they must fall within the deflection patch. For the individual electron, in other words, there will be an uncertainty, not calculable in advance, of its motion after passing through the aperture. Since all the electrons are sent through the aperture with the same velocity, this thought-experiment illustrates the impossibility of simultaneously determining both an electron's velocity and location with arbitrary great precision.

If we make the aperture in the screen smaller, we reduce the precision of our knowledge of the direction of velocity. But if the aperture is made so large that it produces almost no deflection, this means, conversely, that the direction of the electron's velocity after passage is fixed with great precision, but on the other hand the uncertainty of determining its location becomes great as one cannot say through which point of the aperture the electron has passed, but only that it has gone through at some point or other.

The uncertainty of an electron's location is thus inversely proportional to the uncertainty of its velocity. The one becomes larger as the other is made smaller, and vice versa. Bohr elaborated this uncertainty relationship and applied the term complementarity to the phenomenon described by the concepts of velocity and location, because in certain respects they exclude each other but nevertheless each individually expresses essential aspects of particle behavior. But it will help us to determine the respective roles of Bohr and Heisenberg correctly if we locate and date the events prior to this point. At the end of February, 1927, Bohr went to Norway on a skiing holiday and Heisenberg, who was left alone in Copenhagen, could give his thoughts free rein. He decided to make the uncertainty relationship the central point of his interpretation, and it occurred to him to try, with the help of an imaginary γ-ray microscope, to investigate the possibility of a determination of electron location. After a fairly short time he sent a draft of a paper to Pauli, who soon replied in positive terms.

In Norway in the meantime Bohr had been steeping himself in the complementarity concept, which would make it possible to take the dualism between the wave and particle concepts as the starting point for his interpretation. On returning home, therefore, Bohr was nettled that Heisenberg had not taken dualism as the starting point. But after some weeks of discussion, "which were not without tensions," they were able to conclude, with the assistance of Oskar Klein, that the uncertainty relationship was merely an expression of the general complementarity relationship. Heisenberg could then send his revised paper to be printed, while Bohr revised a publication on the concept of complementarity.

Bohr and Max Planck in 1930 at the Institute.

Just as Bohr, in his letter to Rutherford, had emphasized so clearly Heisenberg's breakthrough with his new mathematical formalism, so did Heisenberg for his part stress Bohr's contribution. Heisenberg wrote afterwards quite without reservation: "We owe this clarification of the physical principles of quantum theory to Bohr, who through his general philosophical approach toward the problem of reality, not only created the intellectual climate (for his colleagues too) in which an understanding of this new and extraordinary system of relationships could grow, but also, via his own contribution, was the first to arrive at a complete and clear perception of the quantum theory's place in the broader scheme of things."

Bohr maintained that just as it is only the quantum effect that keeps the electron and the atomic nucleus from forming an infinitesimally small neutral particle, the quantum effect also requires the abandonment of the causal connection between physical phenomena—previously the very basis of all descriptions of nature. Any attempt to analyze this individuality with the aid of the methods of classical physics will fail because of the impossibility of distinguishing between the independent behavior of atomic particles and their interaction with the

A meeting at the Institute in 1930. From the left in the front row: Klein, Bohr, Heisenberg, Pauli, Gamow, Landau, and Kramers. Perhaps the trumpet in front of Heisenberg and the cannon in front of Pauli were used to express either approval and disapproval during discussions.

Heisenberg and Bohr in the lunchroom at the Institute in 1937.

instruments of analysis used. To determine where the electrons in an atom are located at a given moment will unavoidably involve an exchange of quantities of motion and energy between the atom and the apparatus with which the phenomenon is being observed. This exchange will make it impossible for the scientist to locate the individual electrons in the atom both spatially and temporally. Thus the different quantum phenomena exclude each other under experimental conditions, which is not to say that they are contradictory, but rather that they are complementary. There is no question at all of abandoning further analysis of atomic phenomena. Quite the reverse; the complementarity principle offers the possibility of a wide range of experiments which cannot be performed at all using the methods of classical physics.

Soon thereafter Paul Dirac finally succeeded in overcoming the remaining difficulties. He devised an equation which took account of certain corrections contingent on the theory of relativity. Some Dutch physicists had propounded the theory that all electrons have the property known as spin. They revolve on their own axes like small tops. Now Dirac's equation also gave the number of stationary solutions which the spin of the electrons could be expected to involve. Dirac's theory accounted in every detail for the interaction between the components

Heisenberg and his wife with Bohr in 1937.

of an atom and so completed the theoretical treatment of the mechanics of atoms.

Dirac's theory of the electron brought to a conclusion the heroic years during which an entire generation of theoretical physicists from many lands, led by the pioneers Heisenberg, Pauli, Dirac, with Bohr at the center, collaborated selflessly to make their way, step by step, to the understanding of quantum mechanics.

Rutherford was to write later: "This was in truth a triumph of mind over matter, or rather—over the rays. Considering the extraordinary complexity of even a single spectrum, I thought, before Bohr's contribution, that it would require centuries to get to the bottom of this complex, and yet, led by Bohr's thoughts, this was achieved in a little less than a decade."

The solution to the problem of atomic theory, coming at a point where Newtonian mechanics had failed, took the vast majority of physicists completely by surprise, but Bohr himself was better prepared. This is best shown by reporting on a conversation which took place on Bohr's boat that summer. Heisenberg, who was among the guests, relates:

Bohr was full of the new interpretation of the quantum theory, and as the boat, without much help from us, was carrying us southward at full sail in the sunshine, there was ample opportunity for discussing this scientific event and for philosopical reflections on the essence of the atomic theory. Bohr began talking about the difficulties of language, about the limitation of all our means of expression, which must be allowed for from the outset if one wants to engage in science at all; and he explained how gratifying it was that this limitation had already been demonstrated in a lucid mathematical way in the foundations of the atomic theory. Then one of his friends said dryly, "But Niels, this is really nothing new: you were telling us exactly the same thing when we were young."

Thus Bohr's special qualifications for grasping these revolutionary new conceptions were foreshadowed from the days of his youth by his indomitable drive to uncover the dual nature of existence.

18

Electromagnetism

The theory of quantum mechanics enables us to see the forces that are at work upon the particles in the atom. But the theory was still incomplete with regard to electromagnetism, the theory of the spatial distribution of forces in the form of electrical and magnetic fields. In their enthusiasm for the quantum mechanics, many physicists believed that once electrodynamics as the framework of electromagnetism had been explained, it would only be a short step to the understanding of the atomic nucleus, after which physics would be a closed chapter in the history of science. Bohr held quite a different view, however.

The description of quanta had given a consistent description of the behavior of atomic particles within the limits where their velocities are much less than that of light, and where, therefore, the effects of the special theory of relativity can be ignored. Dirac's relativistic electron theory (of 1928) was the first step toward the development of a relativistic quantum theory. In order to realize this project, however, a quantum description of the electromagnetic field itself would be needed. This was indeed a very important task because the wave particle duality of light was the oldest of the paradoxes of quantum physics.

Although Heisenberg and Pauli had made several important contributions, Bohr could still see many questions that were obscure and he was anxious for further elucidation of certain aspects of quantum mechanics. During Heisenberg's and Pauli's initial work on electrodynamics, a crisis arose which led to further progress. The Russian physicist Lev Landau, who had spent a year at Bohr's Institute, published an article in collaboration with the German physicist Rudolf Peierls in which they suggested that the concept of electrical and magnetic fields itself must be abandoned within the framework of the quantum theory because of the occurrence of random fluctuations. During his stay in Copenhagen Landau's exchanges of ideas with Bohr were as likely to be hilarious as profound. They could become so involved in their discussions that nothing else affected them. One day they were arguing at the blackboard, when suddenly Landau lay down on the floor by the lectern and continued to gesticulate in order to illustrate his argument, while Bohr leaned over him intently arguing the opposite. They themselves were not at all aware of the comedy of the incident.

Both Bohr and Pauli, who had also read proofs of Landau's and Peierls' paper, were sceptical about some of the key arguments. However, at that time, Bohr was not sufficiently familiar with Heisenberg-Pauli's formal description of quantum fields, so it became Rosenfeld's task, as he modestly described his contribution, to initiate Bohr into the mathematical aspect of the problems. As soon as Rosenfeld had done so, Bohr began to work on these new problems.

We have reached 1931. For countless hours over a period of two years Bohr and Rosenfeld discussed and analyzed the epistemological problems confronting them. They demonstrated that Landau and Peierls were wrong and, as so often before, this clearing up of a misapprehension led Bohr on to new advances. If the atomic theory was Bohr's first great achievement and the periodical system of the elements his second, he now rounded off his third major achievement—his contributions to quantum mechanics—with the analysis of field measurements in quantum electrodynamics. He finished the paper on this subject in 1933. But new challenges presented themselves. Heisenberg, who had doubts at first about the calculations, moved during a visit to Copenhagen from "passionate unbelief to passionate enthusiasm." Pauli once again urged Bohr to keep going in order to try and resolve the remaining questions.

"As Pauli correctly pointed out," wrote Rosenfeld,

Bohr was the only one to master the peculiar methods required for such analyses of ideal measurements; even to this day, no physicist can boast of approaching Bohr's virtuosity in this respect. We did yield to Pauli's exhortations; and although this new investigation suffered many interruptions, and only reached the stage of publication in 1952, it did not take us very long to complete a first survey of the ground, which led us to conclusions rather similar to those we had obtained in electrodynamics. Pauli received these provisional results with expressions of great satisfaction, tempered by the fear (justified by the event) that the further course of the work would be slow. "However," he added in his usual sarcastic fashion, "since you have managed to publish the work on the electromagnetic field, it has become impossible to state with certainty that the other work will never be published." This mild derision, of course, was only a cloak for really deep feelings of grateful admiration; Pauli did also tell Bohr, at that time, that the analysis of the measurability of electromagnetic fields had meant a great deal to him, by deepening his understanding of quantum theory and strengthening his faith in the soundness of its foundations.

19

The Honorary Residence,
Old Carlsberg

Just at the time when Bohr began to work on electromagnetism, the Royal Danish Academy of Sciences and Letters, following the recommendation of the Carlsberg Foundation, honored Niels Bohr by offering him the honorary residence, Old Carlsberg, in Copenhagen. Harald Høffding, who was the first occupant after the Jacobsen family, died in 1931. The will of the founder of the Carlsberg Brewery, J. C. Jacobsen,

Margrethe and Niels Bohr outside the garden entrance to the honorary residence in 1954.

Bohr at the garden entrance of the honorary residence in 1935.

A corner of Niels Bohr's study in the honorary residence, with paintings (top row, left to right) of Christian Bohr, Harald Bohr, and Harald Høffding. Under the painting of Christian Bohr is a portrait of Niels' mother Ellen Bohr. In the corner is the cabinet where the chocolate was kept, and a carved toy monkey hangs from the chandelier.

had provided that his home, the building called Old Carlsberg, should be made over as a gratis residence for life to be occupied by a man or woman who deserved to be honored by Denmark because of his or her activities in science, literature, art, or some other field. This provision took effect after the death of his widow and of his son, Carl Jacobsen.

Bohr had often visited Harald Høffding during the years when the latter had lived at the residence, and he was familiar with the building,

Margrethe Bohr's room in the honorary residence.

In Bohr's favorite sofa corner at Old Carlsberg in about 1960. The painting on the wall above Margrethe Bohr is of their son Christian.

A reception in the Pompeii salon at the honorary residence in the 1950s.

which J. C. Jacobsen had had built in the Roman style. Bohr had undeniably been accustomed to living quarters on the grand scale, from the elegant mansion on Ved Stranden where he was born, to the Academy of Surgery in Bredgade where he grew up, and the summer home in the country, Nærumgaard. Therefore he was quite up to the task, along with Margrethe, of exploiting the spacious setting by filling the walls with art old and new, arranged with the good taste of generations—but above all by making Aeresboligen, the honorary residence, into a rendezvous for all the family's Danish and foreign friends. Scientists, artists, politicians, and heads of state were soon to imbue it with life at large social gatherings which, held in the garden during the summer and in the large room called the Pompeii salon during the winter, acquired a legendary reputation. Bohr's own favorite spots were the sofa corner in the small living room, where the family sat when they were by themselves, and the study, the little room with the blackboard, behind the Pompeii salon.

20

In Jest and in Earnest

The challenges of quantum mechanics made very heavy demands on everyone's powers of concentration, and there were periods when the Institute was charged with an atmosphere of latent tension. Such a condition demanded interludes of total relaxation, so the Institute became renowned for the frequent jokes and pranks that could erupt quite unexpectedly and in the midst of great seriousness.

As one way of relaxing tension, a trio consisting of the two Russians, Gamow and Landau, and the Dutchman Casimir, used to amuse themselves by going to the movies, preferably to B-movies. Now and then they succeeded in getting Bohr to go with them to see a cowboy film or even a gangster film. One day he accompanied them to an indescribably fatuous Tom Mix movie, which was made unforgettable for the trio, however, by Bohr's comments on it:

> That the villain runs off with the pretty girl is logical: it happens all the time. That the bridge collapses under their wagon is unlikely, but I am willing to accept it. That the heroine continues to hang over the precipice is more than improbable, but I will also go along with that. I am even willing to accept that Tom Mix comes riding past at that very instant, but that at the same time there should also be a person with a movie camera recording the entire story—that is more than I am willing to believe.

Bohr could certainly find an interesting point in almost every little incident. For example, he also became celebrated for a theory on the advantage of shooting in self-defense versus drawing first. He advanced the theory one evening when they had been watching a gangster film in which the hero shot down every gangster who tried to shoot him. Bohr considered the psychological reason for this success to be that every action resulting from a definite decision that has to be formed will be carried out more slowly than an action which is a response to an external impulse. If a gangster decides to pull out his revolver in order to shoot the hero, then his action is slow enough for the hero,

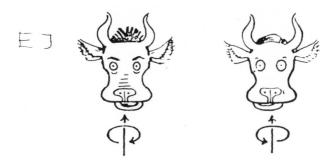

The need for relaxation from the demands made by quantum mechanics on the concentration could lead into quite unexpected paths. One summer's day in 1927 Pascual Jordan and Ralph Kronig were watching cows lying in the fields chewing their cuds. This resulted in a paper published in Nature *in 1927 in which they concluded that nearly as many cows rotated their jaws clockwise as counterclockwise.*

who sees what is about to happen and realizes that he must act instantly in order to save his life, to draw his own revolver faster and shoot first.

The other three cinemagoers would not accept this without further proof, so some toy pistols were bought in order to test Bohr's theory. All four were equipped with a pistol, the doubters being the villains while Bohr was the hero. Cap pistols were used so that the shots could be heard clearly, and to everyone's astonishment Bohr was always able to shoot first.

According to Dirac, Bohr later gave the theory a general form. It no longer centered upon a hero and a number of gangsters but on two bandits—two armed bandits facing each other, who both want to shoot but are unable to do anything but talk, because they both know that the one who decides to draw first will be killed.

On Bohr's decennial birthdays a humorous paper called the "Journal of Jocular Physics" was produced, which everyone at the Institute helped write in which everyone poked fun at everyone else. For Bohr's fiftieth birthday Hendrik Casimir wrote a poem about shooting first. Here are the last 12 of the 32 lines of verse of Casimir's own translation into English:

We, arrogant youngsters, we ventured to doubt
This thesis of Bohr and we wished to find out
If really a deep psychological facet
Of criminal law does make virtue an asset.
So the three of us went to the center of town
And there at a gunshop spent many a crown
On pistols and lead, and now Bohr had to prove
That in fact the defendant is quickest to move.

Bohr accepted the challenge without ever a frown;
He drew when we drew . . . and shot each of us down.

This tale has a moral, but we knew it before:
It's foolish to question the wisdom of Bohr.

The last line was paraphrased and often used at the Institute when doubt
arose: "Bohr always wins."

The spirit of the Institute embraced another style of jest as well. There
are some things which are so serious that we can only joke about them,
Bohr used to say. He would emphasize this with an aphorism of which
he was very fond, concerning two kinds of truths, "Profound truth is
recognized by the fact that the opposite is also profound truth, in contrast to trivialities where opposite are obviously absurd." He added
that, "in a new area of experience the progression is frequently one in
which step by step we are bringing order out of chaos. But the intermediate stages, where one falls back on profound truths, are often the
most exciting, because the imagination is constantly encouraged to seek
a firmer grip." Here he was faced with the question of whether it is
possible at all to say what truth is, and to this he answered, "At first at
any rate one might be tempted to say that the truth is something that
one can attempt to doubt. By great exertions one may then gradually
come to recognize that at least some part of one's doubt was unwar-
ranted." In this he was adumbrating his entire method of working, and
from this it could also be understood what anguish it could be for him
to complete even the smallest manuscript. One day at the Institute when
they were trying to find the contrary term to "truth" and no one really
wanted to be so trite as to suggest the most obvious word, Bohr surprised
them by exclaiming, "It is clarity." By this he did not mean to place
clarity and truth in opposition to each other, but rather to suggest that
clarity can have a form which excludes the nuances of the complete
truth.

Among Bohr's favorite stories was the anecdote of Socrates and the
Sophist. Socrates is standing in the market in Athens, talking to some
young people, and the Sophist, who has just returned home from a
journey, goes over to him and says, "Socrates, are you still standing
there saying the same about the same things?" To which Socrates answers, "Yes, but you who are so clever, I suppose you never say the
same about the same things?" Another one of Bohr's favorite stories is
very simple but expresses a multiplicity of meanings. It is the story of
the three Chinese philosophers tasting vinegar, which in China is called
the water of life. The first, Mencius, says, "It is sour." The second,
Confucius, says, "It is bitter." And Lao-tzu, the third, finds that "it is
fresh."

Everyone who came into contact with Bohr realized how eager he

always was to provide solace and encouragement, and he often found
inspiration in such simple stories. He was also very fond of telling the
story of Buddha, who was visited one day by an unhappy woman who
had lost her child and was heart-broken. Buddha said that perhaps he
could help her, but first she had to bring him a mustard seed grown
by a person who had never known sorrow. The woman departed, but
no matter how far she wandered and how many people she met, her
search was in vain, and she returned to Buddha and said that she understood his intention and had now found peace in her heart.

Bohr could be sharp enough in his verbal replies, but he disliked the
polemical form, and to avoid making a direct criticism, he would often
use a circumlocution. His modes of expression in such situations eventually became so well known that the moment he began to say the
familiar words it was at once clear that someone was in trouble. During
discussions at the Institute and in colloquia at which colleagues presented their work, upon occasion Bohr would pronounce the dreaded
words, "That is very, very interesting. . . ." and follow it with "but"—
whereupon the work just presented would be more or less annihilated.
Little by little Bohr came to realize the effect of these words, and one
day he contented himself with saying, "Very interesting," and then left
off, while the entire audience waited in vain for the familiar "but."
When it failed to make its appearance, this was too much for Bohr's
old friend Paul Ehrenfest, who evidently felt that what had been presented was sheer nonsense, and therefore exclaimed, "Herr Bohr, Fan-
gen Sie gleich mit dem Aber an" ("Mr. Bohr, won't you just get on with
the 'but'?").

Another ominous expression of Bohr's was: "We are much more in
agreement than you believe. . . ." Bohr was anxious to be considerate
but also truthful, and so it was in the main clause that the criticism
came.

Bohr did not really need to say much for his presence to have an
effect. But he was often unaware of just how much he influenced those
around him. The mathematician Asger Aaboe tells the following incident about a visitor at the Institute, a young researcher who was presenting his work for the first time. He was writing on the blackboard
when Bohr suddenly remembered a meeting he was supposed to attend.
He got up and crept out as quietly as he could, believing he could go
unnoticed. But after Bohr left the young researcher was quite disconcerted, and stood silently for several minutes. Had what he had been
saying been so wrong that Bohr left? Bohr's personality produced such
a strong effect that a single unlucky incident at the blackboard disheartened this young physicist so much that he went home, never to
reappear.

Another story has some features in common with these and is described in a volume of memoirs published recently by the German physicist Carl-Friedrich von Weizsäcker. He had taken part in a conference at the Institute in 1933 along with Landau and the Welsh physicist Evan James Williams, and Bohr asked him afterwards to prepare a summary of the discussion. This he did over the course of a few weeks and then he gave the paper to Bohr's secretary. At the time Bohr was very preoccupied with taking care of the German emigrants. Two weeks later Weizsäcker and Bohr met to discuss the paper. Bohr arrived late and looked extremely tired. When Weizsäcker brought out his manuscript, Bohr said, "Yes, very, very . . . it is a very fine piece of work . . . yes, now it is all clear . . . I hope you will publish it soon. . . ." Weizsäcker thought, "Poor man! He simply has not had time to read it." But then Bohr said, "Just so we can learn a little what does the formula on page seventeen really mean?" "I explained it," writes Weizsäcker. Bohr said, "Yes, I understand that. But then the footnote on page fourteen must mean the following." Weizsäcker replied, "Yes, that is what I intended." "But then. . . ," and thus Bohr continued. He had read the whole thing. An hour passed, and he became fresher and fresher, while at one point Weizsäcker had difficulty in explaining himself. After two hours had passed Bohr was still sparklingly fresh, concentrated, and full of artless zeal. Weizsäcker, conscious of his own tiredness, felt his back to the wall. After three hours Bohr said triumphantly, but at the same time innocent of ill will, "Now I understand! Now I understand the point. The point is that the whole thing is the exact opposite of what you said it was. That is the point!" And with some appropriate scaling-down of "the whole thing," it was true enough. Concluding his description of the episode, Weizsäcker writes, "When one has had this sort of experience a few times with one's teacher, one has learned something one would not have learned otherwise."

"Just so we could learn a little"—this phrase of Bohr's was often the prelude to a long discussion. He took stock of every contribution to physics, including his own, with the words, "what have we learned?" and his passion for learning always remained undiminished as the trigger of his curiosity.

One of the many light-hearted stories about Bohr is the one about Fredensbro ("The Peace Bridge") in Copenhagen. Hendrik Casimir recounts it in his memoirs in order to show that Bohr's breadth of view encompassed not only atomic physics but everyday practical affairs as well. Bohr and Casimir came to the bridge during a walk one evening in the early 1930s. It is necessary now to give a detailed description of the bridge's parapet as it was at that time. Stone pillars one meter in height were spaced three to four meters apart and connected by an iron pipe driven into the pillars and going from one to the other. Halfway between every two pillars was an iron ring anchored in the masonry

Weizsäcker (left) wrote in his diary after his first meeting with Bohr: "I have seen a physicist for the first time. It is his destiny not to be able to stop thinking." Casimir (right) still recalls the words Paul Ehrenfest said when they went to see Bohr in 1921: "Now you will get to know Niels Bohr, and that is the most important thing that can happen in a young physicist's life."

of the bridge, and from both sides of each ring a stout iron chain went up to the iron pipe close to each of the pillars. In this way the chains hung in a series from pillar to ring and from ring to pillar, but all were linked to the iron pipe going through all the stone pillars.

When they arrived at the bridge that evening, Bohr suddenly took hold of a chain and made it swing back and forth. "To my great surprise," relates Casimir, "the next chain began to swing likewise." "A noteworthy example of resonance," explained Bohr quietly. The phenomenon made a tremendous impression on Casimir, but then Bohr laughed. Obviously resonance could be ruled out as the connecting forces were extremely small, and the amplitude of the swings must inevitably decrease sharply. What had happened was that the moment Bohr set the first chain swinging, he simultaneously—and without Casimir seeing it—turned the iron pipe, which was indeed driven into the stone pillars but was not made fast. By turning it he also set the second chain in motion. "I was thunderstruck at having shown so little common

sense, but Bohr consoled me by saying that he had also tricked Heisenberg in the same way, and Heisenberg had even given an entire
lecture on resonance!"

The bridge was afterwards known as the Resonance Bridge among
atomic physicists, and the name stuck until the chains and iron pipe
were removed during the enlargement of the bridge a few years later.
The staff of the Institute was well aware that many of their humorous
caprices must have seemed somewhat sophomoric to outsiders. But they
were necessary diversions between the periods of intense work. From
time to time some almost childish piece of absurdity could reveal an
unknown trait in one of the participants. For example, a battle that
amused Bohr took place one day between Heisenberg and the young
Paul Ehrenfest. This was at the time when workers at the Institute had
discovered that individual particles in cosmic radiation could release
whole showers of other particles. Casimir thought up a nonsensical
competition in the "production of showers." Heisenberg and Ehrenfest
were each placed in a chair a few meters apart, and above each of them
a can full of water was suspended by a seesaw arrangement which could
easily be tipped. The two competitors were each supplied with a basket'
full of tennis balls, and at a given signal they would each try to hit the
other's can so the water would fall in a shower over the opponent.
Both missed on the first throw. Heisenberg's next throw missed too,
but Ehrenfest's was a bull's eye. Heisenberg was drenched—and looked
very upset. Casimir muttered to Weizsäcker that he thought Heisenberg
was less annoyed about getting wet than about losing. "You know him,"
was Weizsäcker's reply. But they realized afterwards that they actually
should have disqualified Ehrenfest, because he had risen halfway up
from his seat when throwing, and that was against Casimir's rules.

When Casimir told the story to Heisenberg's widow not long ago, she
was very amused; she quite agreed that Heisenberg did not enjoy losing
even in a silly jape, and he would certainly become irritated over losing
by a foul. Heisenberg could also become distressed if he had to give
in during important scientific discussions, but this was seldom necessary.

"Even Bohr," wrote Casimir, "who could concentrate better and had
greater staying power than any of the rest of us, needed to relax now
and then." He had a predilection for crossword puzzles, and regularly
bought the Sunday *Berlingske Tidende* (a Danish newspaper) for that
reason (and also in order to chuckle at a favorite comic strip whose
baroque humor appealed to him). When it was time to solve the crossword he liked to have a colleague to work with him. Now and then his
sons would have to oblige, but perhaps mainly in order to train their
ingenuity.

It could happen that in solving a crossword puzzle a single word might be missing which could clear up an entire area. Casimir was frequently successful in finding just the right word, and then Bohr would exclaim delightedly: "Now it's all coming!"

Another time when Rosenfeld was helping he discovered how tireless Bohr could be when it came to solving a crossword puzzle. It was getting late, and they were stumped by one word, a name with three letters. Finally Rosenfeld went to bed exhausted. But no sooner had he fallen asleep than there was a knock on the door. Quietly opening the door, Bohr put his head round and said apologetically in German, "Rosenfeld, es ist nicht die Meinung zu stören, aber der Name ist Yin." ("I don't want to disturb you, but the name is yin.") The crossword was solved, and with one of Bohr's favorite concepts ("yin" and "yang"). At last the house could settle down, and Rosenfeld went to sleep again, this time smiling. Once again he had heard Bohr say, "Es ist nicht die Meinung zu stören, aber. . . ." Everyone at the Institute knew this phrase in Bohr's special variety of German. Everyone said it whenever they had an excuse to do so, in the same way as they often used another celebrated Bohrian reply. "Es möchte schön sein, ob. . . ." ("It would be nice if. . . .").

Bohr was familiar with Conan Doyle's stories about Sherlock Holmes, but was less fond of some of the detective stories which many of his colleagues found relaxing. And when Conan Doyle became involved in the occult in his later years, Bohr's comment was, "Of course he is more easily duped than the rest of us. We know that we know nothing about solving crimes and exposing criminals. Conan Doyle does not know either, but he thinks he knows, and now this reveals itself as an enormous disadvantage for him."

Bohr had no interest at all in occultism and clairvoyance. When a "medium" appeared in Copenhagen after World War II and gave séances which became popular in fashionable circles north of Copenhagen, Bohr was asked what he thought about it. He replied, "If anyone believes in it, why do they not ask what Stalin is going around thinking about, which is really the most important thing to find out just now?"

A paradoxical coda may be added to this Bohrian utterance in the form of the following anecdote—which again would probably have amused Bohr in the present context. One day at Tisvilde Bohr was putting up a horseshoe over the doorway, and a guest asked in surprise if he really believed that a horseshoe brought good luck? No, replied Bohr, but I have been given to understand that it does bring it even to those who do not believe in it.

This is how Gamow tells the story in his book *Thirty Years That Shook Physics*. But when Iørn Piø of the Danish Folklore Collection wrote to Bohr asking if the story was true, Bohr answered that it was a story which Gamow had made up. However that may be, it was a story

which Bohr himself enjoyed telling. Bohr recalls that he first told it
when he came home from the United States after the war. If Bohr found
little amusement in superstition generally, he did enjoy the cunning
ambiguity in Gamow's joke. And now, just so that we shall not feel too
sure about Bohr, we include a picture from Tisvilde showing that a
horseshoe actually did hang over the door to the woodshed. But maybe
Bohr's true attitude toward mysticism manifests itself in the fact that,
as you can see, the horseshoe is upside-down. For those believing in
superstition it means that the good luck will fall out.

The photograph shows the horseshoe over the door to the woodshed at Tis-
vilde. Bohr is on the right, sawing with Kramers.

21

Jest for Jest's Sake

Apart from the numerous anecdotes which had a deeper meaning and which even Bohr related, there were many which were purely and simply playful anecdotes *about* Bohr. They amused him too, if they were correct. Among them are stories which are construed by some as indicating that Bohr was abstracted and impractical—in other words, that hackneyed old figure the absentminded scientist. But as Jørgen Kalckar said in his essay on Bohr, it is questionable whether this stereotype actually does fit any of the pioneers of natural science; at all events Bohr definitely does not conform to it. "To be absentminded and to be preoccupied do not always mean the same thing." To begin nevertheless by taking that banal view of Bohr, he taped with a great deal of laughter, an anecdote about an incident from his childhood when he and Harald were on a streetcar with their mother. As they rode along their mother was telling them a story in which both boys are quite absorbed. They were probably sitting with their mouths open, and then their mother overheard a couple at the other end of the streetcar talking about the boys, and the wife said to her husband, "That poor mother!" But above and beyond the preoccupied expressions that troubled the couple on the streetcar, what was happening was simply that the children were concentrating very hard in order to take in every tiny detail of the story. In later years Bohr's colleagues at the Institute learned to watch out for his preoccupied expression when the solving of a problem had apparently reached a deadlock. One day Bohr's expression was so distant that his colleagues thought that he was feeling sick, but then all at once his face brightened and he exclaimed, "Now I have it!" Bohr had concentrated so intensely that in a flash he had seen the solution to a point which they had been discussing for hours.

Many people have witnessed Niels Bohr's ability to shut out everything else in order to concentrate on a single specific matter. The poet Hans Hartvig Seedorff tells of a day when Bohr visited him at his home

Bohr's fondness for Goethe's Faust *inspired Max Delbrück to write a humorous version of it with the motto "Not in order to criticize." Gamow drew the characters: (from top to bottom) Bohr is God, Ehrenfest is Faust, Pauli is Mephisto, and Einstein—the bottom two drawings—appeared as the King in Gretchen's song.*

in Tibirke. Seedorff's young nephew was visiting there and accompanied the two friends when they went for a walk in the hills. The nephew wanted to hear about the atom, and Bohr, who was always glad to meet young people who showed curiosity, began to talk to him. They had now reached one of the narrow paths through the heather along which it was only possible to walk in single file, but Bohr failed to notice this, so that he stumbled and fell down in the heather. When he fell down and while lying in the heather and even while he was getting up, he kept on talking uninterruptedly and eagerly, as if nothing had happened.

The first time Niels and Harald went on a trip abroad together, their father accompanied them to the boat with many admonitions. They were going to Oslo, and he told them to be sure to check the place and time when the boat was to sail home again. The day came, and Niels and Harald arrived at the quay just after the gangplank of the ship had been raised. With frantic gestures they persuaded the sailors to lower it again. They went on board, and the boat set off. But after a few minutes they discovered that they were on a ship bound for America! This time they were rescued by the pilot boat which took them back to the quay.

Bohr has recounted what happened when he was on his way to visit Japan for the first time, and the ship was ready to sail from Honolulu to Yokohama. Margrethe Bohr and their son Hans were accompanying him, but the family arrived at the pier late. The reason for the delay was that enroute to the pier Bohr started to film some surfriders and he could not bear to stop. Both Margrethe and Hans attempted in vain to remind him of the time. In addition they had an immense amount of luggage as well as long sugar canes and other "curiosities." All their baggage formed a vast heap on the quay when they finally arrived there. Margrethe hurried on board, while Bohr ran up and down the gangway bringing up the suitcases one at a time, the sugar canes, and everything else. This was accomplished with the customary interruptions during which Bohr would use several matches to relight his pipe. When he finally picked up the last suitcase, a harbor policeman exclaimed, "You are the most foggy gentleman I ever saw!"

Toronto is the city from which comes the anecdote about the briefest, but not the dullest, newspaper report of a lecture delivered by Bohr.

Lev Landau on Aage Bohr's tricycle, Aage, George Gamow on the motorcycle, Ernest Bohr, and, on skis, Edward Teller.

(a)

(b)

A popular toy in the 1950s was the tipping top, which can turn upside-down while spinning and continues to twirl on its peg. (a)Bohr and Pauli study the phenomenon in 1954. (b) Bohr entertains the King of Sweden and the Prime Minister with the top in 1951. (From the Danish newspaper Jyllandsposten.*)*

His visit was the event of the season, and all the luminaries of the city were assembled along with students and researchers. During the lecture, which Bohr had prepared with his usual thoroughness, he also showed slides with diagrams and equations. When he needed to point to the topmost of the diagrams and could not reach high enough, he pulled down on the screen in order to get the diagrams closer. His facial expression, when he realized that the figure had not moved, was seen in a photograph in Toronto's biggest newspaper the next day. The picture was the only report of the lecture, and it carried the brief caption: "Mr. Bohr reached for the moon."

Another true story is told by Bohr himself from his sojourn in the United States during the war, when he used the alias Nicholas Baker. Bohr is one of the main characters in the story, but the other one, a lady, must be introduced first. The Austrian physicist Hans von Halban had worked for a time at Bohr's Institute in Copenhagen. At the beginning of the war he was in France, and when the Germans were approaching Paris, it was he who carried the heavy water out of the city and had it brought safely to England. What directly concerns our story, however, is that at one time he had been married to a very beautiful and prodigiously wealthy woman. They divorced, however, and she remarried, and her second husband was also a well-known physicist, George Placzek.

One day in New York Bohr entered the elevator at Rockefeller Center, and a woman in it exclaimed, "Well now, aren't you Niels Bohr?"

"No, my name is Nicholas Baker,"—he paused, and looked at her and then said:

"But aren't you Mrs. Halban?"

"No, I am Mrs. Placzek!"

During their stay in America, Bohr and his son Aage, who went under

In the humorous newspaper the Journal of Jocular Physics, *which came out on Bohr's decennial birthdays, Gamow immortalized Bohr as Mickey Mouse in a series about memorable events. Ping, Bohr's favorite character from a newspaper comic strip, has been given Heisenberg's initials. The cartoon is captioned "The Juggler."*

Students cheering Bohr on his fiftieth birthday.

the name James (Jim) Baker, were always guarded by two plainclothes detectives. The latter had their work cut out looking after Bohr, with his penchant for crossing on the red light, and on several occasions they had to rescue him from the heavy New York traffic. One day their superior asked them whether Aage could watch over his father, and both detectives responded in unison, "The young one, he is even worse!"

Finally the favorite stories of Margrethe Bohr and Lèon Rosenfeld concern both Bohr personally and his popularity in "wide circles." Margrethe's story is about an occasion when Bohr came home after buying a raincoat and asked her if they had shopped in that store before. She said, "No, she did not think so," to which Bohr replied, "We must have, because the assistant knew my name."

Rosenfeld's anecdote concerns one morning when he and Bohr went to the lecture hall early to see that everything was ready for the day's colloquium. When they opened the door, a bum was lying on the stairs sleeping. Rosenfeld was nervous over what might happen next, but the vagabond got up, took his hat off, bowed to Bohr and said politely, "Good morning, Professor Bohr."

22

Tisvilde Again

It was not only at holiday times that the Bohr family went to their house at Tisvilde. Whenever the burdens of administrative duties at the Institute became too heavy and hampered scientific work, Bohr would escape to Tisvilde for a few days. But he seldom went alone. Impressions of the summer days there include recollections of visits by many Danish and foreign guests. Bohr, with his constant flow of brain waves, was the inspiring and unifying focus of all these visits. It was not just a matter of being entertaining: Bohr simply could not act in any other way, for he received so many inspirations.

During Heisenberg's first visit to Denmark in 1923 Bohr invited him to Tisvilde. Heisenberg was a good listener, and he liked Bohr's stories. Their scientific discussions were seldom conducted without numerous interruptions by new stories. On this first visit, they took a walk on the beach, where Bohr—as he often did—began throwing stones. Then he suggested that they have a throwing contest.

Bohr had a fondness for philosophical generalizations derived from such simple games. When Heisenberg threw a stone at a distant telegraph pole and, against all reasonable odds, hit it, Bohr exclaimed, "To aim at such a distant object and hit it, is, of course, impossible. But if one has the impudence to throw in that direction without aiming, and in addition to imagine something so absurd as that one might hit it, yes, then perhaps it can happen. The idea that something perhaps could happen can be stronger than practice and will."

Heisenberg was to recall the trivial incident of the telegraph pole during a later visit to Tisvilde. At that time there happened to be three mathematicians visiting also: these were Harald, G. Hardy from Cambridge, and A. Besicovitch from Russia. In the afternoon the four men began playing *boccia*, a lawn-bowling game. "We divided up into two teams, and as both Harald Bohr and Hardy were ardent sportsmen, it was a bitter fight on both sides." Besicovitch, who was quite inexpe-

Bohr and a son cutting wood, in the 1920s.

In front of Johannes V. Jensen's house: Bohr and Else Jensen in the summer of 1943.

rienced, was the only one to have very little success. But the game ended quite unexpectedly. Niels Bohr and Besicovitch were on the same side and were so far behind as to be almost certain to lose. Besicovitch had the last throw, and being fully aware of how hopeless the situation was, he turned round and threw the bowl backwards and over his shoulder—and it landed in exactly the right place. Amid general rejoicing that decided the game in his and Niels Bohr's favor.

These playful traits are perhaps illuminated best of all in notes left behind by Niels Bjerrum, who next to Harald was one of Bohr's closest advisers as well as a lifelong friend. Bjerrum and Bohr met when they were still quite young at Nærumgaard, the summer home of Bohr's mother. Later Bohr and Bjerrum were students together and they had common interests in the area between physics and chemistry.

During their student days, Bohr and Bjerrum went on day-long hikes along the North Sea shore. Later on, Bjerrum had a summer house at Skagen, which is 200 miles north of Copenhagen, and their joint outings continued. The following quote from Bjerrum dates back to that time:

To be able fully to understand Bohr's rare nature, one must be clear that

Family and friends with Niels Bohr (in the white cap) and (extreme right) Margrethe Bohr, in 1943.

through the years he has retained the boy in him, retained the boy's love of play and the boy's curiosity, the latter of course being a very important thing for a researcher in science. The boy in Bohr shows itself in many ways. Bohr has always been capable of throwing stones high and far, and the delight of doing this has never left him. I remember one time when he was visiting us at Skagen, and we went to the abandoned church which was half-buried in the sand. Bohr tried throwing stones over it. When this proved too easy for him, he hit on the idea of trying to get the stones to land outside the shutters of the two peep holes on the first and second story of the tower, but this was too easy as well, and Bohr, becoming more and more excited, then thought of throwing stones in through the small holes in the shutters, and when this was successful he suggested that we try to throw our walking sticks up and get them to stand up outside the shutters, and when this was successful, we had to get them back down again by throwing more stones. In the end he had us trying to get the sticks to hang up there with their handles caught in the holes of the shutters, and we actually succeeded. Now we others gave up trying to get them down again by throwing stones, but Bohr continued and was happy when he finally succeeded.

In 1926, along with Bjerrum, Ole Chievitz, and yet another childhood friend, a wood engraver named Holger Hendriksen, Bohr became joint owner of a sailing boat named the "Chita." They went on many pleasant outings both short and long and often with guests. Niels Bjerrum wrote

The family at Tisvilde in 1928. Christian and Hans hold arrows.

The boys watch Margrethe and Niels on a motorcycle, in 1930.

in a note from one of these trips: "Whenever Bohr was not lying down in the cabin, he was always leading conversations and discussions. Bohr has a remarkable capacity for sparking ideas from his companions, so that they felt cleverer than was their wont. Bohr also had a remarkable capacity for finding interesting problems in everyday observations. When he saw the streak of moonlight on the water, it became a problem to deduce why it was a streak and not simply a large patch. When we used the sail to work our way against the wind, it became a problem to figure out how this could be possible."

Niels and Margrethe's eldest son Christian was born in 1916, and during the 1920s they had four more sons—Hans, Erik, Aage, and Ernest. Being together with the boys was an essential part of summer at Tisvilde. Niels Bohr loved to play with them, and he used to challenge them with small problems which he invented incessantly. One of them, which he himself greatly enjoyed, was the little joke about "The cat which has three tails." "How can that be?" he asked the children. "You see, no cat has two tails; one cat has one tail more than no cat; therefore one cat must have three tails." All the children realized what was wrong with that, but it was just not so easy to explain. Bohr was proud when the three-year-old Aage, waving his arms, said, "Here, father, there is no cat, so how are there two tails?" The story is almost a mirror image of a family story stemming from the time when Niels himself was about three years old. While they were out on a short walk, his father showed him a tree and began talking about how beautifully the trunk divides itself into branches, and the branches into still more slender branches, ending at last in a leaf. Having listened to this for a while, Niels is said to have exclaimed, "Yes, but if it were not like that there would be no trees."

Bohr's son Hans has written about some of the problems which their father set them. For example, there was the one with the two glasses containing wine and water respectively. If one takes a spoonful of the wine and puts it into the water, and then puts a spoonful of the mixture back into the wine, then will more wine have gone over into the water or more water over into the wine? It was seldom that anyone could give the correct answer, which was that exactly as much wine would go over to the water as water over to the wine.

Hans also relates how the dinner table was a family gathering place, where their father was eager to hear about their experiences and to recount his own.

As well as problems he showed us simple physical experiments which could be done with forks, glasses, and napkin rings, and although mother made gentle protests, gradually everybody took part in the exercises. Father had a special trick of transferring the vibrations from a fork to a glass by deftly making use of the table's resonance vibrations, and a glass could be made

An early summer sail on the "Chita."

to "sing" when you rubbed around the edge with a wet finger, and napkin rings were made to roll backwards by twisting, or could be raised in the air without support by rapid rotation around a finger.

What my father wanted to give us, however, was not merely training in logical thinking or problems; to him it was essential that you had thought over life's problems and had made a real effort to reach a deeper understanding.

Bohr also liked to train his children athletically by light-hearted but nonetheless vigorous free-for-alls. Seedorff tells how he arrived on a visit to Tisvilde one day and saw "Niels in battle with his then already numerous offspring. The boys were simply flying through the air and landing in the strangest places. Niels was standing in the midst of them, and when he saw me he said, 'I can still cope with them.' I at once joined on the boys' side and helped to pummel him playfully."

Seedorf also tells of another free-for-all. One day Niels had vainly tried to explain to Seedorff something about atoms, which remained incomprehensible to the poet. At last Seedorff resorted to a challenge and asked, "Niels, is it true, as some say, that you are a second Newton?" Bohr did not answer, but pounced upon Seedorff, turned him over in the grass and rained gentle blows on him. "Then," continues Seedorff,

*Bohr and his mother at Tisvilde in
the late 1920s.*

"I teased him by putting the question, 'What is the practical result of all this splitting you do? For example, can you make gold?' "

" 'I like to believe it is possible,' replied Bohr, 'but it will be dreadfully expensive for you.' "

In all the practical business of the summer, Bohr always wanted cooperation. This applied even to the periodic woodcutting in the extensive grounds. Everyone would take part in both the falling and the sawing. William Scharff has described the tree-cutting operations in a letter of reminescences written to Bohr as a keepsake on Bohr's seventieth birthday:

> Over a number of years you used much energy in cutting down trees, an art you introduced to children as they became old enough to take part. They loved it, and it gave you an opportunity to indulge your need for physical labor and to use your abilities as a practical organizer. Over the years, far too many trees had grown up around your house and the surroundings had quite changed in character. For you, cutting them down grew into an absolute passion. It could happen that the axe struck your leg instead of a tree, and in your zeal some of ours also would disappear occasionally—the trees, I mean.

Before the felling of each tree there was a thorough discussion on whether it should be just this tree or some other, on what the procedure was to be, and what role each individual would play. As a rule, Mar-

This happy picture from Tisvilde was taken by Stefan Rozental at the end of the 1940s.

grethe was called in and asked for advice. For instance, one day Bohr wanted to do some fairly drastic thinning and therefore absolutely had to have Margrethe's opinion. He explained eagerly how the thinning would bring more light to the other trees. Margrethe observed his eagerness and said, "Well, if that is how you feel, I think you should do it." To which Bohr, piqued, replied, "Yes, but Margrethe, you must not just say so, you must really mean it."

Correspondingly, Harald was fond of telling of the time when Margrethe and Niels were buying a baby buggy for one of the children. They were unable to agree on which one to buy, but finally Margrethe gave in, and they bought the one which Niels preferred. But Niels looked gloomy and was asked why, since he had been successful. He answered that it simply did not satisfy him to gain the day in this manner. He did not want a concession but rather an agreement based on real conviction.

Here is a story from Niels Bohr's childhood that tells of his ability and need to get everyone to participate. The rear hub of a bicycle had broken down, and in spite of the protests of the adults Niels resolutely set about dismantling it. A long time passed before he began to put it together again, and the adults renewed their protests, advising Niels worriedly to give up and take the bicycle to a repair shop. But his father only said quietly, "Now leave the boy in peace. He knows what he is doing." And after having studied the individual parts, so the story continues, first in the oral and later the written tradition of the family, Niels was able to put the bicycle together so that it was as good as new. His cousin Paula Strelitz, who has related the episode, and who herself was in the group around Niels and the bicycle, added that even though in fact they were all mere spectators, he gave everyone a sense of involvement—as though the bicycle was repaired by all of them.

There is also a story about Bohr's determination never to speak ill of anyone. One summer's day Bohr was invited to visit a forest ranger who lived some distance away from Tisvilde. Bohr biked there accoompanied by one of his sons and by William Scharff's son, the young atomic physicist Morten Scharff, who told the story to the historian of science Asger Aaboe. It was a strange afternoon during which the guests became increasingly more uncomfortable, although the forest ranger doubtless felt that he had done his best to entertain them as well as possible. What he did, however, was to talk incessantly and with sublime complacency about himself. When at long last the visitors managed to get away, they rode home in much-needed silence. Little by little, however, the silence became oppressive. What sort of comments would Bohr actually make on the encounter with their host? Both his son and Morten, although they knew Bohr's tolerance well, expected an angry outburst, for the forest ranger had certainly been unbearable. However, they went all the way home without a word having been said, but finally, as Bohr got off his bicycle he remarked calmly, "Well, that forest ranger is after all a well-intentioned person."

Thus the forest superintendent was consigned to oblivion, no harsh words were spoken, and the sun shone once again.

The bright summer pleasures in which Tisvilde played so great a part for Niels and Margrethe Bohr also brought them their heaviest affliction. This story furnishes an insight into Bohr's view of death, and the strength with which he could meet it. The account may also be read as a manifestation of his philosophy of life.

Bohr's eldest son Christian showed an early interest in natural science and was also quite artistic. When he was quite young he wrote some poems and showed them to his father, who suggested that he let the poet Seedorff read them. Seedorff recognized in the poems the father's marked sense of lyricism, and he urged Christian to continue writing. Seedorff had no doubt that, as Niels Bohr hoped, Christian would develop into a talented artist.

After Christian had matriculated in 1934, he went along on the first sailing excursion of the summer in the "Chita." The July day was bright, and so were everyone's spirits. Christian was sitting by the tiller. But

Bohr's son Christian on a summer day in 1931, with his cousin Ib Nørlund.

suddenly the wind increased and a heavy sea poured in and washed Christian overboard. A lifebelt was thrown to him but he could not reach it. Then Bohr stood up, and it was probably the most painful moment in the lives of his three friends when they had to restrain him from jumping in after Christian. They then continued to search for him until nightfall without success.

It can be imagined what strength was required to help the family through the weeks that passed before Christian's body was found. And at a memorial service held at home in Old Carlsberg, Bohr showed in the address he delivered that he was also strong enough to hold to the view he had expressed before when death was mentioned. He who in his youth had written, "I believe in all that is fine in life," rejected the idea of death as intrinsically tragic.

Although he spoke about the loss which he felt so intensely and which was so hard to bear, he gave more prominence to the value of the idea that everything a person stands for lives on in the people whom he has been able to influence by his actions and his example. He emphasized first that although Christian would never advance beyond his youth, his life had not been in vain. "On each of us within this home and on those intimately linked with it, he has surely bestowed precious mem-

Niels Bohr photographed in 1937 in New York by the photographer Eric Schaal.

ories purified by pain, which will bind us still more closely to one another, and in which, without aging, he will be living with us."

And the last words of the memorial address offered this consolation:

> The manifold tokens of fidelity to his memory, for which we offer most heartfelt thanks on behalf of Christian and ourselves to his friends young and old, have also given us the sure confidence that even beyond our little circle his spirit will continue to work as truly as each one of us lives out his life most strongly in the thoughts of his fellow human beings.

Bohr was affected by the tragedy for a long time, and it had demanded a superabundance of strength for him to formulate these words of farewell. But they helped both Margrethe and himself through the worst time. And also those nearest and dearest perceived the death in a way they could not have imagined earlier.

One of Christian's friends wrote afterwards: "It was an intense joy to experience the powerful vitality that, in those dark days, entered our hearts so generously and abundantly. We continued our work and included our dead friend in our lives."

23

Bohr and the Great Poets

Everyone who visited Niels Bohr soon realized the importance to him of the great poets, especially Goethe.

Bohr became familiar with Goethe during his formative years. To Bohr's father, this great European poet and thinker meant more than the general cultural grounding that the study of Goethe signified to the majority of the more progressive academics of those days. Harald Høffding wrote that Christian Bohr knew his Goethe well and he often read aloud from the works of Goethe, both in the family circle and among their friends.

As a young man Christian Bohr lived for a time at the Medical-Physiological Institute in Copenhagen. On the top floor of the Institute professor Ebbe Brandstrup, the gynaecologist, was working on his dissertation, when one day he noticed a verse scratched on a windowpane. Beneath it Christian Bohr had written his name and a date which Brandstrup recalls as 1879. Christian Bohr was twenty-four years old then. The verse produced such a strong effect on Brandstrup that he wrote it down, and later he came across it again in the foreword to Goethe's *Proëmion*, written in 1817. In English the verse reads:

> Wide the world and life expanded,
> Long years striving as demanded,
> Always searching, always grounded,
> Never closed off, often rounded,
> Saved in age by being true,
> Friendly, ready for the new,
> Mind serene and pure of purpose:
> Now, one surely will make progress.

Christian Bohr was not the only one to find a deeper meaning in this verse. It is reproduced here because Niels also returned to it time and time again.

However, Niels was not merely influenced by his father's reading of

Goethe. He developed his own relationship to Goethe's poetry, which so affected him during his youth that in later life he could recite verse after verse by heart even though years might have passed since he had last recalled them. He remembered everything that influenced him, and a memory could surface again after a long time in response to the enthusiasm of another. Bohr's love of Goethe came to light again when he invited Jørgen Kalckar, one of the many colleagues with whom he exchanged ideas, to Tisvilde. They spent many mind-expanding hours talking in the pavilion, which were never to be forgotten.

Jørgen Kalckar has written a memoir to mark the centennial of Niels Bohr's birth called *The Incommensurable: Fragments of a Tone Poem/ Antiphon with Niels Bohr*, in which he recalls many conversations with Bohr. Still listening in his mind to the voice of Bohr, he amplifies Bohr's interpretation of Goethe and so opens the way for a greater insight into Bohr's own world of ideas and an understanding of his view of humanity.

Bohr had not merely read the works of Goethe. He was familiar with Goethe's diaries and with the literature on his life, and he had his own view of the great biographies of Goethe from Georg Brandes' to Eckermann's. The individual poems also gave him more than the actual ideas they contained because Bohr had a highly developed feeling for artistic expression. We also know from his schoolfellows his special talent for reciting poetry, which he could recite by heart, "not just a line here and a verse there . . . he could recite stanza after stanza without faltering, his controlled and beautifully modulated voice bringing out the rise and fall of the verse rhythms and the lyrical timbre of the words."

In the midst of the work of dictating and correcting a paper, Bohr could pause and return to where he and Kalckar had last left off with Goethe. It could be that in the meantime he had found a verse or a piece of prose which illustrated what they had just been discussing. During a period when the guest cottage was fully taken up by children and grandchildren, Kalckar had a room at the Tisvildehus pension, and in the evening, after their work was finished and Kalckar had said goodnight to the family, Bohr would say, "I will come with you part of the way just to say one simple thing."

Then they set off together along the path by the fringe of the woods, and upon reaching Tisvildehus they would stand in front of the house for a long time, and then it would be Kalckar's turn to suggest that he would accompany Bohr part of the way back home, and in this way they would stroll back and forth wrapped in intimate mutual comprehension of Goethe, until they heard the cries of a family search-party, equipped with torches, that had come out to rescue them—and were amazed to discover how much time had passed.

Men of letters and enquiring spirits seeking to garner wisdom from the great poets, have now and then, of course, been impelled almost to beg providence for a revelation. What did Goethe mean by this and that? What did he mean by *Faust*? Goethe himself was asked this count-less times all through the almost sixty-year period that he was working on the drama, hiding it away and then taking it out again. But no one ever got an answer. If someone pointed out to Goethe that he had sometimes contradicted himself, he replied, "Should I have reached my old age just to think the same thing all the time?" Bohr would have been more likely to do so: he liked Socrates' laconic answer to the sophists: "You who are so clever, you never say the same about the same thing, do you?" But Bohr acquitted the great poet. And he felt convinced "that Goethe made a point of not allowing *Faust* to end up in stanzas which in the remotest way would permit an unambiguous interpretation."

"Logic" was not what Bohr looked for in a work of *art*, still less a thesis to be "proved." Nor, when Bohr spoke of the wisdom of the thinkers of antiquity, the ancient Hebrew prophets and the Chinese philosophers, was it ever with a view to finding or singling out a specific "idea," some solution complete in itself. "It was not for nothing," writes Kalckar, "that in that sort of context Bohr preferred to use the word 'insights,' which has a mysterious ring to it."

Kalckar's memoir formulates Bohr's understanding of and empathy with Goethe's artistic vision in this way. It is no accident that it is the poetically most accomplished passages which have occasioned the most fruitless speculation and the most futile attempts at analysis. The quite fundamental error is surely that people try to extract from such passages some thought which may be expressed independently of the form which Goethe has given it. This is only possible in the passages which have *not* really succeeded for him. But at the true poetic high points we are not dealing with some thought or other which has first been conceived and then put into verse; verse and thought are here one and the same thing—the one cannot be imagined without the other. This is infinitely more than the harmony between form and content toward which we others, with our feeble capacities, try to struggle. What we are con-fronted with here is the unbreakable unity between perception and form: it is analogous to the impossibility of subdividing the quantum process without having to face a totally different phenomenon.

Kalckar then moved on from Bohr's views on art, to Bohr's irreligious interpretation of Goethe's works and personality. Goethe was probably heathen, declared Kalckar, but not a stranger to religious feelings. To which Bohr replied,

How could such a great poet be a stranger to such a universal feeling? This religious feeling or attitude has always existed and will always exist in every age, and in itself, obviously, there is nothing wrong with that. What is wrong is to try to freeze it in the conceptual world framed at a stage of human knowledge that has long since passed away. *Once* it was not crazy in itself to believe in the account of creation given in Genesis—which may well have more to be said for it than for the Egyptian idea of the world's being balanced on the shell of a tortoise! Goethe's religious feelings—or poetic devotion— were interwoven and in intimate harmony with all the accumulated insight into nature which he had won by unremitting studies, and which at certain points at least were enormously advanced in relation to his time.

Bohr also emphasized that those who have been too occupied with exploring the profundities in *Faust* miss the vital element of *play* inherent in Goethe's conception of the entire work. Play, he said, contains in its essence a typical complementarity relationship: he who stops and enquires the meaning of play has then and there deprived himself of the possibilities of further play. Here Kalckar is reminded of Bohr's wordplay on the question of whether the meaning of existence is entirely meaningless. Bohr agreed with the ancient Indian thinkers that every use of the word "meaning" implies a comparison, and with what can we compare the whole of existence? He countered the assertion of the absurdity and meaninglessness of existence with the words, "The only certainty is that a statement like 'existence is meaningless' is devoid of *all* meaning." But, Kalckar objected, Bohr had also singled out their ability to provide consolation as a vital attribute of the sages of old. How could a person in despair over the meaninglessness of existence find consolation in such metaphysical wordplay?

> Then Bohr looked at me with those clear blue eyes from which emanated such power and expressiveness, and said emphatically, "We are trapped by language to such a degree that every attempt to formulate insight is a play on words. Those who see only the wit in this play naturally feel no consolation from that; but there is consolation for those who really know how to enter into its spirit and have apprehended a feature of the conditions of our human existence."

In Bohr's view *Faust* also contained every conceivable state of mind, with but one exception: hatred. None of the figures in the drama knows hatred. And this applies not only to *Faust*, observed Bohr, but to all of Goethe's poetic works. Bohr did not see in this any limitation of Goethe's poetic gifts or imagination but purely and simply an element that was missing from Goethe's conceptual world. And however much Goethe could mock the folly of men, he never seems to have found them evil— "just as Bohr himself never did."

But we cannot leave Bohr/Goethe without some reference to Goethe as a natural scientist. He was of course also celebrated for his scientific studies of nature, and here, again with Kalckar, Bohr distinguished between, on the one hand, the fundamental sense of the mystical coherence of all things which marks the great philosophical and nature poems, and, on the other, the more concrete elements in which patient observations and studies of natural phenomena are sublimated into high poetry.

Although, as a scientist Goethe made acute observations of nature, his work on optics and color were never regarded by anyone as more than amateur philosophy. But how should one react to this? Bohr again took the poet's side and quoted the poem from *Faust*, drenched in light and color, on the rainbow quivering in the waterfall. And he added, now if Goethe's years of study were a prerequisite for his being able to write these stanzas about the rainbow, should *they* then be written off along with all the nonsense in his scientific writings?

Through Goethe, Bohr came to Schiller, but a long time passed after his youthful days with Schiller before this other great German poet came to the surface of Bohr's awareness again. Here too, Bohr happened to meet someone with whom he could discuss and enjoy the poet. When the physicists had gone home from Tisvilde and Bohr stayed behind on his own, he could go over to the home of the poet Hans Hartvig Seedorff, knock on the double door, put his head in, "and with an affectionate smile" ask, "I wonder if you would find it convenient to take a walk in the hills with Schiller?" Bohr was especially fond of Schiller's epigrams, and Bohr and Seedorff together found great enjoyment in exchanging new discoveries when they had not seen one another for a while. And again and again they could take pleasure in the beauty of such selections as:

> Nature stands in a unique union with genius; what the one promises, the other renders certain.
>
> (Final stanzas from the poem *Kolumbus*, 1795)

> Believe me, it is no fairy tale, this Fountain of Youth, it flows truly and always. You ask, where? In the art of the poet.
>
> (From *Epigrams*, 1896)

Bohr returned over and over again to the Icelandic sagas and he was fond of quoting long passages from *Egil Skallagrimsson's Saga* and *Njal's Saga*. He felt them to be such an essential part of Nordic poetry that he had to pass them on at every opportunity. All the foreigners who became close to Bohr, or with whom he sensed a spirituall affinity beyond physics, became acquainted with the Icelandic epic narratives through him. What enthralled Bohr was the vast drama related without frills but with intense power and with man as a part of mighty Nature. There were also the many utterances on responsibility and justice in a distant world where man took land and had to administer the laws he wrote. Finally Bohr was moved by the way the great figures of the sagas went out alone into the mountains when they wanted to gather "Words and Thoughts" on important questions.

The short, simple sagas also appealed to Bohr, the ones which led via a brief but vivid narrative to a happy outcome in the reconciling glow of justice. He was very fond of the acute psychology in the tale of Endride and Erling Skjalgsøn in which the latter had to overcome his pride and offer his daughter Sigrid—before being asked for her—to Endride as a token of justice inasmuch as Endride had had to bear the ordeal by fire to prove his innocence.

Bohr's sensitive spirit also responded to Herman Wildenvey, the great Norwegian lyric poet of the 1920s. Bohr admired Wildenvey's mastery of language which enabled him to interpret the human condition in simple terms and to summarize the nature of love in the lightest tones.

Both Bohr and Margrethe also very much enjoyed the lyric poems of Sophus Claussen, a Danish poet. They read his poems together but seem never to have met him. The inspiration for Sophus Claussen's great thirteen-verse poem *The Rebellion of the Atoms* therefore probably did not come from any direct meeting with Bohr. It is surprising that this poem, which glows with the power of its vision, could have been written as early as 1925. We have mentioned earlier Hans Kramers' and Helge Holst's popular book *The Atom and Bohr's Theory of its Structure*, which was the first generally accessible book written on the new doctrine of the atom and which was successfully published in several editions in 1922. This book also contains visions, although expressed in more sober language, so it could be this book or a review of it which Sophus Claussen had read before he wrote his prophetic verses. He could also have read the many articles carried in the newspapers when Bohr received the Nobel Prize. Nonetheless it is quite remarkable that of the thirteen verses, the following (rendered here in translation) could have been written at such an early date:

My shoulder slap less heartily, my merrymaking friend,
An atom at its flashpoint shall determine death or day.

Now all the atoms of the world demand to be set free.
I beg you, rushing myriads that our planet tight embrace,
O league of storms! O fire! O water! Atoms all absorbed
In tension's balanced force or working in the growth of life
All elements of light and sound and even my poor frame,

O sea of atoms . . . this I beg: have mercy on our globe!
Likewise do I beseech the Plague and War and Woman too
(Now all the atoms of the world demand to be set free)
And all who can our earth-life harm: have mercy on our globe.

Our planet thin and fragile is: this bubble quick can burst
I fear that one day it will pass, by magic whispered word,

A formula of chemistry for water or for gas
Or unknown substance, numinous in might beyond all words
Ah, formula of formulas! Beware what's in your net!

And the final stanza:

Now all the atoms of the world demand to be set free,
All nations will do battle and their compacts all dissolve
And I, an atom 'neath the sun, will pray to land and sea.
And trees and stones and metals, beasts and birds and all that breathes,
And currents in the deepest sea and fire in heart of rock:
If our poor star can rescued be, let us not do her hurt.

Bohr shared this enjoyment of Sophus Claussen's poetry with Karen Blixen, who used the pen name Isak Dinesen, and whom he met through Johannes V. Jensen. He also enjoyed her own writing. In her *Seven Gothic Tales* he found a continuation of the Danish fairy tale with roots in Hans Christian Andersen and with new inspiration from both Hoffman and Stevenson, with whom Bohr was also familiar. A correspondence between Bohr and Blixen began, but only in connection with her anti-vivisection campaign against experiments on dogs. She wrote to Bohr to ask if he would lend his signature, but he answered her arguments with points of his own and said no, although in very friendly fashion.

Bohr's interest in art was nourished by painters too. The friends of his own age and above in Tisvilde have been mentioned, but Bohr also had a special interest in younger artists. This was in line with his marked awareness of talent among quite young physicists and indeed the great attention he paid to young people generally. He wanted to know what they thought and what they were involved with. His son Christian's friend, the very young painter Mogens Andersen, has described his first visit to Tisvilde and his first meeting with Bohr:

Even at this first short meeting the warmth that radiated from this human person could be felt. It was good to be near him. Here was security, cheerfulness, and you felt that your life and work had become more important.

"What do you young people think of Scharff, Giersing, Isakson and Weie?" was the first question Bohr asked me, and I did not realize that day that his great interest in art and his artistic approach to work would be such a source of happiness for me throughout a generation.

Bohr became more than just interested. It is not very well known that Bohr was Mogens Andersen's patron during the important early years of the latter's development as an artist. The same applied to other young artists. When Henning Koppel, the sculptor and silversmith, went to France and Italy to study, he financed his trip by selling shares. One of the shareholders was Bohr, whose shares were later redeemed in the form of watercolors.

Thirty years after Bohr had asked Andersen about young people's opinions, Bohr gave the answer—so Mogen Andersen relates—by declaring that the work of these painters had been of the most vital importance to modern art. Bohr himself owned a large picture by the French cubist Jean Metzinger, who had based it on the theories he and Gleizes had formulated in *The Cubist Manifesto*. Bohr was intrigued by the ambiguity of the picture's elements, and he also was interested in the work of the first abstract painters. It is interesting that Asger Jorn, perhaps the greatest of these Danish abstractionists, also tried to follow Bohr's thoughts on complementarity. He wrote a lengthy letter to Bohr and a paper (in French) in which he declared the feature of complementarity to be applicable to Stone Age man's relationship to religious mysticism and reality. He also gave explicit form to these ideas by painting very large works filled with symbolic figures. Jorn's letter is still in the Bohr archive, though Bohr does not seem to have taken up the issues raised. But the letter does establish that at this time Jorn was seriously ill with tuberculosis at Vejle Sanatorium, and it was just then— in 1950—that Bohr, only a short distance away from Vejle, spoke on complementarity at a meeting of the Nordic Summer University at Askov. The lecture, which was also reported locally, had not been held in vain, although during the meeting both a psychologist and a biologist were trying to tell Bohr that he was on a wrong track.

24

The Bohr-Einstein Debate

The step-by-step victories of atomic theory and quantum mechanics appear like ridges on the landscape of physics. Superimposed on the massive efforts which enabled the barriers to be surmounted were incidents and events which may appear coincidental, and as such would be unique in the history of science. Perhaps the most wonderful of these happenings occurred in 1927, when Heisenberg was left alone in Copenhagen and Bohr put fatigue behind him by taking a skiing holiday in Norway. At the moment of disengagement, while they were recharging their intellectual batteries, each was viewing in his own way his own sector of the route forward to the clarification of quantum mechanics, the achievement of that goal being consummated by their joint exertions when they met again.

But this event was more than a coincidence: it was the consequence of the fact that the united strength of a multitude of scientists had led to the exciting situation in which synthesis awaited and demanded one final effort.

The achievement of Bohr and Heisenberg was hailed with enthusiasm by all those of the Copenhagen school who had contributed to one advance after another, but it also triggered the now celebrated debate between Bohr and Einstein about their disagreement over our knowledge of the physical world.

Every third year since 1911 a physics conference had been held at the Solvay Institute in Brussels, where the most prominent figures in international physics assembled to discuss the ripplings on the frontiers of physics. The high point of the congress of 1927 was a discussion between Einstein and Bohr. Although Einstein had already shown, by his earlier contribution to quantum mechanics based on Planck's quantum of action, that the emission of light from an atom can sometimes be interpreted as a wave phenomenon and sometimes as a stream of particles, and although in that way, fully in the spirit of Bohr, he had taken part in unveiling the paradox which only the concept of complementarity could resolve, Einstein nevertheless did not break with the accustomed modes of thinking of classical physics.

Among the famous participants in the Solvay Conference of 1927 apart from Einstein and Bohr were Planck, de Broglie, Schrödinger, Born, Lorentz, Kramers, Pauli, Dirac, and Heisenberg. The burning question was whether the quantum theory could at last be regarded as the

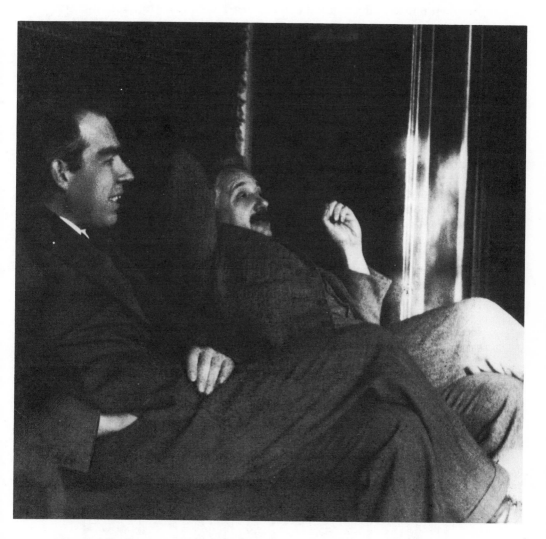

Ehrenfest took this photograph when Bohr and Einstein visited him in Leyden after the Solvay Conference in 1927. Courtesy of the Center for History of Physics, American Institute of Physics.

definitive conclusion of the efforts of many years, and whether its relation to the complementarity concept, introduced by Bohr and accepted by Heisenberg, Pauli, and Dirac, the pioneers of the theory,
could be assented to by Einstein as well.

The main topic for the debate was Bohr's central thesis that if the
conditions under which the behavior of atomic particles is studied
cannot be defined because the crude measuring instruments will themselves influence the particles, then neither the cause nor the effect of
the phenomena being studied can be clearly defined. The individuality
typical of quantum effects is seen in the very fact that every division
of the phenomenon requires a change of the experimental arrangement
that only creates new possibilities for an interchange of influences between objects and measuring instruments—an interchange which, again,
cannot be controlled. Neither, therefore, can the results obtained under
different experimental conditions be combined into one simple picture, though the various results are complementary in the sense that
taken together they do give all the information which it is possible to
obtain. The multiplicity of meanings which can arise from this provide
a parallel to the dilemma with the electron—now presenting particle
properties, now wave properties—of which atomic theory had to take
account. But Bohr realized also that the consequences of quantum mechanics would entail an even more radical break with the everyday
experiences of classical physics than the limitation which it had been
necessary to introduce upon the understanding of atomic structure.

By introducing the concept of complementarity into quantum mechanics, Bohr succeeded in both embracing the individuality of quantum phenomena and clarifying the special features attributable to the
problem of observation itself.

But Einstein was not satisfied. He believed that it had to be possible
to determine the position of a particle without influence from the instrument of measurement. At the Solvay Conference, Einstein started
from an idealized thought-experiment which is illustrated in the experimental arrangement shown here: the electrons (or photons) pass
through a slit in a screen and then through a second screen with two
slits, and finally hit a photographic plate.

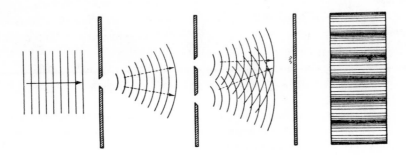

This setup makes it possible to study the wave properties of electrons. The wave train of electrons approaching the second screen will leave it as two wave trains, and these will interfere with each other, as is known from general optical phenomena. The two wave trains approaching the photographic plate are seen in the figure interfering with each other. At the far right of the figure is a front view of the plate after being struck by the wave trains, showing the pattern of interference. The pattern is created by the joint effect of a large number of individual processes, each of which produces a tiny spot on the plate where the electron in question has struck it. In other words, the experiment shows that on the one hand the individual electrons strike the plate at a specific point in accordance with the particle conception, while on the other hand the distribution of the spots follows a law which can only be understood on the basis of the wave conception. Thus far Bohr and Einstein were in agreement.

But Einstein now suggested introducing a certain control which would make it possible to analyze the entire course of the experiment without influence from instruments. In the figure the dashed arrows indicate the momentum transmitted to the screen with the two slits. Einstein suggested that a control of the momentum transmitted to the screen would determine through which of the two apertures the electron had passed before reaching the plate. In this way he felt it would be possible to determine the location and motion of a particle with unlimited precision.

At breakfast in the hotel one day during the Solvay Conference Einstein appeared with this challenge for Bohr, and he and Bohr eagerly discussed it as they walked the way back to the Solvay conference hall, accompanied by Pauli and Heisenberg, who added comments now and then to the discussion.

In the course of the morning meeting, Pauli and Heisenberg began to analyze Einstein's thought-experiment, and they talked it over with Bohr during lunch while Bohr exchanged his own ideas with them. There were numerous breaks later in the day during which the three consulted with each other further, and by the late afternoon Bohr had his answer ready. He gave it to Einstein at dinner in the hotel.

As a rule Einstein was a lone wolf, whereas Bohr collaborated extensively. Such was the situation on this particular evening too; and as almost always it was Bohr who focused on the real nub of the problem and thus pinned down the irrefutable solution.

Let us look again at the experimental arrangement suggested by Einstein with the two slits in the second screen, while recalling the experiment described in Chapter 17 where an electron passes through a small slit and is deflected around the edges of the slit, creating a diffraction pattern and signifying that it cannot be said exactly where the

Einstein and Bohr in Brussels in 1930 on the way from their hotel to the Solvay Conference.

electron will fall, only that it will fall somewhere within the diffraction pattern. In the present experimental arrangement, however, we have two slits in the second screen. According to the theory of light, waves which pass through two such slits will not create the bright diffraction pattern on the photographic plate but a series of alternating light and dark stripes. Interference occurs between the waves from the two slits, because the distance from a random point on the screen to the two slits is different. The light stripes correspond to waves which have reinforced each other, while the dark stripes represent places where they have weakened each other. If one slit is covered, the interference pattern disappears and the diffraction pattern already discussed is created instead.

Bohr now replied that if one were really able to determine the velocity and location of an electron with arbitrarily large precision, before it passes through the slits, then according to the law of causality one must also know through which slit in the screen it would go, and at what place it would strike the plate. That is to say that the electrons which will pass through the lower of the two slits must remain unaffected by whether we cover the upper slit or not. But if we cover the upper slit, then the electrons which pass through the lower slit strike quite different places on the plate, because they are now diffracted around the edges of the slit and create a diffraction pattern instead of stripes. Since it would quite clearly be absurd to imagine that the electrons which are known to pass through the lower slit would be able to observe whether the other slit is covered or not, the analysis of this experiment shows that it is impossible to ignore the interaction between objects and instruments.

Einstein had to give in again, but his heart was not in it. The discussion turned more and more toward the philosophical but now and then Einstein had to resort to humor. He could not reconcile himself to the play of chance revealed by quantum mechanics, and when their exchanges of view came to a head, he exclaimed, "Yes, but do you believe that Almighty God plays dice?" (. . . ob der liebe Gott würfelt). Bohr answered by pointing out that even the ancient thinkers had enjoined caution over ascribing to Providence attributes culled from everyday speech. And Ehrenfest chided Einstein. He remarked jocularly that he was ashamed of Einstein for behaving just like the opponents who in his time had tried to refute his theory of relativity. Nevertheless, Ehrenfest added, for his own part he would not be able to feel completely at ease until agreement with Einstein had been achieved.

The debate reached a dramatic climax during the Solvay Congress of 1930. Einstein came up with another idealized thought-experiment. Now he would show that it is possible to implement control of the interchange of momentum and energy between object and measuring instrument if the requirements of the relativity theory were considered.

All of classical mechanics depends on the proposition that if the location and momentum of a body at a certain time are known, then its location and momentum at another point in time can be calculated if the forces influencing it are known. But since it is not possible in atomic processes to determine location and momentum simultaneously, quantum mechanical predictions become in principle statistical. Many experiments will be required to yield a useful result. We should also remember that in classical mechanics momentum is equal to the mass of the body times its velocity, and the total momentum is a constant quantity for a system which is not influenced by outside forces.

With this new intellectual experiment Einstein introduced a device known since this celebrated battle between the two titans as Einstein's Box.

In one wall of the box was a hole furnished with a shutter, which could be opened and shut at a certain time by a clock also located inside the box. The clock inside the box was synchronized with a clock outside in the laboratory. It was assumed at the start of the experiment that a certain amount of radiation was present in the box; and the box was suspended in a spring balance. The idea of the experiment was to let the radiation out at a certain time weighing the box before and after the release.

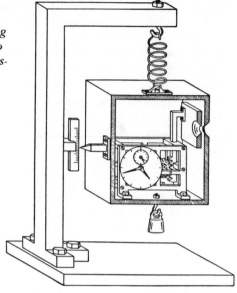

"Einstein's Box" shown in cross section to allow its interior to be seen. The box hangs from a spring and is furnished with a pointer to indicate its position on a scale fastened to the carrying pole.

Let us first imagine the following simple arrangement: a single photon is placed in the box with the clock which can open the shutter over the hole. A photographic plate is placed at a distance of 300,000 kilometers from the hole.

If the shutter is opened at exactly twelve o'clock, for example, the photon will make a spot on the photographic plate precisely one second later, since light travels at a velocity of 300,000 kilometers per second.

However, the indeterminacy relation of quantum mechanics, which says that it is not possible to know the energy of the photon without destroying the time determination, argues against the validity of the experiment. But Einstein's idea was that it must be possible to determine the energy of the photon by measuring its mass, and in principle this mass could be determined by weighing the box in the earth's gravitational field. One of the most important results which Einstein deduced from the theory of relativity was that the energy of a body is equal to its mass times the speed of light squared, and mass is something which can be determined by weighing.

By weighing the box before the photon is released, and again after it has gone, a figure can be obtained for the energy of the photon. But what does weighing mean? Let us take a bag of potatoes. Weighing this is the same as measuring the force which keeps the bag from falling. Weighing, in other words, is a measurement of the force of the earth's gravitational field on the body. (And according to Newton's second law the change in the momentum of the body is equal to the force multiplied by the time during which the force acts. And the weighing in the example amounts to a momentum measurement of the box with and without the photon. But the more accurately we carry out the weighing and therefore the momentum determination, the more uncertain becomes the position of the box in the gravitational field. If the momentum and the weighing are made ten times as accurate as before, then the uncertainty of the position of the box becomes ten times as great.)

Whereas Einstein let himself be led astray by the theory of relativity, Bohr's triumph was that he upset Einstein's experiment with the same theory. Bohr pointed out that one of the many important results of the general theory of relativity is that the functioning of a clock depends on where it is located in the gravitational field. This means that the more the clock is moved in the gravitational field, the more this changes its functioning. The greater the uncertainty with regard to where the box is located in the gravitational field during the weighing, the greater the uncertainty in the functioning of the clock inside the box. The uncertainty is in relation to the experimenter in the laboratory, who therefore is no longer in a position to say that the photon is released at precisely twelve o'clock. And he is also no longer in a position to say that it arrives 300,000 kilometers away one second after twelve o'clock.

Einstein had to agree, but only that his experiment did not prove him right. He no longer entertained any doubt as to the logic of Bohr's argument, but he still felt the same dissatisfaction ("Unbehagen") at being confronted with the strange consequences of the theory with Bohr's introduction of complementarity relations.

Ehrenfest later told Bohr that Einstein had devised more thought-experiments with the famous box, but Bohr was able to refute these as well. The next Solvay Congress took place in 1933, but Einstein was absent, having abandoned a Europe threatened by Hitler. However, he and Bohr met in the United States that same year, "but the differences of our approach and mode of expression still presented obstacles to mutual understanding." Two years later still Einstein published a paper titled "Can Quantum-Mechanical Description of Physical Reality be Considered Complete?" He wrote the paper in collaboration with the Polish physicist Boris Podolsky and the German physicist Nathan Rosen. It was a paper whose postulates Bohr immediately refuted, and of which he said, "They are doing it cleverly, but the point is to do it right." Einstein tried again, however. He refined the intellectual experiment subsequently known as the Einstein-Podolsky-Rosen Paradox, but this too was refuted by Niels Bohr. However, it did inspire J. S. Bell, a Scottish physicist, to formulate another theory, which took the E.P.R. paradox into account, and his theory has been a well-known counter-candidate to the quantum mechanics of the Copenhagen school. In

1983 the theory was reexamined in a French experiment, and the result was in complete agreement with quantum mechanics.

Bohr's reply to Einstein's criticism was summarized by Rosenfeld who wrote the following:

> The refutation of Einstein's criticism does not add any new element to the conception of complementarity, but it is of great importance in laying bare a very deep-lying opposition between Bohr's general philosophical attitude and the still widespread habits of thought belonging to a glorious but irrevocably bygone stage in the evolution of science. . . . It was impressive to watch him thus at the height of his powers, in utmost concentration and unrelenting effort to attain clarity through painstaking scrutiny of every detail—true as ever to his favorite Schiller aphorism "Nur die Fülle führt zur Klarheit." He was particularly well served on this occasion by his uncommon ability to go into the opponent's views, dissect his arguments and turn them to the advantage of the truth. In this, however, he always proceeded with complete open-mindedness, and only rejoiced in victory if in winning it he had also deepened his own insight into the problem.

Bohr and Einstein met only twice more. Once was in 1939, when the world situation probably gave them other matters for discussion than quantum mechanics. Then came their last meeting, which took quite an unexpected course, but which also showed to what a high degree Bohr was affected by Einstein's opposition. When Robert Oppenheimer became director of the Princeton Institute for Advanced Studies, Bohr was nominated as a permanent nonresident member of the scientific staff. He could come to visit at any time and leave again whenever he wished. As early as the time of his flight from Denmark during World War II he had been offered an ideal research appointment there. He had other duties at that time, but now there were two periods when Bohr availed himself of his affiliation with the institute. The episode which concerns us here took place during the first of these periods, in 1948 when Einstein let Bohr use his large room at Princeton. Einstein did not like big rooms and preferred to use instead a small adjoining room which was actually supposed to be for an assistant. Bohr was accompanied on the journey by Abraham Pais, who told about one morning when Bohr asked him to come to his room at the institute. He apparently had something important to dictate. No sooner had Pais sat down than Bohr began walking swiftly around a large oblong table in the middle of the room.

He asked Pais to take down some sentences, little by little as they emerged, while he continued his circling. As so often before, he would linger over one word while considering the next, and he might say the first word imploringly, as it were, while searching for the second. On this occasion the word was "Einstein." Now Bohr was almost running around the table, repeating "Einstein . . . Einstein. . . ." Then he went to the window, gazed out, and repeated now and then "Einstein . . . Einstein. . . ."

At this moment the door opened very quietly and Einstein crept softly in. He put a finger to his lips and signalled to Pais with a roguish smile to remain quite still. He made stealthily for Bohr's tobacco jar, which was on the table, while Bohr stood unsuspectingly at the window muttering, "Einstein . . . Einstein. . . ." Pais was at a loss; should he intervene? But then the following happened:

> With a firm "Einstein," Bohr turned around. There they were, face to face, as if Bohr had summoned him forth. It is an understatement to say that for a moment Bohr was speechless. I myself who had seen it coming, had distinctly felt uncanny for a moment, so I could well understand Bohr's own reaction. A moment later the spell was broken when Einstein explained his mission and soon we were all bursting with laughter.

When Einstein turned seventy in 1949, Bohr at last had an opportunity to sum up their debates because he was invited to contribute to a book in honor of Einstein for an American series of books called "The Library of Living Philosophers." It took Bohr two years to write a 38-page chapter. But it has also stood subsequently—word for word—as Bohr's most outstanding and at the same time clearest (in spite of all the details) description of the apparent paradoxes of quantum mechanics. Bohr was able to include all the essential particulars of the dramatic development of quantum mechanics while at the same time ringing down the curtain on 25 years of debate with Einstein. Bohr felt that this was a unique opportunity for him to summarize his views in order to bring clarity. It is as though he is weaving a picture with two silk threads, each of its own color, but of equal strength. The one describes Bohr's affectionate admiration for Einstein's genius and underlines the latter's revolutionary contribution to physics, while the other equally carefully recounts all the thought-experiments and traps laid by Einstein during his opposition to allowing quantum mechanics to relinquish its foothold in classical physics. Nothing was missing from the rebuttal, although the firmness with which Bohr carries his arguments forward are only an underlying theme and never take on a polemical character.

In this most elegant presentation of a scientific controversy, which is of lasting interest in terms of its description of nature, Bohr invalidates each and every one of Einstein's counter-arguments, but rather than feeling this to be a victory, Bohr continued to find it almost incomprehensible that Einstein's final comment was that "it is so very contrary to my scientific instinct that I cannot forego the search for a more complete conception."

But instead of delaying the development of atomic physics, Einstein's

174 CHAPTER 24

resistance on the contrary stimulated Bohr to elucidate the concept of complementarity with greater and greater clarity. Bohr himself emphasizes this in his tribute to Einstein, in which he writes:

> When I had the great experience of meeting Einstein for the first time during a visit to Berlin in 1920, these fundamental questions formed the theme of our conversations. The discussions, to which I have often reverted in my thoughts, added to all my admiration for Einstein a deep impression of his detached attitude. Certainly, his favored use of such picturesque phrases as "ghost waves (Gespensterfelder) guiding the photons" did not imply a tendency toward mysticism, but illuminated rather a profound humor behind his penetrating remarks. Yet, a certain difference in attitude and outlook remained, since, with his mastery for coordinating apparently contrasting experience without abandoning continuity and causality, Einstein was perhaps more reluctant to renounce such ideals than someone for whom renunciation in this respect appeared to be the only way open to proceed with the immediate task of coordinating the abundant evidence of atomic phenomena, which increased from day to day in the exploration of this new field of knowledge.

This could hardly be expressed in a more self-effacing way. Bohr refers to himself as "someone" and thereby almost conceals, in the references to the abundance of experiences that presented themselves day by day, the role which he himself has played in order to attain—well, a boundary certainly, but at the same time a bright new reconstruction of time-honored ideals.

Bohr concludes with these words:

> The discussions with Einstein which have formed the theme of this article have extended over many years which have witnessed great progress in the field of atomic physics. Whether our actual meetings have been of short or long duration, they have always left a deep and lasting impression on my mind, and when writing this report I have, so to speak been arguing with Einstein all the time, even in discussing topics apparently far removed from the special problems under debate at our meetings. As regards the account of the conversations I am, of course, aware that I am relying only on my own memory, just as I am prepared for the possibility that many features of the development of quantum theory, in which Einstein has played so large a part, may appear to himself in a different light. I trust, however, that I have not failed in conveying a proper impression of how much it has meant to me to be able to benefit from the inspiration which we all derive from every contact with Einstein.

Einstein also was invited to write some recollections for the same book, and just as Bohr formulated his tribute with admiration and affection, Einstein wrote of Bohr's contribution with similar grace. After having noted Planck's discovery and his own contribution to the quantum theory he wrote:

> All my attempts, however, to adapt the theoretical foundation of physics to

this (new type of) knowledge failed completely. It was as if the ground had been pulled out from under one, with no firm foundation to be seen anywhere upon which one could have built. That this insecure and contradictory foundation was sufficient to enable a man of Bohr's unique instinct and tact to discover the major laws of the spectral lines and of the electron-shells of the atoms together with their significance for chemistry appeared to me like a miracle—and appears to me as a miracle even today. This is the highest form of musicality in the sphere of thought.

Léon Rosenfeld and J. A. Wheeler have probably probed the most deeply in trying to find the reason for Einstein's persistent opposition to the paradoxes of quantum mechanics. Rosenfeld tackled the problem in a Festschrift for Max Born published in 1963. He began by singling out the theory of knowledge which had served as a guide for Einstein particularly and for Bohr to a lesser extent, and which goes back to the Austrian philosopher and scientist Ernst Mach.

During his studies of the discoveries of earlier times, Mach found certain common features and in so doing described the standard procedure by which the concepts and laws of science are devised, based upon thought-experiments, i.e., experiments which are not carried out but imagined in an idealized form and supported by experience in similar circumstances. Essentially this implies that scientific ideas can be regarded as a kind of concentrated key to action: they are defined by the use of a predetermined series of appropriate apparatuses and are in that way reduced to a clearly demarcated connection between the senses of the observing researcher. In order to analyze the assumption of simultaneity Einstein thus imagined two observers exchanging light signals at the same time, while Bohr ascribed the absence of a causal connection in atomic phenomena to the interchange between the atomic systems and measuring instruments applied to them.

The weakness of Mach's theory, says Rosenfeld, is its oversimplification of the relationship between ideas and sense impressions. Ideas can be joined together by a tangled web of logical connections which form impressive structures, as in geometry, for example. And when we view such logical constructions we encounter a considerable difficulty: it is not immediately obvious that the sense impressions and the information which we receive from them indicate completely without ambiguity the ideas which are suitable to their description.

How is this situation to be clarified? A thinker like Henri Poincaré, who independently of Mach held views closely related to his, had a cunning way of getting around these difficulties. He simply ignored them. Poincaré reduces the ideas to this passive role inasmuch as he only chooses between ideas which already exist.

Rosenfeld pointed out that Einstein had originally followed the pattern indicated by Mach, and in large measure accepted the functional and fruitful aspects of Mach's philosophy. But gradually, as Einstein lost himself in abstract mathematical speculation, his thinking took a wrong turn. Like Poincaré he abandoned the measurable values in Mach's empirical approach. Certainly he could not imitate Poincaré and confine himself to the already accepted. He regarded scientific ideas and theories as "the free creations of the mind," but he added that in every single case it must be possible to find a final formal theory better adapted to experience than others and in this sense the only one true to reality. What he asserted was that the human mind with its free activity is capable of constructing a true picture of the world. But, says Rosenfeld, we cannot expect Einstein to instruct us how this wonderful harmony between our intellectual constructions and the phenomena of the external world comes about. For this harmony, said Einstein, is a miracle which we shall never be in a position to understand. In this way he ended up in pure mysticism.

How are we to avoid this mystification? asks Rosenfeld. What was Bohr's approach to the problem?

> The most striking difference between the attitudes of Einstein and Bohr is that Einstein stresses the permanence, the finality of scientific thought, while Bohr insists on its unceasing development. This gives the clue to the solution of the difficulty. It makes a tremendous difference whether one looks at a

Léon Rosenfeld.   *John A. Wheeler.*

theory in its final state, or at the imperfect stages through which it passed in the course of its development. The harmony between form and content ultimately achieved may indeed appear wonderful; but it was much less so in the preliminary drafts. The mystical touch, the wonder, is an illusion resulting from a static approach; it vanishes as soon as the process of formation and growth is considered in its development. New ideas are, of course, creations of the mind; but they are by no means free creations. They only arise as a response to the always recurring necessity of adjusting our mental picture of the world to our changing empirical knowledge of it. In its perspective, the interaction between observer and phenomena appears as an inherent part of the process and thereby is also susceptible to rational description. We simply cannot afford to ignore the fact that science is a human activity tied up with the whole process of organic adaptation of man's mind to the external world. Or at least those who choose to indulge in dreams of formal beauty must realize that they cut themselves off from the "solid ground of Nature."

J. A. Wheeler, with whom Bohr wrote a paper in 1939 on uranium fission, and who was one of the few whose name appeared on one of Bohr's papers, had a room at Princeton quite close to Einstein's. He had many conversations with Einstein over the years. "We explained to each other what we did not understand," and Wheeler gained more and more insight into Einstein's "Unbehagen." Einstein also had many conversations with other colleagues in the gardens of the institute at Princeton, where "he talked and walked, and walked and talked," but of greater importance to him were the colleagues he met in books. He was very fond of reading the old natural philosophers, and his greatest hero was Spinoza, who above all others gave expression to a convincing faith in the harmony of nature.

In his *Ethics* Spinoza states: "Nothing in the universe is contingent, but all things are conditioned to exist and operate in a particular manner by the necessity of divine nature." "Einstein," wrote Wheeler, "accepted determinism in his mind, in his heart, into his very bones." God does not play with dice.

In 1939 Wheeler arranged a colloquium at Princeton at which he asked Einstein to speak of quantum mechanics and discuss the disagreement with Bohr. Nothing new came out of this. Einstein maintained that the laws of physics were simple, and to a question from the audience, "But if they are not simple, what then?" he replied, "Then I would not be interested in them."

Bohr too felt that only what was simple was interesting in physics. But he added that simplicity is not there beforehand. At each new stage of development one must fight one's way forward through intermediate complexity before achieving the clarification which creates the new simplicity.

When this book was being written, Wheeler could still remember the conclusion of Einstein's address: "When a person such as a mouse observes the Universe, does that change the state of the Universe?"

If Einstein had an unshakable faith in the harmony of nature, then in truth harmony was no less Bohr's guiding star. But Bohr regarded each new conquest or perception as a springboard for further advance. He expressed it in these words in the speech he made at his fiftieth student class reunion: "Harmony allows itself only to be sensed, never grasped, and if we attempt to grasp it, it slips through our fingers by its essential nature. Nothing is fixed: every thought, yes, every word even, lends itself merely to emphasize connections which in themselves can never be fully described, but can always be amplified."

25

Complementarity

Niels Bohr often declared that our epoch, with its rapid developments in many areas of knowledge, was reminiscent of the Renaissance. And then if he needed to introduce complementarity in a few words, he would do so as follows:

> But even if the natural sciences have contributed so much to technology as we experience it every day, we have simultaneously and unexpectedly attained entirely new possibilities and insights into hitherto unsuspected conditions as observers of the natural world of which we ourselves are a part. Our progress thus contains a message of significance for our approach to common human problems, and therefore the progress of the natural sciences by no means involves any schism between humanism and the physical sciences. The ancient question of the unity of knowledge is put into a new perspective, and complementarity—as a framework broad enough to embrace the explanation of fundamental regularities in nature that cannot be summed up in a single picture—presents itself as a fruitful point of view.

However, it is important to make plain that complementarity is not a philosophical superstructure imposed on quantum mechanics. Bohr's analyses clearly showed that it is logically contained in quantum mechanics. Therefore one cannot accept quantum mechanics on the one hand and reject complementarity on the other. Einstein realized this too, and therefore he did not conceive of any different interpretation of quantum mechanics either. What he dreamed of was its total replacement with something quite different, but what this may be has still not been revealed fifty years later.

In order to facilitate our understanding of the new situation with regard to observation in physics, bound up as it is with complementarity, Bohr took analogies from everyday life, situations well known to us all and such as he himself had been absorbed by since his youth. He cited psychological experiences, for example, which have always been a considerable problem in philosophy. On the question of the

179

freedom of the will it is especially important to have regard to the complementary manner in which such words as "reflection" and "volition" are used.

When Bohr wanted to illustrate the complementarity aspect of psychology, he also pointed out the impossibility of distinguishing through self-observation between phenomena themselves and the conscious perception of them. When we say that we have our attention drawn to one or another aspect of a psychological experience, closer examination will disclose that we are dealing with situations which mutually exclude each other. When we attempt to analyze our own feelings, we hardly have them any more; they are not entirely the same as before we began to analyze them. Such psychological experiences, which can only be described by words like "thoughts" and "feelings," have a complementary relationship with experience in atomic physics.

As has already been suggested, Bohr's own road to the complementarity approach in quantum mechanics seems to have grown out of conceptions originating from everyday observations and his thoughts about them. We recall the sailing trip in 1927 during which Bohr, engrossed in the new interpretation of the quantum theory, spoke about the limitations of our means of expression, only to be interrupted immediately by one of his friends: "You told us exactly the same thing when we were young." With complementarity we find ourselves in the sphere of the paradoxical and when complementarity was first clearly linked with quantum mechanics, Bohr thought that it might also perhaps prove fruitful as a framework for description in other fields of knowledge, where it had not previously been recognized.

Robert Oppenheimer, who became interested in Bohr's ideas early on, gave a lecture on a BBC radio program shortly before Bohr's seventieth birthday in which he discussed the complementarity principle and pointed to the relationship between the individual human being and the community. On the one hand there is the human being as an end in himself, while on the other there is the person whose words and actions only acquire meaning in the context of other words and actions and in relation to other people. He also drew attention to the vast difference between continuous change and renewal, including the transitory nature which is a part of everything earthly—and the element of eternity which is in everything. He cited the antithesis between the constantly shifting and spontaneous as against the existing and enduring.

Bohr himself pointed out the typical complementarity relationship subsisting between concepts like instinct and reason. No human reasoning in the true sense is possible without the use of a conceptual structure based upon a language which each generation must learn from the beginning but the use of such concepts stands in distinct comple-

Bohr and Oppenheimer in 1958.

mentary contradiction to the development of hereditary instincts. And he called attention to a similar observational problem in the study of different human cultures, in relation to which the main difficulty in the way of an unbiased attitude lies in the background of tradition on which a harmonious philosophy of life within every human society is based and which makes it impossible to compare such different philosophies in any simple way. Here are features in common with the psychological problems involved in the impossibility of distinguishing clearly between an objective content and an observing subject. Bohr expresses this in these words:

> A description of our process of thought demands on the one hand that an objectively given content be confronted with a contemplating subject, while on the other hand—as will be apparent from the very mention of it—no sharp separation between object and subject can be maintained when the concept of such separation forms part of our own mental content.

To illustrate the necessity of distinguishing sharply between the means of observation and the system being observed, Bohr had a favorite example of a blind man's stick. If the stick is held firmly in the hand, it can be used as a kind of extension of the hand to explore the surround-

This is how Niels Bohr appeared to audiences when, as he often did, he abandoned his manuscript and alternately wrote on the board and talked. A lively discussion usually ensued.

This series of four photographs was taken in New York in 1937 by the American photographer Eric Schaal.

ings by touch. But as soon as the stick is held loosely in the hand, the stick itself becomes an object whose presence in the hand is divulged through the sense of touch, and thereby the stick loses its function as an instrument of observation. Bohr was so pleased with this example that when he sat down with a new colleague he would get him to try it out with a pencil. Those who knew the example and witnessed the test had great pleasure from watching Bohr's face light up in a big smile at the instant when he saw that the new colleague, sitting with his eyes closed, had realized the surprising result of the experiment.

On every occasion when Bohr wanted to generalize complementarity, he would turn back to the fondly remembered reading from his youth of Poul Martin Møller's unfinished story "The Adventures of a Danish Student." He always had the little book with the story with him, and whenever a young researcher came to the Institute and had learned enough Danish, the book was trotted out and the lines pointed out to him which Bohr would make famous by constantly amplifying them. It was the newcomer's initiation ceremony. Bohr referred to the conversation between the two cousins in the story, of whom the one, Frits, is distinguished by his down-to-earth competence in practical matters, while the other, a graduate student, is given to unworldly philosophical meditations. When Frits upbraids the student for not yet having made his mind up to avail himself of his opportunities of acquiring a practical trade, the student excuses himself by explaining the difficulties in which his reflections have placed him:

> It is because of my endless study of the question that I accomplish nothing. Even now I am thinking about my thoughts about it—yes, I am thinking about the fact that I am thinking about it, and I am dividing myself into an infinitely retrogressing series of I's, which are contemplating each other. I do not know which to stop at and consider to be the real one, and the instant I do stop, it is another I which is stopped there. I become confused and overcome by giddiness as though I were staring down into a bottomless abyss, and the thinking ends up with my having an abominable headache.

By reflecting upon everyday psychological experiences, Bohr maintained, we encounter the concept of complementarity in a choice between two standpoints, which, although they are mutually contradictory, can each still be justified by itself. They are both necessary for a complete (exhaustive) description.

We draw a dividing line between the psychological process which is made into an object for investigation and the observing subject when we direct attention to a specific aspect of the process. Depending on how we place the dividing line we can perceive a state of mind as a part of our subjective feelings or we can analyze it as a part of the process observed. The understanding that these two situations are complementary solves the riddle of the student's I's who observe each other, and in Bohr's view constitutes the only salvation from his torments.

Bohr was amused by another description of the student's anguish. When Frits could not see why it should take the student such a long time to begin writing his dissertation, the latter answered:

> To be sure I have seen thoughts set down on paper before; but since I have come to understand clearly the contradiction inherent in such an undertaking, I feel quite incapacitated for forming any written sentence. But notwithstanding that experience has shown countless times that it can still be done, I torture myself trying to solve the inexplicable riddle: how one can think, talk or write. Look, my friend! A movement presupposes a direction. The intellect cannot proceed without moving along a certain line; but before following this line it surely must have imagined it beforehand. So that means one has always thought every thought before thinking it. Every thought that seems to be a minute's work in this way presupposes an eternity. It could almost drive me mad. For how can any thought be born when it must always have existed before it came into being? When you write a sentence you must have the sentence in your head before you write it. But before you got it into your head you must surely have thought of it; otherwise how could one know out of what a period could be brought into being? And before you thought of it, you must have imagined it; otherwise what could have possessed you to think of it? In this way it goes on into the infinite, and this infinity is bounded by a moment.

"But confound it," said Frits carelessly, "in your very own proofs that thoughts cannot move, your own thoughts go forward pretty briskly."

"That is just the trouble," the student replied. "That makes it an even bigger muddle, which no mortal will ever be able to put straight. Realization of the impossibility of thought itself involves an impossibility, and the recognition of this produces in turn an inexplicable contradiction."

It occurred to Rosenfeld, with his intimate acquaintance with Bohr's method of working, his hesitation over every word and every sentence, that perhaps Bohr was so fond of the student because at certain moments he saw in him something of a caricature of himself. But there was one crucial difference between Bohr and the unhappy eternal student. One day when Bohr was working on the complementary relationships of electromagnetism, he went for a bicycle ride with Rosenfeld northwards out of the city. When they were passing Nærumgaard, Bohr said, "It was here that I finished my first paper." Then he told Rosenfeld about how he had worked on it for a long time in Copenhagen, performing experiments that seemed unending to him. "All the time I kept getting involved in new details which I thought I had to get to the bottom of first. But in the end my father sent me out here, away from the laboratory, so I could finish writing."

It would hardly have helped the student in Møller's story to be sent to the country, but Bohr did complete his work for the gold medal of The Royal Danish Academy of Arts and Sciences. Later on he was able to wrestle with a problem for years, coming back to the same point over and over, and not get lost in a maze. He knew when he had to stop. On the other hand an anecdote about Niels and Harald Bohr may be apt here. It has been told in many variations as far as the external framework goes, but the ending and the point of the story are always the same. Niels and Harald were in some situation where a group of journalists were posing a succession of questions and Niels Bohr did his best to answer as fully as he could. It took a long time, and the journalists' attention began to wander. The most eager of them turned to Harald and asked if he could summarize. Harald did so, briefly, clearly, and precisely, and then asked his brother, "Is that right, is that what you meant?" whereupon Niels exclaimed unhappily, "Oh, Harald, you say it so terribly clearly."

However much Bohr strove for greater clarity and more certain forms of expression, he nonetheless frequently disappointed those who sought for new examples of the wisdom of complementarity. In the parallel case of Einstein's relativity principle, it had been much abused as the saying "Everything is relative" was applied to everyday banalities: Bohr did not want to trivialize the insight of complementarity which can lead a person into the depths of knowledge. But by using the example of Møller's student, Bohr guided the initiate into the core of the problem of unambiguous communication of experience.

Bohr's ideas quickly became accepted by physicists, especially among the younger generation. But at first his philosophical ideas attracted only slight attention from biologists, because the relevance of complementarity to biology was unclear. Among the philosophers there were almost none who had sufficient insight into physics to be able to understand the new ideas.

Bohr's philosophical ideas initially arose when he saw that Rutherford's atomic model could not be married with classical physics. He realized the inevitability of the break, and he had the courage to carry it through. He also had the intuition to make successful guesses as to how further progress could be made, and his guesses sprang from his insight into the germ of the paradox in nature itself:

> If a concept like the Unity of Knowledge is to have any meaning, then all experiences, whether they involve science, art, or philosophy, must be communicated with the aid of our common means of expression. And in face of the diversity of cultural forms one must search out those features in all civilizations which have their roots in the common human situation. However, it is obvious that the single individual's circumstances in society in themselves present aspects that are often mutually exclusive, which at once

opens for discussion the scope of such concept as justice and mercy. All human societies seek to unite such concepts, but if the juridical statues are followed to the letter, no opportunity is afforded for the free display of mercy.

It is equally true, however, he emphasized by referring to the Greek tragic poets, that compassion can bring us into conflict with every clearly formulated conception of justice.

Bohr thought that the harmony inherent in the concept of the Unity of Knowledge would help us to maintain a balanced attitude toward our existence, and he added his own tenet: that we are confronted with a human situation with complementary relationships built into it, as expressed unforgettably in ancient Chinese philosophy, which states that in the great drama of existence we ourselves are both actors and audience.

Abraham Pais has related the following episode from Tisvilde when Bohr was preparing a lecture on the occasion of the 300th anniversary of the birth of Newton.

Bohr stood in front of the blackboard (wherever Bohr dwelt, a blackboard was never far) and wrote down some general themes to be discussed. One of them had to do with the harmony of something or other. So Bohr wrote down the word "harmony." It looked about as follows:

However as the discussion progressed, Bohr became dissatisfied with the word harmony. He walked around restlessly. Then he stopped and his face lit up. "Now I've got it. We must change 'harmony' to 'unity'." So he picked up the chalk again, stood there looking for a moment at what he had written before and then made the following change:

with one triumphant bang of the chalk on the blackboard. Harmony and unity, these were the main points.

It goes without saying that Bohr's contribution of the complementarity principle to quantum mechanics could not be the fruit merely of the inspiration received from Poul Martin Møller. His open-minded approach to paradox and his sympathy with the philosophical point of view of the ancient Chinese sages showed Bohr a more direct way to a swifter understanding of the basic common features of nature than most of his contemporaries would find. And with this insight he would further develop the idea of complementarity into the philosophical concept of which he stands as the father.

As already mentioned, there are scientists today who regret that Bohr did not leave more writings for posterity. Including his articles and published lectures, the total number of his publications is only a little over one hundred and fifty. The countless letters he wrote will not help matters until they have been assembled and edited into an accessible form. But bearing in mind the colossal labor which he put into the repeated rewriting of his manuscripts, the number of publications is understandable. It is also possible that he derived his greatest pleasure from furthering progress through dialogue. Every single thought that he formulated in print was the outcome of a toilsome and at times painful process. We have already observed how he would never give up until he believed that each individual sentence could not be brought to greater clarity. It is said that in one day and evening he could wear out several assistants and colleagues, but for him a manuscript was, as he himself expressed it, a document to be corrected. He compared his mode of thinking and working to that of a sculptor, who hews away the superfluous in order to expose the essential.

At the same time, Bohr's working method precluded in every way the steady flow of a stream of publications. In the midst of exacting deliberations he would abandon the work he was immediately engaged on in order to start on a new task if he felt that the solution to the latter would lead to clarification of a newly arisen critical point. He approached problems—as did Goethe—by willingly yielding to "die Forderung des Tages" (the demands of the day).

But despite the struggle with the subject matter, Bohr availed himself of every opportunity to make plain his ideas about complementarity. This was especially the case when he was invited to speak in connection with some cultural event, congress, or commemoration day. There is a special story about the lecture which he prepared for the inaugural meeting of the Second International Congress of Light Therapy, which took place in Copenhagen in 1932. On the same day that the meeting took place, the German physicist Max Delbrück, who at that time was associated with the Bohr Institute, returned to Copenhagen after a journey. Léon Rosenfeld picked him up at the railway station and by going directly to Christiansborg, where the lecture was to be held, they arrived just in time. "To claim," Rosenfeld wrote later, "that we were fascinated by the lecture, whose title was 'Light and Life', would be a romantic overstatement, but it is a fact that when Delbrück read the paper afterwards and pondered over it, he became so enthusiastic about the vision which it revealed over the far-flung expanses of biology that he immediately decided to take up the challenge."

Max Delbrück, who had worked for Otto Hahn and Lise Meitner in Germany, became a geneticist and molecular biologist from that time onwards, and thirty years later when he was appointed director of the new genetics institute in Cologne, he invited Bohr to speak at the formal opening of the institute. Delbrück suggested "Light and Life Revisited" as a title for the lecture. Bohr said yes reluctantly. He was feeling very tired, as we shall see later. But the thought of the lecture appealed to him for many reasons, and he set about preparing for it with his customary meticulous care. He revised the old lecture at essential points, but the printed version was Bohr's last, but incomplete, work. This essay is prized, however, as a clarified revision and further development of the earlier lecture, and was published in the new volume in which selected chapters are now assembled under the title *Essays 1958/1962 on Atomic Physics and Human Knowledge.*

In the first "Light and Life" lecture, Bohr had a heaven-sent occasion for pointing out the obvious ambiguity in the concept of light: the complementary relationship in the discovery that all light effects can be traced back to individual processes each of which includes a quantum of light and which are apparently in conflict with a picture of the propagation of light as a continuous wave. In the second lecture, "Light and Life Revisited," he returns thirty years later to the quantum of light as the fundamental element of atomic physics and as an allegory for biologists on the existence of life itself. In the first lecture it was an especially fruitful inspiration for Bohr that his approach to the significance of the complementarity principle for biology could be grounded in his father's standpoint at the close of the previous century. It was in those years that the advocates of mechanistic materialism felt the foundations shaking under the impact of the new finalistic views, which said that only by knowing the function of an organ could one hope to elucidate its structure and physiological processes. Niels Bohr's father Christian Bohr was keenly interested in the new ideas but felt a loyalty to the body of practical experience which biology hitherto had attained; at the same time, however, he was anxious to analyze the life processes as far as the technical means permitted.

Niels Bohr sensed here a complementary relationship between the physicochemical and the purely functional aspects—the two approaches that were sharply at variance with each other. He considered that this contradiction was merely a consequence of the kind of logical conceptions which in physics had been recognized as too narrow, and that the broader framework of complementarity had room for both approaches. Both could be turned to advantage without any conflict, and this could lead to new developments in which the possibilities for scientific analysis could be fully exploited, just as his father had advocated. He considered that a continuous exchange of matter must take place between organisms and the surrounding medium in order for them to be able to maintain life, so that a clear demarcation of the organism as the physicochemical system is not possible. Therefore it may well be that every experimental intervention to make the distinction sharp enough to allow an exhaustive physicochemical analysis of an organism would obstruct the metabolic process to such a degree that it would lead to the organism's death. In saying this he wanted to illustrate the fact that the physicochemical concepts on the one hand, and the concepts describing biological functions on the other, refer to conditions for observation of organisms which are complementary to each other. And he suggested that the existence of life itself perhaps must be accepted as a fundamental fact in biology just as the quantum effect in atomic physics must be regarded as a fundamental element which cannot be reduced to the concepts of classical physics.

When Bohr took up this conjecture for reexamination in "Light and Life Revisited" in 1962, he revised it at one crucial point. He stressed that it cannot be the task of biology to account for the fate of every single one of the countless atoms in a living organism. Instead, the situation is that in the study of biological regulators no sharp distinction can be made between the detailed structure of these mechanisms and those functions they fulfill in maintaining the life of the organism as a whole:

> Many expressions used in practical physiology reflect a research method based on knowledge of the functional role of the parts of the organism and aiming at a physical and chemical account of their finer structures and of the processes in which they participate. As long as one speaks of "life," whether for practical or for epistemological reasons, such finalistic expressions will be employed to supplement the terminology of molecular biology. However, this circumstance in itself does not involve any limitation on the application of the well-substantiated principles of atomic physics to biology.

Bohr also interpolated into the lecture one comment which was not included in the manuscript: "Finally, there is a question of how we are now to advance further in biology. I believe that the wonder which physicists felt thirty years ago has taken a new direction. Life will always be a source of wonder. But what does change is the balance between this sense of wonder and the courage to strive for understanding."

The basis for the complementary mode of description in biology is not connected with the problems of controlling the interaction between the object and the measuring instrument but with the practically inexhaustible complexity of the organism. This is the crucial new issue raised in "Light and Life Revisited." Bohr had realized during his revision that he had really gone a step too far on the earlier occasion. The development of modern molecular biology had shown that the situation was more subtle than could have been suspected in the 1930s, and he arrived at a clear and concise point in his view of biology: in the description of living organisms we need to use words and concepts which are alien to physics, such as "purpose." We can analyze a liver into its atomic components; we can account for all the chemical and physical processes which take place in the liver; and there is still the obvious question: what purpose does this organ serve in the living organism? This is a question one would no longer put with respect to a star in the Milky Way.

As an indication of the possible application of the complementarity concept in elucidating the human psychological situation, Bohr pointed out how the close link between psychological experiences and physical and chemical processes in our bodies finds outward manifestation in the use of medication for mental disorders. That physiological processes can at no time be left out of consideration is clearly reflected by the degree to which everything that has ever penetrated our consciousness can be remembered. And Robert Oppenheimer added:

> Despite all the progress that has been made in the physiology of the sense organs and of the brain, despite our increasing knowledge of these intricate marvels both as to their structure and their functioning, it seems rather unlikely that we shall be able to describe in physicochemical terms the physiological phenomena which accompany a conscious thought, or sentiment, or will. Today the outcome is uncertain. Whatever the outcome, we know that, should an understanding of the physical correlate of elements of consciousness indeed be available, it will not itself be the appropriate description for the thinking man himself, for the clarification of his thoughts, the resolution of his will, or the delight of his eye and mind at works of beauty. Indeed, an understanding of the complementary nature of conscious life and its physical interpretation appears to me a lasting formulation of the historic views called psycho-physical parallelism.
>
> For within conscious life, and in its relations with the description of the physical world, there are again many examples. There is the relation between the cognitive and the affective sides of our lives, between knowledge or analysis and emotion or feeling. There is the relation between the aesthetic and the heroic, between feeling and that precursor and refiner of action, the ethical commitment; there is the classical relation between the analysis of one's self, the determination of one's motives and purposes, and that freedom of choice, that freedom of decision and action, which are complementary to it.
>
> Whether a physico-chemical description of the material counterpart of

consciousness will in fact ever be possible, whether physiological or psychological observation will ever permit with any relevant confidence the prediction of our behavior in moments of decision and in moments of challenge, we may be sure that these analyses and these understandings, even should they exist, will be as irrelevant to the acts of decision and the castings of the will as are the trajectories of molecules to the entropy of a gas. To be touched with awe, or humor, to be moved by beauty, to make a commitment or a determination, to understand some truth—these are complementary modes of the human spirit. All of them are part of man's spiritual life. None can replace the others, and where one is called for the others are in abeyance.

Bohr became involved time and time again in discussion of these ideas with philosophers and psychologists but he seldom encountered understanding. He retained grateful memories of the polymathic Harald Høffding, who frequently and strongly asserted the close connection between philosophy and natural science. Although Høffding lacked detailed acquaintance with natural scientific thinking, he evinced a lively interest in the new perceptions. When Bohr as a young man was attending Høffding's lectures in formal logic, he became aware of a latent error in Høffding's exposition, and by now it can hardly surprise the reader that he quite openly brought it to the notice of Høffding, whom he admired and of whom he was very fond. Neither will it occasion any amazement that Høffding took note of Bohr's correction in a later revised edition of the lectures, in which he even wrote that his attention had been drawn to the error by one of his students.

When ideas about complementarity came up for discussion Bohr was gratified by the receptiveness of Johannes Witt-Hansen, professor of philosophy at the University of Copenhagen. But he had no success at all with Jørgen Jørgensen, author of the book *Psychology on a Biological Foundation*. They had long discussions, for Jørgensen really wanted to understand Bohr's ideas. Indeed he was convinced that natural science and philosophy had to be closely linked in the endeavor to arrive at a theory of human knowledge. But it was as though they spoke two widely different languages. Jørgensen was not particularly familiar with physics, and if Bohr was dismayed after these discussions, Jørgensen did not want for words to express despair. There is a very eloquent story, from the summer of 1950, when Asger Aaboe, Jens Lindhard, and Jørgen Jørgensen were all staying not far from Bohr in Tisvilde. Piet Hein had stayed with Bohr for a time that same summer and, as noted earlier, had helped with the polishing of a number of short papers. When the papers had been retranscribed, Piet Hein was again on a visit to Tisvilde and had a copy with him one day when he went to visit Jørgensen in Vejby. As soon as Jørgensen had read the paper, he asked Piet Hein whether he would ask Bohr some questions on his return to Tisvilde. Piet Hein, who knew how far apart the two of them were and how futile it would be, replied, "I will ask Bohr just one question." Jørgensen pondered for a long time, and finally he said, "Then I will say please ask Niels Bohr what he means when he uses the word 'reality' on the first line of the first page of this paper." On Piet Hein's return some time passed before he put Jørgensen's question to Bohr. Only when he was on the point of leaving did he blurt it out. Bohr's first reaction was silence and quiet sighs and smiles over the difficulty. Piet Hein goes on,

> Then he pulled himself together and said, "Well, I think I must ask you to explain to me . . . how Jørgen Jørgensen's mind works." So I did so. The main theme of this was that in order that the conclusion should be indisputable, Jørgen Jørgensen had to proceed from premises of which he entertained no doubt whatsoever (in contrast to Niels Bohr, who kept a problem open from all angles) and that for him, words had a meaning in themselves—for example, words such as "reality" and "actuality." After a brief silence Bohr replied, "Yes, then please tell Jørgen Jørgensen that when I or any other physicist ever say reality, then we mean . . . nothing."

Asger Aaboe, who heard this conversation, recounted it to Jens Lindhard, who recalls how Bohr came and said to him one morning when they were working together, "I have made a great discovery, a very great discovery: anything which any philosopher has ever written is sheer nonsense." Bohr was capable of expressing himself thus bitingly in conversation, but Jens Lindhard knew well that what Bohr had in mind were the various schools of philosophy which spent all their time defending their doctrines against one another rather than opening themselves to new ideas.

"No one who calls himself a philosopher understands the significance of the complementary mode of description," Bohr said. "At all events they cannot, or a few years ago could not, see that this is a question of the only possible objective description." There must come a day, he believed, when a direct understanding between philosophers and natural scientists would come about through education.

"Those who thought that Copernicus' system was elegant were killed, Bruno was burnt and Galileo was compelled to retract his words. But in the next generation the school children did not find anything crazy in it, and thus a situation was created where the new ideas had to be taken for granted. I believe the same thing will happen with the complementary mode of description."

Bohr often quoted and also enlarged upon the facetious characterization of the difference between a specialist and a philosopher. The specialist concentrates on learning more and more about less and less and ends up knowing everything about nothing, while the philosopher, with his wide-ranging interest in garnering experiences from wider and wider fields, ends up knowing nothing about everything. "But we"—Bohr always said "we" not "I"—"usually say that an expert is a man who by personal painful experience knows a little bit about the grossest errors one can commit in the tiniest possible field."

In his admiration for Bohr's capacity for achieving breakthroughs, Heisenberg remarked one day that Bohr was more a philosopher than a physicist, but Heisenberg knew that the clarification of quantum mechanics would never have been accomplished without the philosopher and the physicist in one and the same person. On this subject Bohr himself said, "I believe that never in the entire history of science have so many people worked so intensively for so many years in so small a field"—they were all experts.

There are many accounts of how intense the discussions were when the Copenhagen school was working on quantum mechanics, but there is one anecdote in particular from the later years which says a great deal about what was special about Bohr. One day, as so often before, the discussion at the Institute had been a long one. Bohr wanted to get to the core of the problem they had run up against. Many people took part, but gradually they all gave up and went away, until at least there were only two people left—father and son. When Aage Bohr advanced what he thought had to be the final argument, Niels Bohr answered, "Yes, but Aage, that is logic, you know, but it does not have anything to do with physics."

Of course Bohr attached the greatest importance to logical stringency, but formal logic plainly did not have his heart. When Rosenfeld was a student he was as interested in the humanities as in science, and the choice of physics as a research field was both an expression of his unique ability and of his feeling for the fruitfulness of interchange between the humanities and science. His approach as a scientist was that what really counted was to learn from nature by putting the right questions, and here he and Bohr were on common ground. But as he later related, his admission into complementarity and the circle around Bohr could not take place without the pain that is part of a true initiation.

Rosenfeld's first message from Bohr was a telegram he received in Göttingen in 1929. It said that the Easter conference in Copenhagen to which Rosenfeld was invited had been postponed for a few days. When he arrived in Copenhagen, Bohr met him at the railway station and explained that the reason for the postponement was that he must first complete the translation of a paper to be published in the university Festschrift. Bohr recounted the venerable traditions of this Festschrift and gave Rosenfeld to understand that it would have been a catastrophe if he had not been able to deliver the paper on time. Rosenfeld for his part thought that this was probably a considerable overstatement of the situation. But "how feeble at that moment was my conception of the tragedy concealed behind the apparently simple procedure of giving a paper its final polishing. And how little did I sense that it was to be my fate to be involved in countless such tragedies!''

Rosenfeld relates also of his meeting with Bohr at the station that what made a special impression on him was the fatherly benevolence radiating from Bohr's whole being, which was further underlined by the presence of some of his sons.

> I speculated a good deal over these sons. When I saw Bohr again at the Institute the next morning, there were also a couple of sons around him, but they were not the same ones. I thought he must have a whole host of them. That same afternoon I was utterly confounded to see yet aother son at his side. He seemed to conjure them up from the ground or pull them out of his sleeve like a magician. In the end I learned to distinguish between them and found out that despite everything there was only a limited number.

The Easter conference began with Bohr's opening lecture. Rosenfeld continues his description: "I do not know what the Athenian delegation felt on their return from consulting the Delphic oracle, but I imagine that it would have been akin to my feelings after having heard Bohr's introduction." And Rosenfeld relates how the subsequent exposition "made all our heads swim (except Pauli)."

On the last day of the conference several of the participants expressed ideas which Rosenfeld felt were quite mistaken, and he whispered that they seemed to be incorrect, whereupon Bohr whispered back, "No, it is sheer nonsense." However, since Bohr now realized that Rosenfeld was interested and eager, he took him to a nearby room, where Rosenfelt sat down at an oblong table

> while he himself began to walk around at a lively pace in a "Keplerian ellipse," all the time explaining in a low voice his thoughts on "complementarity." He walked with bent head and knit brows: from time to time, he looked up at me and underlined some important point by a sober gesture. As he spoke, the words and sentences which I had read before in his papers suddenly took life and became loaded with meaning. It was one of the few solemn moments that count in an existence, the revelation of a world of dazzling thought, truly an initiation.

Bearing in mind the expected traditional discomfort associated with a real initiation ceremony, the present one left nothing to be desired. "For since I had to strain my ears to the utmost in order to hear the words of the master, I was compelled to keep rotating in time with his wanderings around the table. The real purpose of the ceremony, however, first became clear to me when Bohr at last emphasized that complementarity cannot be glimpsed without feeling completely dizzy. When I heard this, I understood everything."

One of the physicists who visited the Bohr Institute was the Japanese Nobel Prize winner Hideki Yukawa. When Rosenfeld met him in Kyoto in 1961, he asked him whether Japanese physicists had had the same difficulty as western physicists in coming to terms with Bohr's idea of complementarity. Yukawa answered: "Bohr's argumentation has always appeared obvious to us. . . . You understand, in Japan we were never led astray by Aristotle."

When Rosenfeld wrote this in 1963, it was thirty years after quantum electrodynamics had been completed in essentials via the complementarity principle, and he summed up the situation in this way: "On the face of it, physicists at large have reconciled themselves with this intrusion of dialectics into their traditional modes of thought. Who among us, however, could boast of having mastered all the intricacies of complementarity arguments to the point of being prepared for any situation?" Here Rosenfeld recalls an episode when one of Bohr's faithful and distinguished students, Victor Weisskopf, had undertaken, not without much effort, the exposition of a difficult problem involving complementarity, and when one of his colleagues expressed doubt he at once admonished him with "Bohr always wins." Rosenfeld adds,

> Too few even now realize the earnestness of the epistemological issues with which Bohr had to contend single-handed; too few fathom the depth of the problems he had solved and appreciate the revolutionary significance of his contribution to a better understanding of the dialectic process and the development of a truly scientific philosophy. Complementarity is no system, no doctrine without ready-made precepts. There is no via regia to it; no formal definition of it can even be found in Bohr's writings, and this worries many people.

And further Rosenfeld wrote: "He often evoked the thinkers of the past who had intuitively recognized dialectical aspects of existence and endeavored to give them poetical or philosophical expression; our only advantage over these great men, he would observe, is that in physics we have been presented with such a simple and clear case of complementarity that we are able to study it in detail and thus arrive at a precise formulation of a logical relationship of universal scope."

Perhaps Bohr gave the most poetic expression to the idea of complementarity when he returned home after his visit to Japan. One evening, enthralled, he had looked up toward Mount Fuji at sunset, when the topmost peak was hidden behind a curtain of gold-rimmed clouds. The great mass of the mountain under the brilliant crown left him awestruck by its majesty. But the next morning the scene was quite different. Now the highest peak of the mountain could be seen, covered with sparkling snow and reaching upwards above the billowing morning mist of the valley. The landscape radiated joy and gaiety. In this way, said Bohr, the two views of the mountain did not represent one single mountain at all. Each of them had its special individual character: the two were complementary.

For his coat of arms Bohr chose the symbol of Taoism, the ancient Chinese Yin and Yang, two similarly shaped figures that fit together and form a circular disc. As two opposing elements, Yin and Yang are complementary to each other, and together they form the world.

Yin and Yang each have a dot of the other's color within themselves as a symbol that each contains the germ of the other, that they mutually imply one another. In this way the sign also became a symbol of Niels Bohr's human and scientific attitude. Harmony and unity were for him the condition of our being and knowing.

26

Aiding the Refugees

Until the beginning of the 1930s, little was talked about among the physicists at Bohr's Institute except physics, philosophy, art, and literature. A common mode of thinking and feeling was created. The group included people from many European countries as well as from the Soviet Union, Japan, and India. "No world war," wrote Victor Weisskopf, "no political gulf, nothing could shake the basic unity of this group, whose members always felt themselves to be 'priests of a church'. . . . This spirit grew out of pure science, even when science is understood in the deep sense in which Bohr pursued to it with his friends."

But with Hitler's assumption of power in 1933 a new period began in the history of the Niels Bohr Institute. During a journey through Germany that same year, Bohr made enquiries through his colleagues to find out which scientists could expect dismissal as a result of the new "racial laws." His continuing help for scientists who were already in difficulty or whose lives were threatened made the Institute a transit point for many men and women fleeing to the free world.

Perhaps the following incident which occurred in 1933 during Bohr's trip to Germany tells more than any longer account. In Hamburg, Bohr sought out Otto Robert Frisch, a fairly young Jewish physicist, who later related that Bohr went straight over to him when he entered the laboratory, took him by his waistcoat buttons and said, "I hope you will come and work with us for a while. We need people who can carry out intellectual experiments."

Frisch had just finished an experiment on the sodium atom which few people had believed to be possible, but he had little hope for the future. That evening, however, he went home and wrote to his mother: "You are not to worry about me any longer. Our Lord Himself has taken me by the waistcoat buttons, and He smiled at me."

Bohr also involved himself in practical questions of how help could

198

Left, Gerda Ploug Sarp's drawing from 1935, and right, Homi J. Bhabha's drawing from 1960.

be organized on a larger scale. At home in Copenhagen "The Danish Committee for Support of Intellectual Workers in Exile" was established in that same year, with Professor Aage Friis as chairman. Harald and Niels Bohr were both members of the Committee along with their former schoolfellow Albert V. Jørgensen, barrister of the Danish Supreme Court, and Dr. Thorvald Madsen, director of the State Serum Institute. The very active secretary was Gerhard Breitscheid, son of a prominent German social democrat. Working alongside were the Jewish aid committee known as the "Committee of May 1932" and the social democratic Matteotti Foundation. They all merged later to form "The United Danish Emigrant Aid Committee," which dealt with all German emigration problems.

Through his colleagues in other countries, Bohr was able to get posts established and to have vacant appointments filled by refugees, chiefly in England but also in the United States. In Scandinavia, Sweden was the destination of many. There were others whom Bohr was able to keep in Denmark through the good offices of the Carlsberg and Rask-Ørsted Foundations and a good many physicists thus became associated with the Institute as long as they were able to stay in Denmark. It was not possible to establish positions equivalent to what they were used to for everybody, however, and especially not for scientists accustomed to directing entire institutes with considerable staff. Bohr was anxious too about their future in Denmark, and even before the end of 1939 he managed to get positions for most of the Jewish refugees who were under his roof in either Sweden, England, or the United States. All the records relating to these activities were destroyed in the early hours of the morning of April 9, 1940, when the German occupation of Denmark began.

Those who lived through that period have never forgotten the amount of time which Bohr devoted to the personal problems of many individuals. He was tireless in arranging everything for the best. If a refugee did not find the post Bohr had procured to be attractive, then Bohr sought energetically for another one—and usually succeeded in finding one.

One of the most famous refugees was the German physicist James Franck, who had collaborated with Hertz to develop an apparatus for electron impact experiments, which could measure impact energies for the lowest stationary states. In this way they had provided incontrovertible proof of Bohr's postulates in the atomic theory.

Franck traveled first to the United States but returned to Denmark for a time in order to work with Bohr. In Germany he had had a large institute in Göttingen with many staff members so his visit was not without problems. However, Bohr managed to secure as an assistant for Franck, the young physicist Hilde Levi, who had arrived in Denmark in 1934. She was the last Jewish student to receive a doctorate in Berlin, slipping through with the aid of the physicist Max van Laue, who like Bohr, worked very hard on the behalf of many Jewish scientists.

Levi had collaborated with Frisch to build the Institute's first "homemade" Geiger counter and amplifier. She remained in Denmark after the German occupation, and was safe for a while because at first the Germans were not paying much attention to female Jewish researchers. In the years before her final flight to Sweden in 1943, Hilde Levi experienced Bohr's incredible solicitude. On Christmas Eve for several years she was invited to his home and made to feel a part of the family. She has said of these evenings that they were "the quintessence of closeness and human warmth." After dinner they would sit in the middle of the room, with Bohr in the sofa corner. And then he would read Hans Christian Andersen's fairy tales. The whole family—sons, relatives, Aunt Hanna, and all the guests—every single one enjoyed and loved these evenings. "For me they were the most beautiful adventures: I shall never forget them."

And after the war Bohr's solicitude continued. When both he and Levi had returned to Copenhagen after the war, he took steps on his own initiative to enable her to visit her aged parents, who had escaped from Germany to Belgium and were living under great privation. Travel was difficult for a long time after the war but Bohr arranged to get Hilde

Levi onto a military flight, a courier plane with a sack of mail from the Danish foreign ministry to the Danish ambassador in Brussels.

The Polish-born physicist, Dr. Stefan Rozental, who has been mentioned earlier, also came to Denmark before the war began and remained at the Institute until 1943. After Léon Rosenfeld left in 1940, Rozental became Bohr's closest collaborator and his right-hand man during the final difficult time before Bohr himself had to leave the country.

A vital contribution was also made by another refugee, Sophie Hellman. The history of her association with the Institute is a story in itself and also shows what great care Bohr took of his staff. She arrived in Denmark in 1935 to visit Hilde Levi, whom she knew from Munich, where she had been a scientific secretary. Levi told Bohr about Hellman's secretarial abilities and her knowledge of languages. However, since she did not have a resident permit for Denmark, she could not seek work there. But then a fortunate situation arose for her: Bohr was in need of help. He had to make arrangements for a conference to be held at the Institute and his secretary was very young. She was well-meaning but not equal to the task, and so Harald Bohr intervened. On the pretext of his own need for help, he asked Sophie Hellman whether she could assist him occasionally. He got others at his institute to do the same, and since everyone was exceedingly satisfied with her work, Harald was able to report to Niels before long that Mrs. Hellman would be the perfect secretary for him. She was not aware of this when to her surprise she was invited to a garden party at the honorary residence. Margrethe introduced her to the guests in the garden, and then she went to talk to Bohr in his study. He asked her if she would consider becoming his secretary? She agreed and Bohr handed her a piece of paper and a pencil—and so she began. The conference was organized perfectly, and after the war she was responsible for all major events at the Institute, and known and esteemed by all the scientists who came to visit. But at first Bohr had great difficulty in securing a work permit for her. In order to obtain one he had to document that she was able to do something which no one else could do. Since the post was only described as a secretarial one, it was difficult even for Bohr to convince the Danish officials. Only the initiated could appreciate how hard it was to be Bohr's secretary from early morning to late at night. Sophie Hellman could do it, and she remained Bohr's secretary until his death. She became almost an institution and she created a protective barrier around Bohr, who became ever busier. She also began to systematize his extensive scientific correspondence, which was more or less a jungle of letters; and it was also characteristic of her care that she had Bohr's collected works bound, and presented them to him on his seventieth birthday (with later supplements). For a long time this was the only bound set in existence.

George de Hevesy, the friend of Bohr's young manhood in Manchester, was another of the greats whom Bohr welcomed when it became intolerable for him to remain in Germany, where he had been at the University of Freiburg. Hevesy "inherited" Hilde Levi as his colleague when James Franck left the Institute.

For his doctoral thesis at John Hopkins University in 1984 the Norwegian scientific historian Finn Aaserud described the major factors underlying the progress made in atomic physics in the 1930s. He found that one of the main factors was that the racial laws in Hitler's Germany forced the pace of development in many other places because so many prominent scientists had to flee the country. The refugees sought each other and settled wherever their research could thrive. Aaserud also notes the fact that the arrival of particularly distinguished scientists at the Bohr Institute meant that Bohr had to find new problems to enable people like Hevesy and Franck to flourish, and this also led to rapid developments. With quantum mechanics one epoch was concluded; with Hevesy, Bohr inaugurated isotope research, and with Franck, nuclear physics.

In addition, through an indiscretion, Bohr also helped to save a great Italian physicist from Hitler's allies. In the fall of 1938 he told Enrico Fermi, who was visiting the Institute, that he probably would receive the Nobel Prize that year. In almost any other circumstance it would have been unthinkable for Bohr to have broken the confidence which the Nobel Committee expected from him and others perhaps might have hesitated. But Bohr took the responsibility, and Fermi and his family grasped the opportunity to flee Italy. He took his wife and children with him to the Nobel Prize ceremony in Stockholm and then flew straight from there to New York. Everything was well prepared. He was received with open arms at Columbia University.

27

The Isotope Adventure

Enrico Fermi had already made his mark both as a theoretician and as an experimental physicist when the free world received him with open arms. It is commonly known that by bombarding an element with neutrons, a radioactive isotope having the same properties as the corresponding, nonradioactive element can be produced, which will enter into the same chemical compounds. If an isotope is introduced into a living organism, it can be readily followed because it is radioactive and can be traced with a Geiger counter. This gives information about the behavior of the nonradioactive matter normally present in the organism.

It was Fermi who first bombarded a whole succession of elements with neutrons in order to see whether radioactive isotopes would be created. Until 1934, only the naturally occurring radioactive substances were known, but all of them are heavy metals and are so poisonous that they cannot be used for studies in living organisms. But then Fermi was successful in producing radioactive isotopes of the light elements, which are suitable for experimental purposes. One of the isotopes was radioactive phosphorus, which led to the great isotope adventure at the Bohr Institute.

It is one of the singular events in the history of science that Fermi's production of the radioactive isotopes of the light elements took place just at the time when George de Hevesy realized that he could no longer remain in Hitler's Germany. After his discovery of hafnium in Copenhagen, Hevesy had become a professor at the University of Freiburg, believing that his role now was to guide the young physicists rather than to throw himself into further original research. But matters transpired differently. In 1933 he visited Bohr in order to discuss his own future with him, and afterwards he wrote to a friend, "I found Bohr greater and more magnificent than ever. Most people stop growing when they get into their forties (here he was thinking of himself in Freiburg) . . . Bohr's fabulous personality constantly develops further and further.

Left, Enrico Fermi. Right, Niels Bohr, James Franck, and George de Hevesy at the Institute in 1935.

My final impression was that regardless of the unhappy turn of events in Germany, my real place must be in Copenhagen." He left Freiburg the following year and for the second time he began to work on a brilliant new achievement at the Bohr Institute.

Fermi had produced radioactive phosphorus by bombarding sulphur with neutrons, and after J. Ambrosen at the Bohr Institute had repeated the experiment, Hevesy became involved in earnest. In this way, at Bohr's prompting, the era of work with radioactive isotopes began in Copenhagen. The ideas were hatched at the Institute, but the pioneering effort was soon followed up all over the world. Hevesy and Bohr became particularly involved in the biological experimentation by following the telltale isotopes in animals and plants. At first Ole Chievitz made rats and mice available for them at the Finsen Institute, but the analyses were carried out at the Bohr Institute, and soon Hevesy enlisted the cooperation of several other laboratories and institutes in Copenhagen. Experiments on maize were carried out at the Carlsberg Laboratory, studies of phosphorus conversion in the teeth took place at the Dental College, and at the Zoophysiological Laboratory the transfer of salt through the skin of frogs was investigated. At almost the same time, medical studies were beginning with the aid of radioactive isotopes.

These were conducted in hospitals on thyroid patients, for example, and formed the basis for the subsequent treatment of cancer patients.

Hilde Levi was associated with the work on isotopes from its inception. At Bohr's suggestion, she and Frisch designed the necessary measuring equipment, which became the first Danish-built Geiger counter. It is now kept at the Technical Museum in Helsingør and is still in working condition today. The counter itself, which was supplied by the Copenhagen Telephone Company, was the same type as the one used on telephones to keep track of the number of calls.

When the construction of the first counter was finished and a small particle of uranium salt was placed under the Geiger tube, so that the counter began to click, Bohr was invited to inspect it. He beamed with pleasure when he saw and heard it functioning, but Levi relates,

> Bohr really loved playing around with things like that. I do not remember whether the counter was vertical or horizontal, but in any case Bohr felt it should be the other way. With his powerful hands he proceeded to pull all too hard on the little Geiger vacuum tube, and then it went bang. Our Geiger tube was shattered and Bohr was thoroughly unhappy. It was really the worst thing that could have happened. But I took it lightly, because I knew that we could build a new detector in a few hours.

Left, Hilde Levi. Right, Denmark's first Geiger counter, which Levi constructed in 1935. The amplifier is in the middle and the Geiger tube is clamped in the holder at the right.

When Hevesy first set to work on this new method of exploring the unseen—which was eventually to earn him the Nobel Prize—progress was slow. The amount of radioactive phosphorus he could obtain from the radiation source at the Finsen Institute were quite small, and Bohr decided that the Institute needed a larger source. The experimental physicist Ernest Lawrence had built the world's first cyclotron in Berkeley, in which atomic nuclei of many elements were bombarded producing radioactive isotopes. If a cyclotron could be built at the Bohr Institute, it would be possible to produce all the isotopes of the greatest interest. But large sums of money would be needed, far beyond what it would be possible to raise in Denmark.

Bohr saw a solution, however, for just at this time the Rockefeller Foundation had decided that the advances in physics would benefit biological research. In view of the enormous significance of isotopes for biology, all Bohr needed to do was to formulate the right proposal. The fact that the cyclotron would also be of the highest value for research in physics was scarcely mentioned when it was written, but there can be no doubt that with his customary foresight Bohr was aiming to kill two birds with one stone.

By this time Hevesy had already developed a close collaboration with the director of the Zoophysiological Laboratory in Copenhagen, the great physiologist August Krogh. So it was the trio of Bohr, Hevesy, and Krogh who drew up the proposal and Bohr signed it after he talked to the President of the Rockefeller Foundation personally. The reply was not long in coming, and it was affirmative. The Rockefeller Foundation allocated a large sum for the cyclotron itself and considerable further funds for the biological experiments and for the salaries of scientific staff.

In addition to the Carlsberg Foundation, the Thomas B. Thrige Foundation had often supported the Bohr Institute, and now too it gave money for the cyclotron's large magnet, which Thrige Manufacturing in Odense constructed using a special new technique.

This cyclotron was the first one in Europe, and in 1938 it began operating using neutrons for producing radioactive phosphorus.

Generous donations from the Rockefeller Foundation continued right up to the time of the German occupation. Then the Carlsberg Foundation took over responsibility for the staff remaining in the country, but a few years after the end of the war, when there were no longer any obstacles, the Rockefeller grants were resumed for a number of years.

28

Nuclear Fission

The succession of events has now brought us to the Christmas of 1938, and through the long arm of coincidence to the discovery of uranium fission that was to occur as the fateful prelude to World War II. The theoretical explanation of the mechanism of fission and the events immediately following this event were certainly not lacking in those same elements of drama that had abounded during the elaboration of the atomic and quantum theories.

The Austrian physicist Lise Meitner had been forced to leave Germany in 1938, and she had taken a position at the Nobel Institute in Stockholm. Her nephew was Otto Robert Frisch, who was working with Bohr in Copenhagen at the time. Meitner and Frisch decided to spend the Christmas holiday together as had been their custom, and they did so with friends in a small town in Sweden.

Lise Meitner had worked for more than thirty years with the chemist Otto Hahn before leaving Germany, and they had most recently been studying the radioactive products created when uranium is bombarded with neutrons. Just before Lise Meitner fled in July of 1938, she and Hahn had observed the surprising fact that three of the elements created were of the same chemical nature as radium, although in the table of the elements radium is four places below uranium. This result had to be investigated and they knew they must begin new experiments. When Frisch emerged from his hotel room on the first morning in Kungsälv, Lise Meitner was studying a letter she had just received from Hahn. Hahn and Fritz Strassman had carried out the experiments which Meitner had helped plan before she left Germany. Hahn reported, to her great surprise, that the three elements that had been created were not radium at all. Hahn and Strassmann had added nonradioactive barium in order to make the chemical separation easier, and now they found that the mysterious fragments were isotopes of barium. This was quite strange because no one before had split off parts of the nucleus of the atom larger than an alpha particle. The question therefore was where the energy came from for this quite unforeseen result. Could it be the uranium nucleus which was split in two and had given off sufficient energy? If so, it was not immediately apparent. In Bohr's model, the atomic nucleus was compared to a drop of liquid, and the surface tension on a drop of liquid prevents its division into two smaller drops. Still, the atomic nucleus has an electrical charge, which is known to reduce the effect of surface tension.

Lise Meitner and Otto Frisch remembered this, especially because Bohr's theory for the model of the atomic nucleus was based on drops of liquid. In a later account Frisch wrote:

> At that point we both sat down on a tree trunk (all this discussion had taken place while we walked through the wood in the snow, I with my skis on, Lise Meitner making good her claim that she could walk just as fast without), and started to calculate on scraps of paper. The charge of a uranium nucleus, we found, was indeed large enough to overcome the effect of the surface tension almost completely; so the uranium nucleus might indeed resemble a very wobbly, unstable drop, ready to divide itself at the slightest provocation, such as the impact of a single neutron.

However, when the (uranium) drop divides into two, mutual electric

The workbench at which Otto Hahn and Fritz Strassman split the uranium atom in 1938.

Bohr during a visit to Berlin in 1921. Lise Meitner stands next to Bohr and Otto Hahn is standing behind her.

repulsion will drive the fragments away from each other, releasing energy of about 200 million electron volts. Where did this energy come from? Lise Meitner remembered how the mass of atomic nuclei is calculated, and determined that the sum of the masses of the two nuclei formed by the splitting of the uranium nucleus are about one-fifth of the mass of a proton mass lighter than the original uranium nucleus. According to Einstein's law, whenever mass disappears, energy is created, and one-fifth of the mass of a proton is equal to about 200 million electron volts.

Frisch returned to Copenhagen a couple of days later and immediately went to see Bohr, who had already heard about the three mysterious elements earlier in the year, before any clear understanding of them had been achieved. Bohr was on the point of sailing to the United States, and there was only time for a few minutes' conversation before Bohr had to leave for the boat. But scarcely had Frisch revealed his and Meitner's speculations—"it was not really more at the time"—than Bohr slapped his forehead with his hand and exclaimed, "What idiots we have all been!" He told Frisch that he and Meitner should submit a paper to *Nature* immediately, and he promised not to say anything about the subject before the paper was published. Over the telephone Frisch in Copenhagen and Meitner in Stockholm quickly put together a short paper in which the term subsequently used for the splitting of uranium appears for the first time. Frisch asked an American biologist who worked with Hevesy at the Institute for the name of the process in which a bacterium divides itself in two, and he answered "fission."

Rosenfeld accompanied Bohr on the voyage, and on board the ship they immediately began to make calculations based on this new concept. They worked through all the possibilities in order to ensure that Meitner's explanation was correct. The fact that the drop model could be used to explain nuclear fission was, of course, a great triumph for Bohr's theory. Bohr stayed in New York for a few days before following Rosenfeld to Princeton, only to learn on his arrival there that Rosenfeld had been interviewed by journalists about news from Europe and that he had already let out Meitner's and Frisch's conclusion. When Rosenfeld realized how foolishly he had acted he was appalled, but Bohr had not told him of his promise to keep the fission affair a secret until their paper appeared, and Rosenfeld was under the impression that Meitner and Frisch had already written their paper. Bohr was equally dismayed. Such an important discovery ought to carry the names of Meitner and Frisch, and since he knew the eagerness of American physicists, he sent several telegrams to the Institute asking the staff to begin experiments in order to corroborate the fission hypothesis. In Copenhagen this haste was not understood, but fortunately the report on the confirming experiments reached Bohr just before the *Washington Evening Star* was able to announce the result of the same experiment which two Americans had carried out immediately. Many other American physicists had begun to work as well, and Bohr and Rosenfeld later recounted how they were invited to the American laboratory which was the first to get results where a physicist was observing the counter while simultaneously shouting into the telephone to an eager journalist, "Now there is another one!"

In Copenhagen the Danish physicist Christian Møller was the first to advance the idea that the fission process could emit one or even two neutrons, to which Frisch immediately replied that in that case uranium ore deposits would not exist at all, as they would have exploded a long time ago. But then he realized that uranium ore also contains other elements which could absorb the neutrons.

In the meantime, scientists had begun thinking about the implications of fission. With sufficient care it might be possible to collect a quantity of pure uranium big enough for large amounts of nuclear energy to be released by a controllable chain reaction. Bohr and the American physicist J. A. Wheeler had already made a detailed study of one approach to the problem. And in the paper on atomic fission which Bohr wrote in collaboration with Wheeler, they showed that most of the neutrons emitted from the fission fragments would be too slow to produce fission in the most common form of uranium, uranium-238. Bohr ascribed the fission which Hahn and Strassmann had observed, and which was immediately repeated in many experiments, to the presence of the rare uranium-235.

In the same paper, Bohr and Wheeler showed how the chain reaction could be controlled, and the development of the first atomic reactors followed the guidelines which Bohr had already foreseen a few months after the discovery of atomic fission. At the end of 1939, after returning to Copenhagen, he gave a lecture on the release of atomic energy to the Danish Society for the Advancement of Science. During it Bohr also referred to the possibility of producing a bomb. But he believed that the necessary separation of isotopes would be a technical problem of such vast dimensions that it would take a long time to solve.

The specter of nuclear warfare had appeared on the scene, however. It was in Hitler's Germany, moreover, that fission had first been observed, and when Bohr doubted an early solution of the technical problems, he had not foreseen the fantastic ingenuity of American and British physicists and engineers, who were driven by the fear that Hitler might develop the ultimate weapon before they themselves had done so.

At the beginning of April 1940 Niels Bohr was in Norway, where he had been invited to deliver lectures on the transformation of atomic nuclei. On April 7 he was at a dinner with King Haakon along with members of the Norwegian government, who foresaw the impending German attack. On April 8 Bohr set off for home and arrived in Copenhagen on the morning of the ninth, just as the German aircraft were drawing their black trails in the sky over Denmark.

29

The Call from
America and Britain

Immediately after the German occupation of Denmark, Bohr addressed an appeal to the rector of the university and other Danish officials to protect those colleagues still at the Institute whom the Germans might try to persecute. Although the scientific staff shrank and no more foreigners could come, the work was kept going for a long time, and Bohr continually came up with new ideas and thoughts to maintain morale. However, the German occupation authorities entertained no doubts about Bohr's attitude toward Nazism, and they attempted in various ways to set traps to catch him out. Some were so stupid that they were immediately revealed, while others were more cunningly carried out by people with considerable acting talent. All of them failed, but it was obvious that the danger to Bohr was increasing.

The resistance movement urged him again and again to leave, and there was much anxiety for him outside Denmark as well. But Bohr remained in Denmark until September 1943. Already in 1940, immediately after the occupation, many appeals came from the United States with offers of the most eminent research facilities there. At the same time the American ambassador offered to assist with travel arrangements. But Bohr felt that he should remain in his own country. He believed that he could still be of help in various ways there. He was also concerned lest his departure should cause difficulties for others if the Germans realized that he had in fact fled. He was not just thinking of his Institute: it had made a strong impression on him when Peter Skov of the Foreign Ministry, a friend of his youth, with whom he had discussed his situation, had said that his departure would also cause deep concern and disquiet among Danish Jews.

The very close and harmonious family relationship that was so essential to Bohr could be perceived as a markedly Jewish trait, but it is a question whether this need was more the result of Bohr's warm disposition, for he was not bound by Jewish traditions. His humanity alone

212

impelled him to assist in any way he could, but first and last it was as a Dane that he did not want to forsake his country. His deeply rooted sense of identity with Danish culture is expressed in his foreword to the work *Denmark's Culture in the Year 1940*, published in 1941 by the Danish Institute, which Niels Bohr had helped to found. The work was intended to be a cultural bulwark against the Germans and an inspiration to Danes, while simultaneously establishing their openness to the world. In the foreword Bohr quotes Grundtvig's words on "Citizenship only for Danes, hospitality for all on earth," and Hans Christian Andersen's lines: "In Denmark I was born; there I have my home; there I have roots; from there my world proceeds," and Bohr elaborated,

> Both of these pronouncements, so different in style as well as meaning, express an attitude to the question of our relationship with the world to which it is hard to find any parallel. The heart of the matter is that the question of what Danish culture is can neither be dismissed nor decided but is to be perceived as one which must constantly be asked with respect to great issues and small. The most characteristic aspect of Danish culture may very well be a direct combination of receptiveness to the knowledge brought to us from outside Denmark and insistence upon the philosophy of life, conditioned by our memories and our destiny, which joins us so firmly to one another in face of the greater world to which we indissolubly belong.

Even at the beginning of 1943, when relations with the Germans were becoming extremely critical, Bohr did not want to leave Denmark. But then he received a secret message from England, conveyed by the British intelligence service via the Danish underground and delivered hidden in a bunch of keys. One of the keys had been hollowed out and a piece of microfilm measuring only one-half-millimeter on a side had been placed in the hollow and then covered over. The film had been exposed under a microscope, and Bohr had to combine three exposures in order to read the message. It was a letter from Bohr's close friend, the British physicist James Chadwick, who had discovered the neutron in 1932; he was now one of the leading figures in the English atomic energy project.

Aage Bohr has already given a detailed account of all this in his war memoirs. Chadwick's letter was an urgent appeal to Bohr to come to England. "There is no scientist in the world who would be more acceptable both to our university people and to the general public," wrote Chadwick, and held out the prospect that Bohr could work freely on scientific questions; but between the lines it was obvious that there were certain special problems where Bohr's contribution would be of the greatest assistance.

Chadwick wrote that he did not want to press Bohr but asked him to weigh all the various factors. Bohr's feelings, however, were still the same as when he had refused invitations from the United States. He understood well enough the hints about the special problems in which his cooperation was desired, and in his reply he expressed how strongly he wished to be able to contribute to the common cause in the battle for freedom and human dignity, but:

> I feel it to be my duty in our desperate situation to help resist the threat against the freedom of our institutions and to assist in the protection of the exiled scientists who have sought refuge here. Still, neither such duties nor even the dangers of retaliation against my collaborators and relatives might perhaps carry sufficient weight to detain me here, if I felt that I could be of real help in other ways, but I do not think that this is probable. Above all I have to the best of my judgment convinced myself that, in spite of all future prospects, any immediate use of the latest marvellous discoveries of atomic physics is impracticable.

Only a few months after Bohr's reply to Chadwick, rumors reached Copenhagen of increased production of metallic uranium and heavy water in Germany. Bohr immediately reported this to Chadwick. In the letter, which again was sent through the intelligence service, he discussed the possibility of utilizing chain reactions in slow neutrons for the production of atomic bombs. He concluded, however, that such explosions would hardly be effective—for such a purpose fast neutrons would be required. But he remained generally sceptical about the possible military use of atomic energy because he believed that there would not be adequate technical resources for separating the rare uranium isotope U-235 in the large quantities which would be needed. He had no way of knowing that the Americans had begun work on such separations even before the Japanese attack on Pearl Harbor had brought the United States into the war. As early as 1941, Frisch and Rudolf Peierls, in an English report that became the starting point for the Anglo-American project, had suggested the feasibility of a bomb based on fast neutrons—as foreseen by Bohr—if at least ten kilograms of the rare U-235 could be produced.

The Americans also quickly produced giant reactors for the production of plutonium, based upon the slow neutrons present in the more common isotope, U-238. It is then converted to plutonium, which can be chemically separated from uranium. According to Bohr's and Wheeler's paper of 1939, plutonium could also give a chain reaction with fast neutrons.

The effort was enormous on all sides, and after the war it would come to light that the German atomic physicists had made a similarly promising start but then came to a standstill, partly—as some have asserted—because of lack of ability, and also because of the priority given to the development of the V2 missle.

30

Bohr's Escape to England

Bohr was soon to take part in the Anglo-American effort. At the end of September, 1943, the Swedish ambassador in Copenhagen told Harald and Niels Bohr that they faced immediate arrest by the Germans in connection with the deportation of all the Jews in Denmark.

During the Nuremberg trials after the war it was disclosed that the Germans would have taken Bohr to Germany a month previously—shortly after August 29, when many Danish intellectuals were interned. However, internal conflicts between German authorities postponed action on the planned deportation of the Jews. The Germans who favored postponement thought that an arrest order against Bohr would attract less notice in the confusion that would be produced by mass arrests of the Jews.

Bohr's principal contact people in the Danish Resistance were Heinz Holter and K. Linderstrøm-Lang at the Carlsberg Laboratory, and P. Brandt Rehberg at the Zoophysiological Laboratory. They immediately arranged for Bohr and his family to flee across the Sound, the narrow channel between Denmark and Sweden, that very night after the message had been received. However, since the boat could not carry the whole family, Hans and Ernest Bohr went into hiding until the next night along with Hilde Levi and Sophie Hellman, while Aage Bohr had to remaining in hiding for two days.

Bohr's own crossing of the Sound was successful, although it was not free of anxiety. The boat had to stop several times when patrol boats were heard, but it arrived safely at Limhamn in Sweden on the morning of September 30, and Bohr immediately contacted the Swedish foreign minister. He reached Stockholm that same evening, totally preoccupied by the idea that the Swedish government might possibly be able, by some suitable démarche with the German government, to save the Danish Jews. But the Swedish cabinet secretary E. C. Boheman told Bohr that the Swedish government, prompted by reports of the impending arrests of Danish Jews, had already made representations to the German government and had warned them that such a step would provoke acute anger among the Swedish people. The German reply had been reassuring, saying that the reports were only rumors. But by October 2 a report was received from Denmark that the action had been launched the previous evening and the Jews were being taken to ships in the port of Copenhagen which were awaiting sailing orders for Germany. The Swedish government at once notified Germany that Sweden was prepared to accept the Danish Jews, and Bohr persuaded the Swedish foreign minister to suggest to the Germans that the ships should simply be redirected to Sweden.

In order to leave no avenue unexplored, Bohr secured an audience with the Crown Prince and the Swedish King, Gustav V, who told him without much hope that a similar appeal from the Swedish government at the time the occupying Germans were deporting Norwegian Jews had been rejected as unjustified interference in internal German affairs. But after the advances made by the Allies, Bohr thought that perhaps it would have some effect if the Swedish government announced publicly that Sweden was prepared to receive the Danish Jews. The King immediately contacted the government, which issued the official communiqué a few hours later, and at Bohr's suggestion the King also promised to consider making a personal appeal to Hitler.

Although the proposal for rerouting the ships was rejected by the Germans, the action did render easier the dangerous task of bringing across the Sound the large numbers of Danish Jews who had managed to hide from the Germans. In repeated radio announcements the Swedish government emphasized that Sweden was prepared to receive the refugees, and Swedish vessels were sent to the limits of Swedish territorial waters to pick up the refugees from the Danish boats, which were then able to return quickly for further loads. It was at Bohr's prompting that the radio announcements were broadcast. He also got the police on the Swedish coast to stop questioning new arrivals about how and with whose aid they had crossed, as no one could know where such information might end up.

Bohr's sojourn in Stockholm was very short. Through Ebbe Munck, Bohr received a telegram from Churchill which the latter had sent via Lord Cherwell, his scientific adviser. Ebbe Munck was the leading figure in contacts between England and Denmark via Sweden. It was also his responsibility to get Bohr to England, but Bohr tried to persuade him to postpone the journey, if only for one day, to allow Bohr to make further efforts for the Jewish refugees.

We know from Ebbe Munck's memoirs *The Door to the Free World*, that Bohr eagerly suggested that Aage Bohr should go to England first, because "he knows everything that the English need to know in the first instance." But Ebbe Munck insisted that only if the storm raging just then over the North Sea should continue could a delay be countenanced. Everyone responsible for Bohr was anxious about his safety. The Germans knew of course that he was in Stockholm. The city was swarming with German agents, all entirely official since the German embassy employed hundreds of staff. Bohr was therefore guarded both by Danish officers and by the Swedish police, and although he was staying at a secret address and could only be contacted by a code name, the danger of abduction was real. If the Germans could manage to get him to Germany, they could hope to extract important information from him, and in any case such information would not reach England. Therefore it came as a relief for many that on the evening of the same day when Bohr had asked for a delay, the green light was received from Scotland. The bad weather had blown over and Bohr was taken to the airport outside Stockholm, where a Mosquito airplane was waiting. This little bomber could fly very fast at high altitude and was therefore used for all courier services between England and Sweden.

Bohr serenely allowed himself to be placed in the bomb compartment, where he sat on a pallet over the bomb doors, dressed in the same clothes, Munck related, as he had worn when he fled from Denmark: brown suit, checked wool sport shirt, black tie with red stripes, oil-finished leather boots, and cloth cap; as luggage he was carrying his pipes, a briefcase, and a few toilet articles. He was also given a flying helmet and an oxygen mask.

As is well known, the flight had its moments of danger. The only contact the two crew members had with their passenger was via a telephone connection to the earphones of the flying helmet. The plane gained altitude immediately for safety when passing over German-occupied Norway, and when the pilot reached a height of 30,000 feet he instructed Bohr to use the oxygen mask. But Bohr's helmet was not properly adjusted. It was too small for his head, in fact, so that he did not hear the order—and he fainted. When the crew in the cockpit received no reply, they realized that something was wrong, and as soon as they had crossed Norway they quickly descended over the North Sea. Fortunately, by the time they landed in Scotland their passenger had regained consciousness and was unharmed.

As soon as he arrived in London Bohr was astonished to learn how far the atomic project had progressed. The project's headquarters were in London, but there were laboratories and industrial plants scattered all over England, and Bohr's earliest days were spent visiting them all. Although it was the English results which had set the Americans going in earnest, the collaboration between the two allies crumbled as soon as the Americans knew enough themselves. But after a meeting in Quebec between Roosevelt and Churchill in the late summer of 1943, cooperation again became effective. The English historian Margaret Gowing relates that Bohr's arrival in London, and soon thereafter in the United States, contributed to a high degree to the close British and American collaboration. At the end of October, 1943, many of the British physicists went to the United States, and Niels and Aage Bohr traveled as members of the British party. In Los Alamos they immediately met good friends from Copenhagen, including Frisch, Teller, Weisskopf, and Peierls. As the English scientist and author C. P. Snow wrote:

> Because the United States was rich and at the same time the most secure place of refuge, America got the greatest share of Jewish researchers and thereby the most significant influx of talent which was recorded at any time in history. America, of course, was already producing its native-born Nobel Prize winners. The refugees made it, in a very short time, the world's dominant force in pure science.

31

The Manhattan Project

The Manhattan Project made a tremendous impression upon Bohr. But at the same time as he admired the almost incredible effort it represented, he became more and more concerned over the problems that would arise the moment the atomic bomb became a fact, and he realized that this moment was not far off. But no one knew how far the German had gotten, so in the months Bohr was in Los Alamos he worked on both theoretical considerations and practical advice and direction. His feeling for and ingenuity in experimentation were reawakened, and he clarified certain open questions such as the velocity distribution. He also participated in practical experiments in connection with the assembling of the bomb and the design of the device for initiating the chain reaction. As Aage Bohr later explained: Niels Bohr had a very clear insight into practical and technical matters, in which he made good use of his intuition.

Niels and Aage Bohr's sojourn in Los Alamos lasted for a total of over eight months, with brief interruptions, but even after his first visit, Niels became concerned over the question of effective future control. These thoughts are embodied in a letter he wrote to the British chancellor of the exchequer, Sir John Anderson, who was responsible for the British side of the atomic energy project and with whom Bohr had already had his first conversations on an open world. Control, he now wrote, ought to cover not only a wide array of administrative and technical problems but also such an exchange of information and such openness concerning industrial efforts and military preparations that its scope would far exceed that of the agreements existing between nations before the war.

Bohr was well aware of the great difficulties that would have to be overcome to achieve progress in high politics. But he believed that governmental confidence would be strengthened if Russia were informed about the bomb before there could be any question of using it. If this were not done, then the consequences of the mistrust which would be created on the part of the Russians would be incalculable. Bohr could not see any risk at all in telling the Russians, since in all probability they would be able to construct an atomic bomb themselves very soon. Bohr received support for this idea as early as April, 1944 in a letter from the Russian physicist Peter Kapitza, who was an old friend of Bohr's. Kapitza was a strong personality of whom Rutherford also had had a high opinion and who had had his own institute in England in the 1920s. After Kapitza was forced to return to the Soviet Union in 1934, he eventually received a special position and even became Stalin's scientific adviser—and a boldly freespoken one. His letter, written at the time when the rumor of Bohr's flight to Sweden had reached Moscow, had been on its way for six months before it finally caught up with Bohr in London. In the letter, Kapitza invited Bohr to settle in Russia. This invitation was the origin of the very considerable problems for Bohr to which we shall refer in a little while, but Bohr replied as noncommittally as he could without revealing in any way why he was in London, and he showed the correspondence to British intelligence at once. The invitation convinced him, however, that the Russians already knew a lot about the American project, as indeed was confirmed subsequently by the spy Klaus Fuchs.

Niels Bohr's thoughts now turned more and more toward the postwar era, when the existence of a weapon of total destruction would demand mutual trust between the nations. The efforts he had already started early in 1944 to win over Roosevelt and Churchill are described in detail by Aage Bohr in the commemorative book edited by Stefan Rozental which first appeared in 1963, the year after his father's death. But certain important items of information were still not available at that time. These give a greater understanding of the events surrounding Bohr's race with the atom bomb in the service of peace. Therefore the salient points of Bohr's endeavors will first be outlined and then set in relief against the knowledge which has come to light since. Particularly relevant in this context is Margaret Gowing's account, published in 1964, of Bohr's negotiations with the British and American authorities. She had access to the British government's records and had previously heard Bohr's personal account in the course of conversations with him during her numerous visits to Copenhagen. Most recently she has written a more detailed version for the hundredth anniversary of Niels Bohr's birth, under the impress of the increasing appreciation in many countries of the ideas to which Bohr was the first to give expression.

During a visit to Copenhagen in 1985, Margaret Gowing offered her own response to the question which many have asked since the war: did Bohr's endeavors reflect naiveté; was he the scientist in an ivory tower venturing out into high politics without comprehending the realities? Her reply was a straight negative. After the many hours of conversation she had had with Bohr every day for more than a month, she was convinced that what Bohr had said and done on this great issue during the war had been manifestly realistic, and that his ideas, far from being naive, had been thoroughly considered and forward-looking.

32

The Fight for
an Open World

When Bohr went to the United States, Sir John Anderson (later Lord Waverley) had arranged a regular contact for him with the British ambassador to Washington, Lord Halifax, who knew very little about the atomic project but who quickly became very interested in the future perspectives outlined by Bohr. Bohr himself got in touch with President Roosevelt's close friend, Supreme Court Justice Felix Frankfurter, with whom he had been in contact before the war concerning refugee problems. Having first carefully made sure that Frankfurter knew about the project, so that he would not be betraying anything, Bohr brought up the problems of *realpolitik* associated with the new weapon.

Frankfurter too was impressed by Bohr's ideas and informed Roosevelt, who became so concerned that he said straight out that it "worried him to death" to find the right way out; he proposed that Bohr should take Churchill the message that Roosevelt would gladly receive suggestions from the prime minister on how he thought the matter should be approached.

Sir John Anderson in London was kept informed of the progress of the talks in Washington, and he had tried, even before Bohr's return to London, to convince Churchill of the need to make rapid preparations for international control of atomic energy. But his efforts were unsuccessful: Churchill would not be moved. Unfortunately Bohr knew nothing about Anderson's talks with Churchill. Perhaps out of a sense of discretion toward Churchill, Anderson did not mention his unsuccessful endeavors, and Bohr was therefore quite unprepared for Churchill's opposition when they met at last. Their meeting came about in response to pressing representations from the president of the Royal Society, Sir Henry Dale, who admittedly was sceptical as to its outcome, even beforehand. He feared that Bohr's mild, somewhat hesitant and philosophical mode of expression and his almost whispering voice level would prevent him from establishing a rapport with the desperately

222

preoccupied Prime Minister. Their meeting took place on May 20, 1944, and the British physicist Lord Cherwell, who was Churchill's adviser on questions of atomic energy, was also present. It was the latter, along with Field Marshal J. C. Smuts, whom Churchill esteemed highly, who had urged the meeting on Churchill.

If the groundwork of obduracy had already been laid during Anderson's preparatory talks, matters became even worse during the meeting when Cherwell made some remarks which Churchill misinterpreted as a criticism of the agreement which he and Roosevelt had reached over Anglo-American atomic collaboration. The conversation was sidetracked as a result, and Bohr's concerns were not addressed. By the time the meeting was over, Bohr had not even been able to give Churchill any real impression of how worried Roosevelt was by the problem. When he was about to leave, therefore, Bohr groped for a solution to this dilemma by asking to be allowed to write to Churchill, who answered, "It would be an honor to receive a letter from you," adding, "but not about politics."

It may be surmised from this that Churchill believed that the construction of the atomic bomb could be kept secret. To Bohr this was an obvious delusion. His trump card against Churchill's *realpolitik* was that the leading Russian physicists appeared to be working on the atomic bomb already. Bohr's point, therefore, was that openness would offer a *chance*, and that nothing would be risked thereby, since the secret could not be kept anyway. If nothing was said to the Russians, this would breed mistrust on their side in their relations with the allies after the war. Bohr set forth these arguments in the letter which he wrote to Churchill immediately after the meeting. Then Bohr went to Washington, where he urgently sought another interview with Roosevelt. This was granted, and the failure of the earlier conversation with Churchill was the measure of the success with Roosevelt, who spoke enthusiastically of "a new era in human history." Roosevelt too believed that an approach to the Soviets had to be attempted, and had hopes of a favorable result. Stalin was sufficient of a realist to understand the implications of this scientific and technical revolution. Roosevelt, who had heard of the unsuccessful meeting in London, even thought that he could win over Churchill, and explained that at first Churchill often reacted as he had. He would take the whole matter up with him in the course of their forthcoming meeting in Quebec.

Bohr was so encouraged by the talk with Roosevelt that he himself was prepared to be sent to Russia. He entertained a slight hope that perhaps through Kapitza he could get to speak to Stalin. Shortly before the war he had sent a personal letter to Stalin when the physicist Lev Landau had been imprisoned. Kapitza had done the same, and the result of the appeals was that Landau was released.

Bohr waited excitedly for the result of the meeting between Roosevelt and Churchill. But all hopes failed. Immediately after the Quebec meeting Roosevelt invited Churchill to make a farewell visit to his Hyde Park estate, where they discussed atomic problems and decided that considering the stage which the project had then reached, proposals for any initiative toward other nations should be dropped. Niels Bohr never learned whether and why Roosevelt changed his mind, nor anything about the course of the negotiations. Not a word of these matters is to be found in Churchill's work *The Second World War*. He mentioned that the visit to Hyde Park took place on September 17, but he does not say what was discussed, though he does reproduce a telegram dispatched to the war cabinet in London after the first day's meeting in Quebec on September 13. It reads: "The conference has opened in a blaze of friendship."

From documents which have become available since, however, it appears that Roosevelt and Churchill signed a memorandum at the meeting in Hyde Park containing a paragraph to the effect that an investigation of Bohr should be launched, and that steps should be taken to prevent him from letting any kind of information leak to the Russians.

Lord Cherwell had to listen in consternation to this outburst from Churchill when he returned home afterwards:

> The President and I are much worried about Professor Bohr. How did he come into the business? He is a great advocate of publicity. He made an unauthorized disclosure to Chief Justice Frankfurter who startled the President by telling him he knew all the details. He said he is in close correspondence with a Russian professor, an old friend of his in Russia to whom he has written about the matter and may be writing still. The Russian professor has urged him to go to Russia in order to discuss matters. What is all this about? It seems to me Bohr ought to be confined or at any rate made to see that he is very near the edge of mortal crimes.

Churchill's charges were answered immediately. Cherwell, Anderson, Halifax, and Gerald Campbell all came to Bohr's rescue. Cherwell sent a sharp note in which he told Churchill of Bohr's qualifications for concerning himself with the question, of his conversations with Frankfurter, and of Kapitza's appeal and Bohr's reply, which British Intelligence had approved. He sent the same information to Roosevelt. Churchill, who now realized his mistake, dropped the matter, and Bohr's sense of humor took care of the rest, though now he looked with even greater gravity toward the future.

Bohr was not the only scientist who was worried, of course. In December 1944 Einstein sent him a *cri de coeur* on the prospects of an arms race after the war. He thought that all the influential scientific researchers in all the leading countries of the free world should meet in order to put pressure on the political leaders to implement an internationalization of the world's military might. "Do not say it is impossible," wrote Einstein to Bohr and added, ". . . but wait a few days until you have accustomed yourself to these strange ideas."

How responsibly and realistically Bohr looked at questions involving politics is evident from the fact that he at once met Einstein in order to explain to him what unfortunate consequences there could be if anyone with confidential knowledge of the bomb took matters into his own hands. Einstein accepted Bohr's arguments and refrained from action.

33

Bohr and Churchill

If Churchill's recalcitrance is to be understood, the question inevitably arises whether Niels Bohr had any chance at all of influencing Churchill.

One explanation that has been given for Churchill's negative attitude is that the meeting unfortunately took place immediately before the invasion of France, and Churchill's thoughts were wholly devoted to the gigantic and crucial effort of the allies in their struggle against Hitler. But is this the whole explanation? In the search for a clue in Churchill's memoirs, with their wealth of citations of documents and conversations, one looks in vain for Bohr's name. But for an understanding of Churchill's attitude there are explanatory commentaries to be found in the reminiscences published by Churchill's physician under the title *Churchill—Taken from the Diaries of Moran.*

Charles Moran, who was president of The Royal Medical Society, was charged as early as May 1940 with the duty of being at Churchill's side at all times. He accompanied him on all of his numerous journeys to the historic wartime meetings. He attended most of them, received reports on all of them, and wrote diligently in his diary. He had no thought of publishing his notes, however, and for many years after the war he resisted repeated invitations to have them published. But in the end he felt his duty was clear. It cannot be denied that criticisms of Churchill were raised especially in the final years of the war, and Moran thought that it would be unjust to withhold certain extenuating circumstances which required "the doctor's account of Churchill's medical background" to be heard.

For those who lived through World War II, regardless of their political affiliation, Churchill was the colossus in whose hands the strength of Great Britain was gathered. But more than once in the last critical years when fateful decisions had to be made, Churchill came to Moran and complained of exhaustion. "It was clear that he was almost burnt out." Much that would otherwise be inexplicable, Moran wrote, could be

226

ascribed to exhaustion both of mind and body. Both illness and disappointments sapped his powers. Moran reveals that Churchill received his first warning of heart trouble, in the form of angina pectoris symptoms, as early as December 1941: this was soon followed by repeated attacks of pneumonia and continual anxiety about an irregular pulse that interfered with his sleep.

It is well known that both Roosevelt and Stalin wanted the invasion of France, "the second front," long before Churchill considered it to be possible, and Churchill had to fight—in the end in both directions—for his own viewpoint. He wanted first to exhaust the Germans on the continent and in Africa, while at the same time building up war matériel to sufficient strength for the invasion.

Churchill's relations with the United States on the one hand and the Soviet Union on the other point directly toward the posture in which he must have found himself at the time of his encounter with Niels Bohr over the "open world" issue.

Churchill felt himself to be not only an Englishman. He was proud of being able to say that his mother was American born, and when he was with Americans he emphasized that he was half American. He showed spontaneously on many occasions that this was not merely a polite phrase.

When he was to receive an honorary doctorate from Harvard in September 1943, he prepared one of his major speeches. He knew their effect when he was at his best. While preparing a speech, therefore, he would shut himself off from the outside world and tolerate no disturbances. The whole night could be spent on it; and so it was now. The speech at Harvard would be an academic event, and slowly he approached "the full scope of the working of his mind." Churchill began by quoting Bismarck: "The essential factor in human society at the end of the nineteenth century was the fact that the British and the American people spoke the same language . . . this gift of a common tongue is a priceless inheritance and it may well some day become the foundation of a common citizenship." He continued in his own words:

> I am here to tell you that nothing will work soundly or for long without the united effort of the British and American people. If we are together, nothing is impossible. If we are divided, all will fail. I therefore preach continually the doctrine of the fraternal association of our peoples, not for any purpose of gaining invidious material advantages for either of them, not for territorial aggrandisement or the vain pomp of earthly domination, but for the sake of service to mankind and for the honor that comes to those who faithfully serve great causes. And here let me say how proud we ought to be, young and old, to live in this tremendous, thrilling, formative epoch in the human story.

Here, wrote Moran, Churchill went as far as he dared in proposing a closer union after the war. On the return journey to Washington,

Churchill said that only a short time before he would not have ventured so far, and Moran adds, "I do not doubt that he tried 'common citizenship' on the President before he launched it at Boston."

As early as the end of 1941, when Churchill visited Roosevelt in Washington for the first time, he delivered a speech to Congress which he began with the words, "I cannot help reflecting that if my father had been American and my mother British, instead of the other way round, I might have got here on my own."

But in his visions of a world brotherhood did Churchill dream of including Russia in its blessings? How did his meetings with Stalin go? Churchill took the initiative for the first meeting, which took place in August, 1942. In June, Rommel had beaten the English forces in Africa back to El Alamein, and Tobruk had fallen. This hit Churchill hard. At this time both Roosevelt and Stalin had already been pressing for the invasion of Normandy to be expedited, but after the fall of Tobruk Churchill, with fierce stubbornness, persuaded Roosevelt to postpone the invasion of France in favor of a joint invasion of North Africa. He knew that it would not be easy to explain the change of plan to Stalin, but it had to be done. So Churchill traveled with his retinue to Moscow, and if one reads the volume of his memoirs entitled *The Hinge of Fate*, it seems as though this visit went well, but Charles Moran presents us with quite a different picture. He describes the visit in detail: On the first day in Moscow, Stalin said plainly that he could not accept Churchill's grounds for delaying D-Day, and after the next meeting the same evening Churchill came back "downhearted and desperate." He complained to Moran, "I have come a long way and made a great effort. Stalin lay back puffing at his pipe, with his eyes half closed, emitting streams of insults."

Stalin's wrath arose from the loss of so many Russian soldiers. He felt that if the British soldiers had fought with the same tenacity against the Germans as the Red Army had, they would not be so afraid of them, and now we had broken our promise of a second front.

Churchill went on, his face set in anger, "I can harden too. I am not sure it would not be better to leave him to fight his own battles." The next day, however, Churchill went to a dinner which passed off without any quarrel, and when they got up, Stalin took the initiative for having himself and Churchill photographed together. But then everything went awry. After the photography session, Stalin sat down next to Churchill, who however proceeded to read some documents he had brought with him. He hardly spoke to Stalin. Moran writes:

> I received the impression that Stalin wanted to be friendly, but that the P.M. would not meet him halfway. At last the P.M. got up and said "Goodbye," and moved off. He walked very quickly, with countenance overcast. His face was set and resolute. Stalin accompanied him through the vast and empty

halls which separated the dining room from the door by which we had come into the Kremlin. I had never seen Stalin move except in a slow and measured fashion. Now to keep up with the P.M. he had almost to trot. Watching him, I thought of the importunity of the small boy who is asking for a cigarette card and will not take "No" for an answer. Perhaps Stalin realized that he had gone too far.

In the car Churchill's fury burst forth in earnest. In the car with him was the British ambassador to Moscow, who described him as a bull in the arena, enraged by the picador's lances. He declared that he would go home and not see Stalin again. He emphasized to Moran that he had said "goodbye" to Stalin, not "good night."

However, the ambassador was able to persuade Churchill to try one more meeting with Stalin. Afterwards Churchill told Moran that this time he had attempted to be very cordial, but there was no response from "this hardboiled egg of a man."

The next meeting with Stalin took place during the Teheran conference in November, 1943. Stalin had arranged for Roosevelt to be quartered in the Russian embassy, and there the two had a meeting without Churchill, during which full agreement was reached that the invasion of France was now more important than anything else. Churchill argued for bringing Turkey into the war first and for bringing the war in Italy to a conclusion prior to the invasion of France. Stalin refused flatly. "If we are here in order to discuss military matters, then Russia is only interested in OVERLORD" (the code name for the invasion of France).

During an interval when Churchill was sitting with his military advisers and the British foreign secretary Anthony Eden, he said with his thoughts on the future, "We must be supreme in the air, not merely in numbers, but we must lead in everything." He went on, "If we are strong in the air, other countries, remembering this war, will hesitate to attack us. Moscow will be as near to us as Berlin is now."

Churchill was completely disheartened by Roosevelt's support of Stalin. Now Stalin was in a position to do as he wished. "Will he become a menace to the free world, another Hitler?" Such thoughts obsessed Churchill, and Moran adds that Churchill was "appalled by his own impotence."

If we go to Churchill's own notes and jump ahead to the days immediately before his meeting with Niels Bohr on May 20, Churchill writes to Eden on May 4 and asks him to consider recalling the British ambassador to Moscow, since "quite evidently we are approaching a showdown with Russia on their communist intrigues in Italy, Yugoslavia and Greece . . . I must say I think their attitude becomes more difficult every day." Two days later he writes to Eden again, irritated that the ambassador to Moscow must personally deliver every note to Molotov or Stalin and sometimes has to wait for days for an audience with "these potentates.'' It would be enough to send an official who would simply leave the note without waiting.

Niels Bohr had no inkling of all this, and two remarks made after his meeting with Churchill form an anticlimax both to the great events in which Churchill was involved and to Bohr's no less urgent strivings against the threat of the atomic bomb. When Bohr, deeply disappointed, returned to the hotel and related that he had been practically scolded by Churchill, he said, ''We were not speaking each other's language.'' And Churchill for his part said to Cherwell, ''I did not like the man when you showed him to me, with his hair all over his head.''

Had the conditions for reaching understanding simply not been there? Had there been any possibility at all for Bohr to propound his arguments? Moran describes various episodes during these historic meetings when views were being exchanged. Even at the first Quebec conference, the American military leaders strove to avoid any discussion with Churchill, whom they otherwise admired. ''We cannot cope with him.'' Moran adds that Churchill pursued his own ideas to such a point that he scarcely heard the arguments of others. Even Roosevelt evaded debate if he could. And Clementine, Churchill's wife, one day said to Moran, ''I do not argue with Winston, he shouts me down. So when I have anything important to say I write a note to him.'' Bohr was not aware of these traits, but he too found himself writing a letter as a substitute for a dialogue.

After the meeting with Bohr, Churchill wrote to Cherwell, ''You may be quite sure that any power that gets hold of the secret will try to make the article and that this touches the existence of human society. The matter is one out of all relation to anything else that exists in the world and I could not think of participating in any disclosure to third or fourth parties at the present time.''

He must have put the argument thus strongly to the ailing Roosevelt. Yet it can scarcely have been this argument that influenced Roosevelt. Perhaps it was the rumor that Bohr was a spy. This was refuted, as we have observed, and all the other influential politicians and scientists who had been involved in Bohr's efforts were still just as eager for a decision to be taken on Bohr's proposals. But, Margaret Gowing tells us, when Lord Halifax and Felix Frankfurter went for a walk in Washington in April 1945 and were discussing how further serious progress might be made, they heard all the church bells in Washington ringing. Roosevelt was dead.

Finally, we come to the only sentence in Churchill's memoirs indicative of Churchill's own standpoint on the atomic bomb problem and, indirectly, of his opinion regarding Bohr's ideas. It is found in the continuation of Churchill's account of how he received the report of the atomic test in the New Mexican desert on July 17, 1945. He quotes his own note from that day, but it is worth remembering that the quotation was edited for publication in 1954. It says, "No one could yet measure the immediate military consequences of the discovery, and no one has yet measured anything else about it."

So much, ten years afterwards, for Churchill's view of Bohr's arguments. Certainly Bohr did not manage to say much during their meeting, but he wrote it all down in his follow-up letter to Churchill. The day after the atomic test explosion, Churchill, Stalin, and Truman (now President after Roosevelt's death) were meeting in Potsdam. Churchill and Truman decided that Stalin ought to be informed of "an entirely novel form of bomb." Truman would tell Stalin about it after a meeting, and he would stress that it was an experiment, for that was to be the explanation in case Stalin should ask "Why have you not told us anything about this before?" Finally, Churchill's report concludes, Truman was firmly resolved to refuse disclosure of the details at any price. And Margaret Gowing's account states that Churchill was so intent on preserving the secret of the atomic bomb that he had not even informed his war cabinet or any of his advisers of Roosevelt's message through Bohr, nor of all that followed afterwards.

34

Roosevelt's Last Speech

There is evidence that Bohr's ideas engaged Roosevelt's attention to the last, regardless of Churchill's opposition. Prominent Democrats take turns delivering the "Jefferson Day Speech" in memory of Thomas Jefferson, the founder of the Democratic party, and just before his death Roosevelt was preparing to make that year's speech. Robert E. Sherwood, who was one of Roosevelt's advisers during the war, describes in his book *Roosevelt and Hopkins, An Intimate History*.

Roosevelt had asked Sherwood to find some quotations from Jefferson for the speech because, he said, "There aren't many people who realize it, but Jefferson was a scientist as well as a democrat, and there were some things he said that need to be repeated now, because science is going to be more important than ever in the working out of the world."

The citation which Sherwood found and which Roosevelt decided to make the starting point of his address was: "The brotherly spirit of science, which unites into one family all its votaries of whatever grade, and however widely dispersed throughout the different quarters of the globe."

"I did not know at that time," wrote Sherwood, "but I realized later that when Roosevelt spoke of the importance of science in the future he was undoubtedly thinking of the imminence of the atomic age." And Roosevelt wrote in this, his last speech, which he did not live to deliver, "Today we are faced with the preeminent fact that, if civilization is to survive, we must cultivate the science of human relationship—the ability of all peoples, of all kinds, to live together and work together in the same world at peace."

In the spring of 1945 Bohr wrote another memorandum intended for Roosevelt, which was given after Roosevelt's death to Vannevar Bush, the head of the U.S. Office of Research and Development. Here Bohr went a step further than the idea of merely informing Russia. Although the atomic project was enormous even at its present stage, he had to

Niels Bohr receiving the first "At-oms for Peace" award at a cere-mony in which President Eisen-hower took part.

give warning of the far greater destructive powers that simpler and more intensive methods than the present ones would make available in the near future to every nation with major industrial resources. And in his memorandum he now put forward concrete proposals for controlling atomic weapons under all circumstances. In May, 1945, Bush and J. B. Conant prevailed on Secretary of War Stimson to set up an interim committee to discuss proposals very similar to Bohr's but whose members agreed only one thing—that nothing must leak out before the bomb was used against Japan.

Niels Bohr never took part in military discussions, and he had left the United States before the test bomb was exploded. Neither was he informed beforehand that the bomb would be used against Japan. Among friends he expressed profound regret at this event and at the spirit in which the decision had been reached. "The frightening thing was," he said, "that it was not necessary at all." These were the words he used when he returned to Tisvilde for the first time after the war was over.

Elements of Bohr's ideas are repeated in the proposals discussed soon after the war by the commission established by the United Nations to consider the control of atomic energy. The ideas were reflected also in the proposals put forward by the International Atomic Energy Agency. But now it was Russia that was opposed.

In 1957, Bohr was awarded the Ford Foundation's "Atoms for Peace"

The front and back of the "Atoms for Peace" award.

award, which he received in the presence of President Eisenhower. These were the days when the "cold war" was worrying everyone, and Bohr scarcely felt great happiness about it. But he accepted the prize in the hope that the attention attracted by the award might stimulate interest in his ideas and the drive for openness, which also formed the grounds on which the award was based.

35

Heisenberg Again and Bohr's Homecoming

The events around the atomic bomb problem during the war cannot be reported without mentioning the name of Werner Heisenberg again. He made an unexpected visit to Copenhagen in October 1941 in order to see Bohr. Considering the close relationship Heisenberg had had with the entire Bohr family, it was difficult for Bohr to refuse to see him. But Bohr was deeply disquieted. Earlier the same autumn, he had learned about a paper written by the German physicist F. G. Houtermans that clearly showed that the German physicists understood how to achieve nuclear fission. He also knew that Heisenberg had recently become the director of the Max Planck Institute for Physics and Astrophysics. So when Heisenberg came to talk to Bohr they only had a short conversation, which took place in Bohr's study at Carlsberg. In the course of the conversation Heisenberg asked some oblique questions which Bohr pretended not to understand.

After the war, however, Robert Jungk's book *Stronger Than a Thousand Guns* was published, in which the author says that Heisenberg's visit was actually "a little known peace-feeler for the purpose of achieving a tacit agreement between German and Allied atomic experts to prevent the production of a morally objectionable weapon." And this suggestion of German moral scruples is accompanied in the book by a letter from Heisenberg to Jungk concerning the visit to Bohr. But regardless of what information or prompting Jungk may have received from Heisenberg, this version of the visit is fictitious. There is nothing to be seen in the entire story other than an attempt to whitewash Germany over an issue that was sensitive for the Allies. Aage Bohr, who knew every move his father made on these questions and every word that was said about them on any occasion, can state with certainty that Heisenberg did not make any proposals, but that he did leave behind him a strong impression that Germany attached great military importance to atomic energy.

Finally, the events of those days included a further appearance of Heisenberg in Copenhagen during the German occupation. After Bohr's flight, the Germans occupied Bohr's Institute in December, 1943, justifying this with rumors to the effect that the Institute had worked for the British and Americans. They intimated that the Germans wanted the work to continue under the direction of German physicists, which immediately caused the staff of the Institute to go underground. They next let it be understood that the cyclotron would be dismantled and taken to Germany. In Stefan Rozental's description of what now happened, Heisenberg started a rescue operation at this point. He had heard of the occupation of the Institute and arranged to be sent to Copenhagen to "investigate" whether the Institute had really worked for the Allies. He came to Copenhagen accompanied by a physicist of high rank in the Nazi party. It was an arrangement which Heisenberg himself is said to have devised with the idea that whatever they reported when they returned to Germany would be believed. When they did get home and said that they had found nothing, the occupation of the Institute was lifted. It had in fact continued for some time, but liberation did at last take place in February, 1944.

Meanwhile behind the scene dramatic events were going on. The occupation of the Institute became known at once in Stockholm, and the Danish Resistance movement thought it must mean that the Institute was of great military importance to the Germans. This immediately brought up the question of whether or not it should be blown up, and preparations for this were begun. The building was successfully undermined through the sewage pipes, but at the last moment Ole Chievitz intervened. He was an active member of the Resistance, and when he heard about the impending operation he asked its initiators to wait for Bohr's answer. The courier lines went into action and both the Resistance and those of the Institute staff who were in Stockholm waited in anxious suspense. Anxiety increased as the hours passed and no answer came. In fact Bohr had replied, but directly to Copenhagen, explaining that there was nothing at the Institute of interest to the Germans. The Institute was saved.

After the war in 1947, Heisenberg visited Bohr again. It was at the request of the Danish Intelligence Service, which wanted to know some more details of his visit in 1941. But it was obvious that Heisenberg and Bohr had divergent recollections. Their conversation took place at Tisvilde, and in order for it to have some positive outcome the talk soon passed on to some of the purely scientific advances in quantum mechanics. Bohr did not condemn Heisenberg. As early as 1943 when he had fled to Sweden he had begun thinking about the future after the war would be over. Ebbe Munck recalls in his memoirs how Bohr had said, "We shall not quarrel." And Heisenberg wrote later of his feeling that the old Tisvilde atmosphere from prewar days soon reappeared. But that was what he wrote, and perhaps he did so in an attempt to convince himself that all was well. But his wife wrote, after his death, that it was a matter of regret for him in the later years of his life that his friendship with Bohr never was the same after the war.

Niels and Margrethe Bohr returned to Denmark at the end of August, 1945, and the very next day Bohr went off to the Institute, arriving as usual by bicycle. That his reception was moving need scarcely be said, and soon the delight over his homecoming was being celebrated on all sides.

His sixtieth birthday came on October 7, and immediately prior to it he was honored by the Danish Academy of Sciences, which at the same time held its first meeting at which he again presided. The Carlsberg Foundation donated a sum of 100,000 kroner for the establishment of a trust, which was to bear Bohr's name and support some field of research selected by Bohr. The gift was supplemented from numerous quarters until the capital sum amounted to 400,000 kroner.

Bohr, who dreaded solemn occasions, felt very relieved when he arrived at the Institute and was feted by the staff with exactly the sort of jesting and joviality that he loved. A second disrespectful issue of the *Journal of Jocular Physics* which then appeared is still treasured by those fortunate enough to have retained a copy. In the evening,

The day after his return from the United States and England, Bohr arrived at the Institute in the morning by bicycle, as usual.

however, Bohr was unable to avoid emotional moments completely. Students from the institutes of higher education came in a torchlight procession to the honorary residence and hailed him, and from the front steps he delivered an inspired speech to the young people about the future.

The next day Bohr was back at work. He especially devoted himself in the subsequent years to three great tasks. For the Institute the important task was the study of atomic nuclei, which would be the next great advance in atomic physics; but equally crucial for Bohr was the elaboration of his epistemological philosophy; and, in addition, he always remained involved in the battle for an open world.

The Institute had to adapt to meet the demands of the new age. Bohr had come home from England and the United States not merely with impressions of the resources which had been assembled for the development of atomic energy. He had also visited institutions—especially at Berkeley—where mighty new apparatuses were inaugurating the epoch of peaceful atomic research by penetrating atomic nuclei in order to study the new particles which were predicted to exist. Therefore it was very clear to Bohr that a small country like Denmark could soon fall behind.

The students' torchlight procession to the honorary residence on the evening of Niels Bohr's sixtieth birthday in 1945.

Almost miraculously, the Institute had made a little progress during the occupation. The oldest high voltage installation from 1935, which could produce voltages of up to one million volts, was replaced, despite the lack of both metal and money, by a new installation, a van de Graaff generator, capable of yielding 2.5 million volts. Bohr's tireless activity once again bore fruit, and personal friendships produced their effect. Both the Carlsberg Breweries and the Helsingfor Shipyard donated scrap-metal, and the shipyard reused it to construct an airtight tank large enough to contain the generator, in order to keep it under high pressure and thus avert spark discharges that would interfere with the operation of the generator.

But particles of even greater energy were needed in order to penetrate into atomic nuclei. A larger installation still was required for this. For Bohr a further question to be considered was his responsibility for training new technicians and scientists. Developments were proceeding rapidly in the world outside, and the training of the new generation was more pressing in Bohr's view than the actual question of the industrial application of atomic energy. It was impossible to know how relevant the peaceful uses of atomic energy might be to a country not itself possessing the requisite fissionable raw materials. But the human and scientific resources would have to be ready for their tasks.

Bohr was able to convince his countrymen of the need for the Institute to expand and build new installations. The Danish government provided about half of the necessary funds, and most of the rest was provided by the Carlsberg and the Thrige Foundations. It had gradually become the custom that when the university submitted applications for large grants, the Ministry of Education, if it approved the project, only did so on condition that the Carlsberg Foundation provided half of the sum requested.

The first stage of the expansion consisted of the replacement of the Institute's small workshop building by a five-story office building. The underground accommodation was enlarged over the entire site, and the local authority lent an area of ground for the large new hall for the cyclotron, from which the radiation was so powerful that the cyclotron had to have thick concrete walls. Room was also provided for a new high voltage generator that could achieve 4.5 million volts.

The expansion project made heavy demands on Bohr's time. As usual he concerned himself with every single detail from the first sketches on the architect's drawing board. Stefan Rozental, who was again at his side daily, has written about how Bohr's love of symmetry in the world of the atom was also in evidence in his planning of the Institute's expansion. When some long-discussed detail was finally fitted into place, his face would light up in a smile and he would say, "You see, that is very nice now, and it is really symmetrical as well." But as during the

The audience at a memorial symposium for Bohr held in 1963 in Copenhagen. Front, from the left: Aage Bohr, Victor Weisskopf, Werner Heisenberg, and Lise Meitner.

first and second stages of the prewar construction, so now: Bohr thought of changes all the time. He moved about everywhere among the craftsmen and climbed up ladders faster than either the architects or the engineers—two steps at a time. In fact, Bohr made corrections on the building the same way he did on a manuscript, and moving a door could become just as vital for him as moving a comma. One day a carpenter exclaimed despairingly, "Maybe Bohr has invented the atom bomb, but never the hot water." Although the architects too were often in despair and felt that as an architect Bohr would be best with a drawing board on a scale of one-to-one, they had to admit in the end that the result of all their pains was a considerable improvement on the initial idea.

Bohr now had to find an answer to the question of whether the Institute should continue to do isotope research. Due to its wide-ranging applications in biology, this field hardly belonged in an institute for atomic physics any more. It was therefore decided, after consultations with August Krogh, to hand the work over to the Zoophysiological Laboratory. Since Krogh was on the point of retirement, it was under his successor, P. Brandt Rehberg, that isotope research flourished. The task of introducing isotope techniques to staff at the Zoophysiological Laboratory fell to Hilde Levi, and the Rockefeller Foundation continued for many years to support the steadily growing efforts in which a particularly important part was played by Hans Ussing and C. Barker Jørgensen.

At the same time, the stream of scientific researchers from the great physics centers around the world continued to arrive. Those who have spent periods long or short at the Institute, from its inception until Bohr's death in 1962, include a total of seventeen winners of the Nobel Prize.

During the German occupation George de Hevesy had gone to Sweden, where he received the Nobel Prize for chemistry in 1944, the same year in which Johannes V. Jensen was awarded it for literature. The prize is accompanied by the right to assume Swedish citizenship, and Hevesy was one of the few who have availed themselves of this opportunity. He maintained contact with Copenhagen, and for a time Sophie Hellman functioned as his secretary in her infrequent spare moments. Her work for Hevesy was not without its surprises. One of the last written communications she received from him was a postcard which he sent asking her to reserve a train ticket to Budapest for him on a certain date. He also stated the day of the week, which did not agree with the date, but worse was to come. Hevesy added a postscript which confounded Hellman even further since it read, "By the way do not bother, I have decided not to travel."

36

The Open Letter

Even though the atom bombs had been dropped on Japan, Bohr did not give up his ideas for an open world—on the contrary.

In 1948 Bohr spoke with General Marshall and also sent him a memorandum. The darker the prospects appeared for international cooperation, the more obviously it is necessary "that a matter is raised which is designed to appeal to the highest ideals of humanity: openness and free access to information on all aspects of existence in every country."

But the cold war intensified, and in 1950 Niels Bohr sent his "open letter" to the United Nations. If the time for confidence and trust through openness had come before the bomb had been dropped, the bomb's very existence in a divided world was now an imminent threat and a most grave heritage for the future. All previous wars in history had ended with one party victorious. Everyone now had to realize that a new war between the great powers would end not in victory but in world annihilation. On June 9, Bohr assembled representatives of the world press to the honorary residence at Old Carlsberg and handed each of them a copy of his letter, which was being delivered at the same time to the United Nations by Aage Bohr, who was in New York at that time. Bohr made a brief announcement to the journalists of what he had done, but he added no further comments. Everything was in the letter.

Anyone unacquainted with Bohr who reads the letter today cannot but admire the extent to which he succeeded in taking all factors into consideration. The scientists who knew him recognized his extreme meticulousness down to the last detail. The argument cannot be amplified even today. Nothing was forgotten. With amazing prescience the letter looks toward the rest of the present century, which has had to recognize the truth of Bohr's words on the need for all humanity to become a collaborative unity toward which world citizenship would carry responsibilities and duties.

The reaction was almost nil, however. The Korean war was just breaking out and people were preoccupied with it, while those who saw the gravity of the increasingly tense world situation were despondent. Others, such as Bertrand Russell and Albert Einstein, set peace actions in motion, but Bohr abstained from taking part in any resolutions because he felt that the key factor was the need for openness; and in 1956 he sent another open letter to Dag Hammarskjöld, general secretary of the United Nations.

Just as Bohr had spent time during the war knocking on the doors of influential politicians, so now he again did not spare himself. His contemporaries would often wonder at the amount of time he would give to official entertaining when prominent politicians came visiting, and at the way he opened his home at Old Carlsberg when heads of state came to Denmark. But this was partly because successive prime ministers and ministers of culture did not hesitate to solicit visits to the honorary residence when representative gatherings were to be arranged and partly because Bohr himself felt that he must exploit every opportunity of discussing his ideas of an "open world" with influential people.

In the same year that his first letter was published, but before it was dispatched, Bohr met Churchill again when the latter came to Denmark on a ceremonial visit. Ebbe Munck accompanied Churchill on the journey, and Bohr was invited to attend a luncheon with the King and Queen of Denmark. Bohr contacted Munck beforehand to inquire about Churchill's spirits and state of health—and whether Munck believed that Churchill was now more ready to listen? Munck was sceptical, for if they did finally succeed in talking to Churchill, his physical condition was poorer than before, because Churchill had gradually become very deaf. Afterwards, wrote Munck, Bohr came to me and said with his most charming smile, "You were right. It did not work at all." Churchill himself said to one of his staff that he "felt as though he was in deep water with no deck to stand on." Such was the symbolism in the picture of one of the most persevering and promising of peace efforts being met with the most negative of receptions.

However, there was an attempt on Churchill's part at a personal reconciliation, although it did not change anything in his or Bohr's divergent viewpoints. Both of them were invited to the palace at Fredensborg by the King and Queen, and after the luncheon they took a walk in the park. Churchill took his leave from there and extended his hand to Bohr with a smile, saying, "Think again, dear friend."

Today, more than thirty years later, the same crucial issues are being grappled with on all fronts. Everyone realizes the necessity for openness and control. And it may perhaps be of some interest that a contemporary historian like Margaret Gowing finds a degree of consolation in the fact

The only known occasion when Bohr and Churchill were photographed together was at the University of Copenhagen in 1950.

that east-west contact in scientific fields is much greater than could have been expected in 1950. What she has in mind here is joint information on high energy accelerators and the work on hydrogen fusion for peaceful purposes. There is still no provision for inspection with regard to atomic weapons. But in both camps, information about numbers and types of weapons is far more accessible than in 1950; and finally, Gowing believes, the feasibility of taking photographs in great detail from satellites has to some degree solved the problem of inspection.

It was not only in scientific research that Bohr had vision and intuition, but also in his approach to the problems of high politics, where he was again ahead of his time.

37

The Atomic Power Station
at Risø

The number of tasks which Bohr had set for himself after the war soon increased. The first experimental atomic power station began supplying energy for electricity production in the United States as early as 1949. England followed soon after, and it soon became a dream that atomic power would be the energy source of the future. There was impatience among Danish physicists and power station engineers: when was Denmark going to begin the peaceful exploitation of atomic energy? Niels Bohr was hesitant at first. There was no real point in making a start before uranium was available. There were scattered deposits in the granites on the island of Bornholm, but they were difficult to separate out; and there was insufficient knowledge about the uranium deposits in Greenland. But could Denmark simply sit idly by while the development of atomic energy was accelerating in the outside world? Moreover, it seemed unfair for that to happen considering Denmark's major contribution to atomic physics through Niels Bohr. The Danish Academy for the Technical Sciences therefore established an atomic energy committee in the spring of 1954, and Bohr was asked to serve as chairman.

When Bohr's friend Sir John Cockcroft, director of the British atomic energy project, offered Denmark some enriched uranium that same year, Bohr made his first appeal to the government. The prime minister, Hans Hedtoft, took the plunge enthusiastically and was supported by his minister of finance, Viggo Kampmann, who was subsequently to become the first Danish minister for atomic energy.

Also in 1954 the United Nations decided to establish the International Atomic Energy Agency, and when preparations for the first Geneva conference on peaceful applications of atomic energy got under way it was obvious that Denmark must be represented.

Hans Hedtoft died in January, 1955, and was succeeded by H. C. Hansen, who had already been faced as foreign minister with the international atomic issue. He and Kampmann agreed on the establish-

Bohr taking a rest during a walk in the Risø area in 1956.

ment of a Danish atomic energy commission. Bohr became chairman, and with the establishment of the commission the government had in principle decided to prepare for an active Danish contribution to the exploitation of atomic energy. The commission was charged both with framing specific Danish tasks and at the same time acting as adviser to successive governments.

In the spring of 1955, there was a promise of both American and British assistance for a Danish program, and when the political parties were asked for their views, two main points emerged. The first was that Denmark could certainly accept the benefits of results achieved abroad, but not without offering something in exchange. The second, in effect was that it would be almost impossible to accept the responsibility of not going ahead. Permanent Secretary H. H. Koch, who became chairman of the commission's business committee, later declared that the decision to go ahead

> rested as little upon Bohr's authority as on anyone's desire to honor him— as has occasionally been asserted. The Danish effort was carefully and comprehensively prepared, partly by a committee under the Academy for the Technical Sciences and partly by the preparatory atomic energy commission with the participation of a broad cross-section of Danish economic and national life, and the necessary legislation was adopted in the Danish parliament with the general approval of all political parties.

Bohr up on the scaffolding at Risø.

The Danish Parliament established a select committee to which the commission would make annual reports and with which it would discuss all relevant questions. Only one month later an agreement on collaboration was concluded with the United Kingdom Atomic Energy Authority and the United States Atomic Energy Commission, and almost simultaneously a decision was reached to explore for uranium and thorium deposits in Greenland. Even before the summer was over, the members of the commission participated along with Bohr in the United Nation's first conference in Geneva on the peaceful uses of atomic energy. And already the British, American, and Soviet delegates described the very first delicate attempts to approach a possible solution to the problems of exploiting hydrogen-based energy. So great expectations were raised. A surprising amount of information was presented, especially on the scientific side and partly also—but only partly—on the technical and industrial aspects. It was a step in the right direction, but the picture was not one of real openness but rather of everyone trying to find out as much as possible about the others' projects while not giving a complete account of their own. Attendance at the confer-

Aerial photograph of the atomic station at Risø, with the reactors in the background. In the middle is the agricultural research area, with greenhouses. In the foreground is the Risø site of the Bohr Institute.

ence was extremely high, however. Atomic power stations were now a fact, and the bigger countries were in full swing.

Now Bohr began to look for a suitable location for the Danish atomic research station. It could not be too far from Copenhagen because large numbers of people from there would be involved in the work daily, but on the other hand, the risk of siting the installation too close to a large populated area must be minimized. The most suitable spot would be somewhere on Roskilde Fjord (directly west of Copenhagen), and as usual Bohr was tireless in investigating all the possibilities thoroughly.

H. H. Koch has described an excursion he and Bohr made to the eastern margin of Roskilde Fjord. They had their eye on a small spit of land called Bolund, which is almost an island in the fjord and is connected to the mainland only by a narrow isthmus which is submerged at high tide:

> We went down to the salt marshes and it seemed obvious that quite apart from being a protected area, the place was not suitable for our purpose. Impressions were not enough to satisfy Bohr, however. We had to see for ourselves: off with our shoes and socks, up with our trouser legs and out into the water, Bohr in the lead over the sharp stones and up the slope to the top of Bolund—our impressions were now excellently documented; . . .

Niels Bohr in Greenland in 1957.

the place was unsuitable, and we could cross off Bolund with an easy conscience and concentrate on other possibilities—at the same time we had
learnt a little more about Bohr's style of working.

Soon the ideal spot was found, however, and by something of an accident. Professor J. C. Jacobsen was on a Sunday outing with his family,
and while they were bathing at Risø it suddenly occurred to him what
a suitable site it was, with good sailing conditions off the point and
with the main road to Roskilde close by on the other side. The size of
the area was ideal, the view wide and open, and it was neither too far
from Copenhagen nor too close to Roskilde.

Bohr too found the site very suitable, and as soon as funds had been
appropriated for the purchase of the land, the project could be put in
train. But by Danish standards an extremely large sum of money was
involved, and at that time the power plant at Risø could not be justified
merely on the ground that the plant would help to secure the nation's
power supply. However, Bohr declared that the nation's interests would
be served through the medium of Danish industry's capacity to keep
up with the new developments. The same consideration applied to the
training of scientists within the new fields of expertise. Regardless of
the atomic research station's practical objects, it was also Bohr's goal

*Bohr and the Greenlander who was the pioneer of sheep breeding in
Greenland.*

At the inauguration ceremony at Risø. From left to right: Bohr; the minister of education, Julius Bomholt; and the rector of the University of Copenhagen, H. M. Hansen.

that by this new research activity Denmark should contribute to international research and thus to the common stock of human knowledge, so enabling Denmark to retain a place in the community of nations in keeping with her traditions. It was therefore natural some years later for Bohr's own Institute to be expanded at the Risø site by the installation of the latest accelerator equipment then available. Some areas were then assigned for College of Agriculture experimental purposes, which opened the possibilities of mutation of grain by radiation. Bohr's friend Aage Berlème could no more have foreseen this than did Bohr when money was first being collected for the Institute forty years earlier.

Bohr played an active part in the developments at Risø and also went to Greenland in 1957—at the same time that the first laboratory was opened at Risø—to examine the uranium deposits there. They turned out to require new methods of separation, which the Risø chemical department under Cecil Jacobsen set about developing. Although exploitation of the Greenland deposits has still not started, the problems have been solved, and it is a fact that Greenland possesses significant reserves.

Risø was inaugurated on June 6, 1958. The brilliance of the silver domes of the two test reactors rivalled that of the sun.

The numerous grave problems raised by the defects and leakages associated with large reactors elsewhere in the world occurred long afterwards and may have delayed for a long time the exploitation of the early gains. But one of Bohr's most important arguments in favor of Risø, the training of technicians to meet the demands of the new age, proved to be sound. The Danish engineers who built the Risø test reactors got the technology right. The installation has functioned faultlessly and under full control. Risø has also assisted with many scientific experiments, and its reactors have produced radioactive isotopes which were soon used for the treatment of patients.

38

The Royal Danish Academy

Niels Bohr was president of the Royal Danish Academy of Sciences and Letters for 23 years, the longest term served by any one person hitherto. We have already noted that he was elected a member of the Academy when he was only 31 years of age. As such it became his task from the beginning to evaluate the physics papers submitted. Over the years, Bohr evaluated no fewer than 90 papers which were found suitable for inclusion in the Academy's publications. He took part regularly in the Academy's meetings all through the years whenever he was not traveling, and he delivered no fewer than 29 lectures himself. (In the usage of the Academy these are not called lectures, but reports.) He himself wrote five papers (three of them with colleagues) for the Academy's publications, and he represented the Academy at many large scientific gatherings abroad during his long term as president. He took part in this capacity in the 300th anniversary celebrations of the birth of Isaac Newton in London and delivered the principal address there. He also spoke at the 400th anniversary of the birth of Tycho Brahe and participated in the festivities for the 500th anniversary of the founding of the University of Glasgow and the bicentennial of Columbia University. He was specially invited to assist at the tricentennial celebrations of the Royal Society in London, and he also represented the Academy on various other notable occasions.

It was on the death of Vilhelm Thomsen in 1927 that Bohr was first asked if he would consent to be elected president of the Academy. Since he was so heavily engaged in the elucidation of quantum mechanics, he had to say no, and the pressure of his work also stood in the way when he was asked again in both 1934 and 1938. However, the Academy awarded him the Carlsberg honorary residence in 1935, and in 1939 he consented to assume the presidency, provided the membership agreed when the proposal was put to them. This agreement was forthcoming when the briefest but most convincing nomination

Niels Bohr represented the Academy at the bicentennial celebrations of Columbia University, where he and Dag Hammarskjöld both received honorary doctorates.

ever heard in the Academy was made by the mathematician Johannes Hjelmslev, in these words: "To make a special case for the proposal would be superfluous." And the Academy's historian A. Lomholt was able to record with satisfaction: "With the election of Niels Bohr as president, we see fulfilled in high degree the Academy's traditional qualifications for president, viz., that he should 'have insight in sciences and be a man of distinguished talent and knowledge'."

The presidential term is five years, but Niels Bohr was reelected again and again. During the German occupation, he presided over meetings right up to the time of his flight in September 1943. On May 4, 1945, an ordinary meeting was held during the last air raid alert (for which the "all clear" was never sounded) and at the end of August in that year the Academy's section chairmen went out to the honorary residence in order to welcome Bohr home. During Bohr's absence they had presided over the meetings at first, and later on one of them, Johannes Hjelmslev, had functioned as president, but at no time was it ever assumed that Bohr was anything other than temporarily absent. He was due for reelection in 1944, but the Academy departed from the rules and postponed the election "in order not to take any step which might

The Norwegian painter Henrik Sorensen working on the portrait of Niels Bohr that now hangs in the Royal Danish Academy of Sciences and Letters.

alter the Academy's relationship with the absent president." It was the second time the rules had not been strictly followed, the first being the ultra-short motion for Bohr's election as president in 1939.

The first meeting in which Bohr participated after his homecoming took place on his sixtieth birthday, during which the Niels Bohr Trust was established as already noted. At the meeting, Johannes Hjelmslev read an address of tribute which closed with these words: "If we take a glance upwards in this hall, our eyes will meet the great picture of Prometheus stealing fire from the gods. It would be impossible to find a better symbol of your work."

During Bohr's presidency the Academy took part in the celebration of the centennial jubilee of the Carlsberg Brewery in 1947. In his speech, Bohr described the sense of social responsibility evinced by J. C. Jacobsen, the founder of the Carlsberg Brewery, in putting the fruits of his life's work to the service of the people of Denmark:

Among the objects to which Carlsberg's founders dedicated their great mission, the progress of science stands in the first rank. Our Academy therefore

This photographic portrait of Niels Bohr hangs in the Academy. It was taken in 1951 by Herdis and Herman Jacobsen.

not only wishes to express its deep sense of gratitude for the support which it has received in diverse ways, but, since J. C. Jacobsen linked his bequest closely to the Academy, ventures to express thanks today on behalf of Danish science generally. Without this grand scale of assistance, the various branches of science in our country would not have the standing which they enjoy, many of their undertakings in past years could never have been carried out, and the planning of tasks for the future would be more uncertain.

Bohr was still president of the Academy on the 150th anniversary of the birth of J. C. Jacobsen in 1961, and on behalf of the Academy he arranged, along with the board of directors of the Carlsberg Foundation, a celebratory social gathering at the honorary residence, where the King and Queen, the prime minister, the speaker of the Danish Parliament, the rector of the University, and the chief burgomaster of Copenhagen all took part, along with the directors of the Carlsberg Breweries and the institutions of the Carlsberg Foundation.

The activities of the Academy during Bohr's presidency were not characterized merely by festivities, however, but just as much by everyday work. In the harsh postwar economic situation, which weighed heavily on Danish science, the character of the Academy's activities came under discussion. One of the participants in the debate was August Krogh, who criticized the Academy's hitherto passive stance. He especially wanted the Academy to elect a number of younger members

In 1923 Bohr received an honorary doctorate from Cambridge University. Bohr (on the left) walking with W. H. Welch of Johns Hopkins University.

"—and now our distinguished guest will repeat his celebrated lecture on chain reactions. . . ." Bohr's numerous honorary doctorates inspired this cartoon in the Danish newspaper Politiken.

in order, inter alia, to represent the cause of science more actively to the politicians. At the meeting on January 14, 1949, Krogh quite unexpectedly resigned from the Academy, simultaneously sending an "open letter" to both the president and the press. As the press said, he slammed the door.

Direct action was simply not Bohr's style, but he challenged the members again, as on earlier occasions, to submit proposals for tasks to be undertaken; and it may well have been as a result of Krogh's letter that a number of young scientists were elected to membership shortly thereafter. But Bohr did things in his own way, and the impact was far-reaching.

A continuous campaign for better conditions for science had been going on in the press for more than a year. It was conducted in close collaboration by Bohr's former colleague H. M. Hansen, who was now rector of the University of Copenhagen, and P. Brandt Rehberg, in whose laboratory many details of the battle were organized. The climax of the campaign, which involved the radio with a talk by Bohr and a powerful program called "Alma Mater is Weeping," led to a protest procession to Christiansborg, where the government is located. The rectors of the institutes of higher education participated, and there was a large turnout of professors and students. The proposal was made that the state

Bohr at the doctoral ceremony at the University of Lund, Sweden in 1954.

should issue lottery bonds to raise funds to be used for the expansion of science institutes and the purchase of equipment. H. M. Hansen endorsed the proposal officially, well knowing that the politicians under the right-wing government of Erik Eriksen would hardly accept it, since it had been advanced by the radical Danish newspaper *Politiken*.

But Bohr, through the Academy and the Commission on Science, had devised another proposal with perspectives reaching far into the future, and his link with the government was still intact. When the protest procession went to Christiansborg, Bohr telephoned the minister of education, Flemming Hvidberg, and asked him to submit Bohr's and the Academy's proposal to the government immediately. The press campaign had aroused public opinion in favor of science, and with this powerful backing Hvidberg saw a chance for success. At the same time it illustrates Bohr's authority in the Danish polity that Hvidberg, when presenting the scheme to his ministerial colleagues, did so with the words: Niels Bohr has authorized me to submit this—which correctly had to be done first through the Academy and the Science Commission. This proposal became known since its adoption as the National General Science Fund. Since then it has been enlarged to form six research councils, which during successive economic crises have been of crucial significance for Danish science.

Bohr at a banquet in 1959 at the Wellcome Trust, the foundation in England corresponding most closely to the Carlsberg Foundation.

When Russian troops invaded Hungary in 1956, Bohr arranged for the Academy not only to contribute to the "Aid to Hungary" fund but also to pledge itself, to the best of its ability, to render much-needed support when information on the plight of Hungarian scientists came out. Through his contacts with the Ford Foundation, Bohr arranged for an offer to be passed via the Academy to the Danish institutes of higher education whereby board and lodging costs for refugee Hungarian students would be defrayed. Representatives of the Academy promptly traveled to Vienna, where the negotiations and selection took place, and five Hungarian students came to Denmark right away. Another twelve arrived at the beginning of the next term.

Ever since the Academy was founded, the reigning king—and now the Queen—has always been its patron. When Niels Bohr's seventieth birthday was celebrated by the Academy, King Fredrik took part. He had conferred the Grand Cross of the Order of Dannebrog on Bohr in a private ceremony just beforehand. During the meeting, the King personally paid tribute to Bohr, while the class chairmen of the Academy also congratulated him and read out the preface to a festschrift comprising fifteen papers that had been written by members of the Academy and by Bohr's colleagues.

39

Bohr's International Efforts

In addition to the expansion of the Institute, the organization and administration of the large new experimental plants, the arrangements for the necessary funding, the care of the fifty or so foreign guests who came every year along with the numerous individual discussions and colloquia involved in these visits, and finally the Risø project and the presidency of the Academy of Sciences—on top of all this came new international responsibilities which placed unending demands on Bohr. He lent his collaboration and participation at every stage of the establishment of the European Centre for Nuclear Physics (CERN), which had neither military nor commerical purposes. This gigantic project was intended to enable Europe to match the biggest American and Soviet installations for peaceful atomic studies. CERN was built in Switzerland, on the border with France, sheltered by a ring of mountains, on a site large enough for the circular, but kilometer-long tunnel in which atomic particles were now accelerated to almost the speed of light.

Planning for this project began in 1950, and during its course many crises arose, but Bohr's abilities as a mediator again came into their own. And when a theoretical group was to be established for the Centre, it was decided to locate its headquarters in Copenhagen, where the traditional international milieu was particularly favorable. A small building was erected on the very last spot available for expansion within the boundaries of the Institute. Niels Bohr was invited to head the group, and the duties made heavy demands on him for five years. During this period, young physicists from the fourteen European CERN countries gathered annually in Copenhagen to participate in research work alongside the Institute's Danish and foreign staff. When working conditions in Geneva permitted it, the theoretical group was moved there in 1957. But the cooperation between CERN and the Niels Bohr Institute has remained close.

No sooner had the CERN group moved to Geneva than a new inter-

The Christmas lunch at the Institute in 1950.

Every year on Bohr's birthday a group picture was taken of the entire staff. This picture was taken in 1960.

Niels Bohr with David Ben Gurion during a visit to Israel in 1953.

national organization appeared on the scene. The initiative this time came from Sweden, which raised the idea of a Nordic institute in Copenhagen to be closely associated with the Bohr Institute and where researchers from the five Nordic countries could also maintain intimate contact with other international activity. Bohr made ready at once. The CERN premises were turned over to NORDITA (Nordic Institute for Theoretical Atomic Physics), which became one of the world's leading centers for exploration of the structure of atomic nuclei and the properties of elementary particles. Bohr was chairman of the board of NORDITA until his death, and he was also the driving force in the organization's growth. Many Scandinavian physicists took part in this collaborative effort, and after some years NORDITA took over Harald Bohr's old mathematical institute.

Bohr's advice was also sought on scientific questions which lay outside the field of physics but on which several countries could jointly carry out important tasks. Bengt Strömgren and the Swedish astronomer Bertil Lindblad attended a meeting in Leiden in 1953 at which the establishment of the European Southern Observatory was discussed for the first time. On their way home, they visited Niels Bohr at Tisvilde in order to obtain his views, and Bohr's support of the idea was of considerable importance. Shortly afterwards Sweden decided to partic-

In 1957 Queen Elizabeth and Prince Philip visited Bohr at the honorary residence along with King Fredrik, Queen Ingrid, and Crown Princess Margrethe.

ipate in this project, while Denmark followed some time later. Since the observatory was established in the mountains of Chile, with headquarters in Munich, its achievements have placed it in the front ranks of astronomy, with Danish scientists occupying several important posts.

In addition, Bohr assumed on behalf of the Academy of Sciences the function of adviser to the Danish national commission established for UNESCO. That he could find the time for all the traveling he did in the postwar period is difficult to credit. He had known the first president of Israel, the chemist Chaim Weizmann, from his Manchester days, and in 1954 Bohr organized the Danish Committee for the Weizmann Institute, which was established in Rehovoth in Israel. He traveled to Israel and took part in the scientific planning, and he also accepted an invitation to lay the cornerstone for a new department of the Institute.

There were many other journeys to countries whose universities wanted to pay tribute to Bohr with honorary doctorates. He did not always find the time to go, but when he did nevertheless go, it was not so much the honorary degree that drew him as his unwillingness to disappoint the expression of friendship conveyed by the award. Bohr became a doctor honoris causa of thirty universities and an honorary

In Japan in 1937 in conversation with the Japanese physicist Y. Nishina, who worked at the Institute in Copenhagen for six years during the 1920s.

Niels Bohr giving a lecture in Peking during his world tour in 1937.

member of twenty-four academies and other scientific institutions scattered all over the world. In addition, during his trip to Greenland in 1957 he was made an honorary citizen of the community of Narssaq.

Niels Bohr's capacity for work and the reserves of energy he could make available for the constant stream of new problems had always astounded those who knew him. But that he found the time for all that he accomplished in the postwar years seems almost unbelievable. Even so, as we have observed, there are those who have regretted since that he did not accomplish still more—which is merely an expression of what he stood for and of how this came to be more and more appreciated. For some years there had been talk of his writing a broadly conceived exposition of the quantum theory. But with all the responsibilities which he undertook this project never came to fruition, and this has been a special cause of regret for many physicists. Everyone was sure that, aided by his incredible memory, he would be able to recount many details unknown to most, and that he could describe more brilliantly than anyone else the greatest scientific advance of our time. His contribution to the Festschrift for Einstein offers more than a glimpse of what a large-scale work might have accomplished, and later on there was no lack of appeals for him to write it.

Bohr and Oppenheimer in New York together with Hideki Yukawa and his wife.

In 1949, the same year that Einstein's seventieth birthday was celebrated, Bohr was invited to Edinburgh to deliver that year's Gifford Lectures, named after the founder of a trust whose sole task was to arrange lectures by prominent personalities and have them published. Bohr prepared a series of no fewer than ten lectures, which were capable of serving as a foundation for the long-awaited overview. He set out with Stefan Rozental in the spring of 1949, with manuscripts, notes, rough drafts, and even a wire recorder (forerunner of the tape recorder), which with its thin steel wire was more trouble than use to him.

Although the founder of the trust, who had been a religious man, had given no directive regarding the content of the lectures, the affair was accompanied by no little ceremonial and tradition. Just to get blackboards put up was a big problem, these not being customary, but Bohr could not do without them. And then an electric socket was needed for the wire recorder. But everything was arranged, and Bohr spent many hours before each lecture drawing on the blackboards to help to illustrate his line of reasoning. One more difficulty had to be overcome, however. The lectures were held in the auditorium of the theological faculty, and the blackboards came into collision with a large lectern which was used every morning for devotions. Bohr did not give up, of course, and with the touch of boyishness which remained in him, he

Adlai Stevenson and Bohr in Copenhagen, 1958.

Albert Schweitzer and Bohr in Copenhagen in 1959.

got Rozental to help him to move the lectern—but only a few centi-meters each day, so that it was not noticed. In the end the blackboards were standing where he wanted them. The sojourn in Edinburgh lasted several weeks, and every day there was work to be done on the next day's lecture, the series as a whole giving a well-balanced picture of the problems of atomic physics and their solution. Bohr's exposition won renown, but although it was one of the rules of the trust that the lectures should be printed, Bohr never had the time to prepare them for publication. In subsequent years he made several tentative efforts at a draft of a book, but some rough notes are all that have survived. It may perhaps also be questioned whether a book would ever have been written even if there had been sufficient time and reserves of energy. As Erik Rüdinger has remarked, a book was not altogether Bohr's style. The short essay, the well-balanced paper, often difficult to com-prehend but still dazzling in its compactness, was really Bohr's form of written expression.

A lecture on Nicolaus Steno, a seventeenth-century Danish anatomist, which Bohr gave at the Danish Medical Society in Copenhagen in 1949, also illustrates his frequently desperate struggles with his manuscripts. Bohr knew that the lecture should be published and it did indeed get

At Risø in 1960 Niels Bohr received Queen Sirikit of Thailand, who was accompanied by Queen Ingrid.

Niels Bohr with students at the University of Moscow in 1961. Here two physics students accompany him to the speaker's stand.

Lev Landau, who learned Danish in Copenhagen, acted as translator during Bohr's speech in Moscow.

printed—but not until eight years later, in 1957, and by then the text was almost completely different.

There were times too when he was asked to deliver a lecture on some less formal occasion, and he would undergo the depressing experience of giving it to a public which had not so much an ear for what he had to say as an eye for the much-honored world celebrity Niels Bohr, one of the world's great figures. Of course Bohr himself could feel this, Kalckar said, and he was amused when jokes were made about it, but in practice he did not accept this state of affairs. He prepared his lecture with the most meticulous accuracy as if it were addressed to an audience of experts, and he was happy if he sharpened a logical point a little more finely or clearly than had been the case before.

The Bohr epoch—the period of Bohr's personal contribution to scientific progress—ended in 1946 when his theories were rounded out, but just as he had been the central figure during that epoch, now he continued to maintain constant contact with all his old colleagues who were still living. In the autumn of 1958, he had a touching exchange of letters with Hevesy, in which they looked back over the forty-five

The large crowd in Moscow listening to Bohr's speech.

years they had known one another. In his letter, Bohr relates that he is preparing a Rutherford lecture to the Physical Society in London, which leads him on to tell Hevesy that in his later years Rutherford evinced a warm interest in the general philosophical views based on atomic physics. "Only a few months before his death," writes Bohr, "I had an unforgettable conversation with him on the subject." Rutherford, the great experimenter, so cautious in his attitude to theories and still more to philosophy, saw in his later years the scope of Bohr's complementarity concept, and a few weeks before Rutherford died, Bohr visited him for the last time and found him thinking seriously about the application of the complementarity approach to biology and ethnology. Bohr's life-long attachment to Rutherford could not have been more richly rewarded, and Bohr's farewell to him may appropriately be recounted here.

When the great figures of the physics world met in Bologna to commemorate Galvani in October 1937, Rutherford was already seriously ill and could not attend, and during the inaugural session the telegram was received: Rutherford is dead. It arrived during Bohr's opening address, so that it fell to him, without preparation, to relay the news to the audience. It is said that he could hardly get the words out as the tears ran down his cheeks.

Rutherford was buried in Westminster Abbey, near Newton's tomb.

40

Bohr and His Family

Any understanding of Niels Bohr's mind and character is indissolubly bound up with his family feeling. One may wonder how he was able, alongside his creative work, his Institute, his travels, his lectures, and the time-comsuming drafting of papers and correspondence, to enjoy in addition a fulfilling relationship not only with his wife but also with five boys and the very intimate circle of his close relatives. If the Institute was a hothouse under his patriarchal care, a rich and warm family solidarity at home was his condition for growth.

Even during his engagement he wrote to Margrethe with longing from England about their future and the time "when you will keep account of my thoughts." It is a mode of expression he returns to over and over again, and for Niels Bohr it implied an immensity of interdependence. It was and remained vital for him, as is revealed by letters written over a period of almost fifty years, that Margrethe should be able to keep pace with him both in his work and in his relationships with their many friends. She had to know all the ideas that came to him during his travels; he had to tell her about everything that he saw and everyone he met, about the thoughts on human life that gripped him when he was absorbed by art or by poetry, or by reflecting on political questions.

The letters to Margrethe are a constant confirmation that throughout his life, she provided the fertile soil for Bohr's creative spirit. But by "keeping account" Bohr did not mean "answer for." For him it was a matter of exchange and reciprocity in his personal life as in all human intercourse. In one of his first letters from Manchester, written on May 13, 1912 while seated at a small and rickety table (with which he excuses his difficult handwriting), he immediately declares his need, above all else, for an intimate fellowship with her. "One little thing I still very much want to say, and that is that you had better not talk to anyone about my paper, as I think I know how I can arrange it" (this refers to the English version of the doctoral dissertation, which the

In the Niels Bohr archive there is a special file of pipe pictures. These are from 1960.

Bohr's seventieth birthday at the Institute. Seventy giant boxes of matches for his pipe were among the presents.

The happiest picture of Bohr—after his son Aage's defense of his doctoral thesis in 1954.

editor of the *Philosophical Magazine* wanted him to abridge). "I shall write to you on how it is going, and so we shall share it—I think it will be so amusing not to tell anyone except you about it until it is ready." As we know, it never did become ready, because in the end Bohr concluded that it would suffer by being shortened.

All his life he sought Margrethe's advice, just as he himself always considered what advice he could give her. He weighed his thoughts against hers. Between them they had tremendous strength, and it became the destiny of their children to try to live up to their example.

Considering the immense pressure that his working methods entailed, Bohr would have had to belong to some race of supermen never to become tired. And he did get tired. Exhaustion could overtake him at the end of a creative period or when he was alone with his thoughts, alone on a trip and due to meet many people, while he was still struggling over the lecture which he was to deliver at the end of his journey. In the early letters—as in his last ones written half a century later—fatigue alternated with the strength to overcome it. When he had spent a long period abroad, evolving new ideas and struggling to clarify them, and then laboriously formulating them in writing, he was often exhausted. His letters home then echo his displeasure at not writing at greater length and more frequently, although the dates show that he

Niels and Aage Bohr at the blackboard in the study at Old Carlsberg in the mid-1950s.

wrote almost every day—sometimes indeed several letters or cards on the same day. At such moments of fatigue he was overwhelmed by self-reproach for spending too little time with Margrethe and the children. And in numerous letters he expresses the hope that when the lecture or the paper or the proofreading is finished, he will try to make up for his neglect. "Then we shall all have a really nice time together at Tisvilde."

A few of Bohr's letters may serve to provide a representative picture. We may take the year 1919, for even at this early date Bohr was feeling the press of work, and at the same time his letters from that year again and again offer impressions of the conditions he experienced when he was traveling to give lectures and an insight into how the days were passed with an excess of meetings and exacting talks.

In April 1919 Bohr was invited, while in the midst of the preparatory work for establishing the Institute in Copenhagen, to lecture at Leiden. He made the journey to Holland via England and had many hours of inconvenience there with passport control, and then immediately took the first morning train to Manchester in order to visit Rutherford. Both were equally surprised, Rutherford because Bohr came without first having written (the postal service was hopelessly slow just after the war), and Bohr when he heard that Rutherford had just accepted the

On board the "Oslo Fjord" sailing to America in 1954. This picture stood on Margrethe Bohr's writing table.

From the mid-1920s. Hanna Adler between her nephews, Harald and Niels Bohr.

professorship at the Cavendish Laboratory in Cambridge after the departure of J. J. Thomson. They had very little time for everything they had to talk about. But Rutherford did manage to tell Bohr of the critical reception his theories were being accorded in England. Bohr wrote home on April 13:

> It seems that my ideas are encountering much criticism in England at the moment. J. J. Thomson has just written a long paper against them in the *Philosophical Magazine*, and Nicholson has written on similar lines in the *Proceedings of the Royal Society*. In itself this does not matter so much, because it just injects life into the whole problem, but there will be some stiff work coming, and I shall really have to keep at it to get my results published and get them out in English in a more easily accessible form.

The letter concludes: "I so much wanted to try to write a nice letter to you yesterday evening, but I came home late and I was so tired. And now I shall have to grapple with the work on my lecture for tomorrow. . . ."

That letter is dated April 13. Two days later he arrived in Leiden: "The whole day today I have had to work on the lecture, which had become far too long." He relates that before leaving England he had gone out into the Sussex countryside in order to work, but he had found

In front of the house at Tisvilde on their golden wedding anniversary in 1962.

no peace anywhere. After the war, England was overflowing with visitors from America and the colonies.

At last, three days later, on April 26, he managed to start another letter:

> Now the lecture is over, and I feel that it went quite well. . . . You may think that the whole thing is a pleasant experience for me, but I am so grieved that I never get to write to you properly, my life here has been more turbulent than can be described. First I had to work on the lecture between all the talks, and since the lecture things have simply gone mad, everyone pestering me with questions and with appointments, and I am so pleased with all the response and the kindness, but I cannot get any rest. I am so upset that I did not manage to write to you yesterday evening straight after the lecture, but it was late in the evening before I was alone, and then I was so tired that I went straight to bed . . . I am writing this hasty little letter in the congress building . . . and now I have to run and take part in the discussions. . . .

Then there is a P.S. "I shall write again this afternoon, as soon as I get a minute to myself."

There was no time to write that afternoon, however—not until the next day, by which time the lecture was haunting him again. It was prepared enough for Bohr to deliver it, but it was not written down. "I only had it in my head. Now it has to be written, as it is to be published down here."

Niels and Margrethe Bohr discuss a question of etiquette on Bohr's seventieth birthday in 1955. Ernest Bohr is in the middle.

The thought of writing down the lecture torments him, and since the situation described has its counterparts in so many other letters, his account of how he spent his time generally will be given:

> After my lecture the day before yesterday I had lunch with Kramers and some of his friends. Next I had a long talk with Lorentz, and I cannot tell you how happy it made me to hear that he, who has so much to think about, had found time to concern himself in great detail with my views and the reason for them. I was so touched that he had also studied my last paper. After that, he and Ehrenfest and I were with Heike Kamerlingh Onnes to see liquid helium, which he is the first to have produced, and which has only been produced at all here in Leiden. Onnes is an extremely likeable man. (I have forgotten to say that I went to such a nice dinner with him the day before the lecture, but I must wait until I come home to tell you everything properly.) After that there was a gathering of physicists at Ehrenfest's place, with uninterrupted discussion of questions to do with quantum theory all afternoon and evening. Ehrenfest is anxious for me to talk to as many Dutch physicists as possible and this is also a great pleasure for me. The next day the congress continued in the morning, and in the afternoon it closed, after which I had a long discussion with Professor Zernets from Groningen. In the evening I was with the Webers in a real Dutch house, and when I came home I had a long philosophical conversation with Ehrenfest until late in the night. Today I first had four hours of talk with Professor Burger, in which I presented my

A consultation on Margrethe's seventieth birthday.

viewpoints to him, and after that a similar conversation with a Mr. Lenluwien, who is interested in spectra from the empirical side. I am learning a lot from all of this, and I am very happy about it, but I do feel that I need some rest, and believe me, I am longing to come home to you and sit alone again and really try to clear my thoughts. But first I am so very pleased also about everything that I shall see down here. Tomorrow I am going with Kramers to Amsterdam to see Zeeman's laboratory. From there we are both going to Rotterdam so as to be there on Friday to see Kramers' family and work on writing the lecture . . . on Wednesday I am coming back here to go to Haarlem with Ehrenfest and visit Lorentz. Furthermore I have arrangements to come to Utrecht and Groningen to give lectures, and to Amsterdam, but I shall tell you about all that little by little as it happens. This evening I only want to try to write a little about how my life is going down here . . . but although everything I have written has been so stupid, it has still felt as though I have been sitting chatting with you. . . .

Passages from another letter which he wrote two days later may be cited to complete the picture of this visit to Holland—and also to tell about Ehrenfest, who first brought Bohr and Einstein together. Ehrenfest was especially esteemed for his critical faculty which frequently helped to simplify and clarify issues. He found a principle which came to play a great role in Bohr's deliberations, and Bohr admired him, although the two were far apart in almost everything. On this journey, Bohr began to look at his own life in comparison with that of Ehrenfest. Ehrenfest suffered increasingly from depression, and however much Bohr and

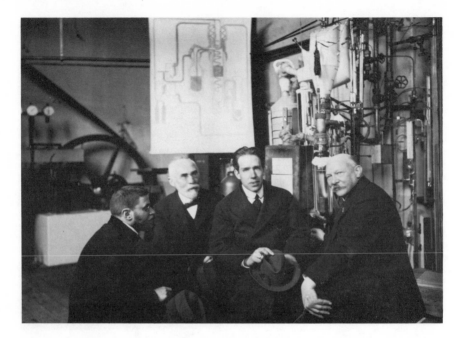

From the visit to Heike Kammerlingh Onnes (extreme right) in his laboratory. From left: Paul Ehrenfest, H. A. Lorentz, and Bohr.

others appreciated him, and however much his students in Leiden loved him, he lost his self-confidence more and more. And it left an abiding sense of loss with Bohr when Ehrenfest committed suicide in 1933.

Bohr writes about Ehrenfest at the end of his letter from Rotterdam:

> . . . he is a very clearsighted man, fertile in ideas, but his temperament is so troubled that I have never encountered anything like it. Apart from physics, I have had long philosophical conversations with him and heard very interesting things about his life, and I have the greatest sympathy for him and compassion for him, but his entire outlook is so different from mine. . . . I have met so many different people all though this trip and have found occasion to think about so many aspects of life and so many questions which we have talked about, and all the time I do not know how I can be thankful eough for all my good fortune in life.

He also refers again in the letter to his stay in England, where he had already worked so hard on the lecture that it became too long. And it appears that here too, where he was otherwise working alone, he had to have someone on whom to try out his ideas. "Richardson most kindly helped me by listening to the whole thing with exceptional patience." Then in Holland it became Kramers' turn; and from Amsterdam Kramers and Bohr went to Rotterdam, where the letter was written, and—as so

Left, portrait of Paul Ehrenfest; right, Ehrenfest at the piano in his home.

often was the case later—we hear how he was ceaselessly making observations during the train journey. The way in which he observes and his mind immediately processes what is seen is very reminiscent of Linné's reflections in his *Travel in Skaane* when he incessantly has ideas about things which others do not see. "The journey was interesting through the flat country," writes Bohr in the letter, "and we also saw from the train some tulip fields; it was quite extraordinary and very beautiful, quite different from what one expects from an ordinary tulip bed. Because of the enormous number of flowers of exactly the same color the colors become so deep . . . but now I had better say goodnight, for it is getting so late, and it is so cold here that I cannot hold my pen properly any longer. . . ."

In Rotterdam, Bohr at last took two days completely free, and the day afterwards wrote, "My head is so full of ideas, and I shall be so very happy to try to rewrite it all when I come home to tranquillity with you. You cannot know how much good the short rest has done me. I am beginning to see the conversations in Leiden in perspective and to create some order in my head again."

After the congress Bohr experienced a great moment about which he immediately wrote home. It was one of his first meetings with the serenity and wisdom of the Orient, and it is a curious coincidence that it should take place in the company of none other than the restless Ehrenfest. They were visiting a museum of Indian, Japanese, and Chinese culture, arranged with great taste in an old Dutch house. "A group of Buddha pictures in the garden under a flowering magnolia tree had such a marvelously evocative effect that I felt I had never seen anything so beautiful."

He also visited other museums and wrote in the same letter, "I have come to love ancient things quite passionately—I feel how a simple piece of beautiful porcelain can jerk one right away from everyday life, open one's eyes to all the abundance of quite different forms under which human life can be lived."

The strong impression which the Buddha pictures made on his mature mind, and which would give him enduring inspiration, are reminiscent of another powerful experience, though of quite different content, which he had one evening on the way home to his room in Cambridge when he was walking past the towers of King's College chapel in the moonlight. It was an October evening in 1911, and he wrote home to his fiancée to give her an impression of the ambience of Cambridge, which

> . . . is dominated by King's College chapel. Not only is it one of the most tremendous things I have ever seen in its interior, but the way it stands against the sky! Like yesterday evening, there was the most menacing October sky—black with silver edges, so terrifyingly menacing. I glanced up in order to see if all its little Gothic spires were not bowing before the threat from the heavens, but no, they held themselves erect, unyieldingly rigid and proud, helping the heavens to frighten the little people doubly. . . . And as in the afternoon when the sky was on fire, and this evening when I walked home in the moonlight, it is always the towers of the college chapel which are sovereign here.

And he adds a further comment: "It is wonderful that people can make something so great that other people feel small by looking at it." The remark recalls the words on the littleness of people in face of the vast forces of nature which are always heard when a hurricane or earthquake rages. But Bohr says something more. He juxtaposes human creativity with the forces of nature, and the point is the paradox that we humans must feel ourselves small even when what we create is great.

The two days of rest, however, were followed by new and intense activity. It seldom happens that almost an entire week passes before he writes again. On the other hand the letter is a long one, and its review of the week is an abundant explanation of why there was no time earlier. One laboratory visit follows another; new talks with new people succeed each other swiftly; but the time is not wasted. The well-equipped physics laboratory in Leiden even has a school for mechanics and glass blowers, and Bohr gets an agreement that the mechanic he will hire when the Institute in Copenhagen is ready will first be "apprenticed" in Leiden. During a visit to the laboratory of the experimental physicist Professor Julius, he further confirms the idea

> which I had already formed at Zeeman's laboratory, viz. to make a major change in the basement of the Institute and dig a deep (10-meter) well in the center of the large basement room, in which to place the optical diffraction grating. I am so pleased about the 10,000 kroner I have received from Johansen, and I believe this will just be sufficient. I am so happy about what you wrote that Harald had said about the possibility of getting money, because I need lots and lots of money.

Just as he is always thinking about the Institute, so also in the jumble of new experiences while traveling he still does not lose sight of his own scientific work. One of the day's numerous conversations begins with a discussion with S. H. Weber about certain calculations in Bohr's thesis. When he finally gets up to his room late in the evening after hours of discussion with Ehrenfest, he sets about thinking over the question he discussed with Weber, and "I managed to hit on something quite neat about that." The day after that comes the conferral of Kramers' doctorate, with a dinner afterwards during which Bohr makes a speech, and then after dinner he finds himself talking to Ehrenfest's eight year-old daughter, who shows him some drawings she has made. She gives him some of them, and he writes enthusiastically to Margrethe how happy it will make him to show them to her. "She is undoubtedly quite exceptionally gifted artistically." (Her drawings hung in the study at Old Carlsberg as long as Bohr was alive.) The evening concludes with a long conversation "on art and various kinds of talent, and I learned so much from it, which we will talk about."

It transpires also, however, that the lecture was still not written, and letters which should have been written did not get written. "I have the most frightful conscience about my correspondence, can you imagine, I have still not had time to write to Nicholson and Rutherford." One day he and Kramers decide to go off into the country in order to work on the lecture, but new items get inserted into the program, and the lecture has to wait again.

Bohr concludes this last letter from Leiden by describing how the evening before, when he was too tired to do anything, he sat down to read the *Tales* of Hans Christian Andersen. He had found a Danish edition in Kramers' house. "I first read 'The Flying Trunk' and then I read 'The Metal Swine,' " but he was so tired "that your silly, silly Niels sat and cried when he got to the end."

In the concluding lines from his Dutch journey Bohr writes, "You do not know how I long to come home to you, I am also longing so much to see the children again. I have been longing so indescribably to be able to talk to you properly and try to tell you about everything

I have seen and thought. Oh, I would so much like to try to share everything with you, every last fiber of my soul, if it would give you any pleasure. . . ."

On Christmas Day 1919, Bohr is en route for Norway, where he is to take a short skiing holiday with Harald. During the journey he writes to try to say "how full my mind is with gratitude for all your ineffably self-sacrificing love, and with sorrow over all my thoughtlessness and neglect toward you . . . but the world is such a meaningless place that he who has deserved nothing for himself receives everything that is good, for although I am distressed to be going away from you, I am still happy as a boy to be getting on a pair of skis and then to be coming home to you and the children again and getting down to work."

Five days later a guest arrived with a letter from Margrethe.

> We were sitting chatting in front of a big fire burning in a corner, and I had to creep right up to the fire in order to read your letter. If you think of me sitting like that, pleasantly tired after a long ski trip and happily reading about all your love and how good the children are, that is the best way of understanding what it is like for me here, better than I can describe it in this hurried little letter which I am writing just before we go for a long ski trip up in the forest. . . .

When Margrethe Bohr read through the letters for the last time in the autumn of 1983 and told of the numerous recurrent journeyings, she

Bohr on a skiing holiday in 1933.

was able to say that the keynote of the letters was the same. But if all through these years the letters were often written in anxiety and always in longing, they were nevertheless always felt as a close contact. However, the spell was broken after Bohr's flight to England and America. Eventually the courier machinery did bring letters frequently to both parties, but delivery was irregular and often in batches, ten or fifteen letters at a time. Censorship restricted the content too, and now Margrethe had the experience of receiving typewritten letters. It was a requirement that letters should be clearly legible, and that was about the last thing one could say of Niels Bohr's handwritten pages. After one or two early attempts from England, in which the censor struck out words here and there, Bohr began to dictate the letters to Aage, who typed them on the machine. But for a year and a half Bohr was unable to tell Margrethe anything about his secret assignment. But his letters do reveal that his thoughts were constantly with the scientists who had fled to Sweden and those who were in difficulties in Denmark. He had hardly arrived in the United States before he contacted the Rockefeller Foundation, which decided to send financial assistance, in the first instance for senior scientists like Hevesy, Buchtal, and Harald Bohr. Next, Niels Bohr was invited also to find out about other refugee scientists in Sweden, young and old, who might need help and he asked both Margrethe and Harald to assist with information. He also thought that Margrethe would probably have come across many young people she would like to help, and he wanted to send something from his own salary. The contact with the Rockefeller Foundation continued the whole time Bohr was in the United States, and plans were already being made to lend support for the work to be done after the war.

The letters also illuminate Bohr's eagerness to make known in both England and the United States what the thinking of the Danes was under the occupation. At the same time that he was a key figure in the negotiations of the American and British atomic energy commissions, and while struggling for an open world and for help for refugees, he was also doing his part to exonerate the Danes from the poor reputation they had gained during the early days of the German occupation. He had confidential talks with the Foreign Office in London, with Christmas Møller and with the Danish minister Count Eduard Reventlow. In the United States he had many conversations, especially with the Danish ambassador Henrik Kauffmann, who wrote home that his talks with Bohr had been of vital importance to him in his effort to draw the right picture of occupied Denmark.

Minor day-to-day events are related in between all this. Aage looks after his father and his father looks after Aage. When Bohr catches a cold in London, Aage sees to it that he stays in bed a day too many rather than a day too few, as he has learnt at home, and Bohr takes advantage of the opportunity to darn all their socks. At one point the exchange of letters discloses a hope that the whole family can be assembled in the United States via England; but then the events of the war gather momentum, and not until the war is over are Niels and Margrethe reunited in London.

After his homecoming at the end of August 1945 we have to jump forward to 1951 before we find a travel letter again. But the pace now becomes more frequent with the numerous new activities, such as CERN, the Geneva conferences, and all the other international gatherings. The pressure of work now only becomes heavier, and the keynote of the letters remains the same. He hopes they will be able to find time for a proper holiday together someday. But the journeys always lead only to meetings: London, Paris, Brussels, and London again.

Before tying up the bundles of letters again, Margrethe read out fragments of the very last travel letters, from Bohr's seventieth year, written in pencil because "in all my hurry and forgetfulness in the morning I left my fine new fountain pen on my writing table." And he continues with the same warm affection as is apparent in his letters from the days of their engagement: "I think about so many things and first and foremost about you, yes just since you smiled farewell to me at the bus outside Dagmarhus." And again he writes about his neglect, but finds consolation, "Quite apart from my inadequacies, however, it is wonderful to think about how well all the boys are doing" . . . and then he goes on to his happiness over the grandchildren, "whom I shall really try to help you in gathering around us." He discusses the year's many strenuous meetings, during which he

> could be simply gripped by fear of failing the great confidence which has been shown in me in so many quarters. It will be specially necessary for me to try to get the Institute on the right lines, so that when its new form emerges it will give the impression that conditions have been created for useful and vigorous work worthy of the great sacrifices made, and will help to get the further support that is needed if we are able to keep pace.

But how did the family view Bohr's worries over not giving enough of himself at home? The sons were certainly aware that their father was often tired, but they never had the feeling of being deprived of anything. "Father always had time for us." And the many friends and guests who came to Tisvilde or to Old Carlsberg are unanimous that Margrethe was always cheerful, always understanding, and never the tired housewife. Scientist friends knew well enough that she had no actual insight into atomic physics, but she had the capacity to listen and an understanding of the demands which Bohr placed on himself.

The many glimpses of mutual dependence afforded by the letters include countless situations where Bohr, occupied by his thoughts,

Bohr and a grandchild in 1954.

Bohr in a sofa corner in 1957, playing with some of his grandchildren.

Bohr and Margrethe with some of their grandchildren on Bohr's seven-tieth birthday.

forgot the time. Or he misplaced a manuscript, and Margrethe always helped. One of the numerous examples is the episode of the forgotten watch, which Margrethe had given him for one of his trips so that during his lecture he could keep track of the time that passed when his thoughts sidetracked him. At the Copenhagen airport one day he realized that he had left it at home. Her concern in promising (with no trace of

Margrethe and Niels Bohr, photographed in Tisvilde on Bohr's seventy-fifth birthday in 1960.

irritation over the forgotten gift) to find the watch as soon as she gets home is touching as also is his anxiety, when he is sitting in the aircraft and discovers the watch in his pocket, to let her know so that she will be spared the worry of making a vain search.

There were many episodes of a similar nature, and Margrethe's daily patience and understanding show the depth of her love. She could call him over and over again to tea or a meal when he was absorbed in conversation with a guest, but she was still just as self-evidently the hostess no matter how long it was before Bohr and the guest made their appearance. She was likewise cheerfully understanding when conversations at Tisvilde extended long into the evening and Bohr had said goodnight to the guest, but then later crept out of the bedroom in stockinged feet to say just one more simple little thing.

The evidence provided by the letters of the harmony and unity of family life can be supplemented by much oral testimony. The physicist Hendrik B. G. Casimir perhaps expressed it with the greatest sensitivity, in these words:

> I believe that the elements of his life were in no way a matter of coincidence, but that they were deeply rooted in the essence of his personality. Of course the fact that he had such a close friend in his devoted and deeply understanding brother Harald, who himself at the same time was a man of great human and scientific stature, was almost entirely a piece of good luck; at all events it was of notable importance. But it was profound insight rather than good luck that led him when he was young to find a wife who, as we all know, was to be so crucially instrumental in making the whole of his scientific and personal development both possible and harmonious.

41

The Last Days

Niels Bohr's last major scientific paper was written in collaboration with Jens Lindhard in 1954. It was an extension of a work from before the war. In addition he was thinking about superconductivity, on which an unpublished article exists. He was appealed to from so many quarters, but although he could not respond to all of them, he did follow closely the efforts of his colleagues to understand the behavior of the many newly discovered elementary particles.

When a long time elapsed with no real progress in the theory of the new fundamental particles, Bohr felt that it was because nothing had yet been encountered that was sufficiently in conflict with what was expected—as when the very sharpness of the discrepancy had given him absolute confidence in the correctness of the quantum postulate.

Léon Rosenfeld summarized his view of Bohr in these words:

> He was fully conscious of his abilities, but his profound humanity, his constant awareness that scientific truths are a common good and the search for them a common endeavor, saved him from the defect which is so prevalent among great men: shutting themselves in with their own picture of the world with neither the will nor the capacity to understand other points of view. On the contrary, Bohr was always eager to "learn" from the ideas of others. He considered every suggestion carefully, and he sedulously encouraged criticism of his own views.

And Robert Oppenheimer said of the era that created our insight into the world of the atom: "The atomic revolution was not the work of one person, but depended on collaboration between scores of researchers from many different countries. Still from the first to last it was Niels Bohr's original, creative, penetrating, and critical spirit which guided, defined, elaborated, and finally transformed the entire work."

But is this now all history in the sense that it does not directly affect physics today? Let Robert Oppenheimer, as one outside the Copenhagen

Bohr in his study after his seventieth birthday party. (Photo by Lund Hansen.)

school, answer this question too. He wrote in 1962, the year which marks the end of this book:

> When instruction in quantum theory began to be given at universities and institutes, it was taught by those who had participated in or had been actors involved in its discovery. Something of the excitement and wonder of the discoverers was in their instruction; now, thirty years later, the instruction is attended to not by its originators, but by some who have learned from others who have learned from these originators. It is taught, not as history, not as a great adventure of human knowledge, but as a piece of information which is set apart by methods, as a scientific discipline, of use to researchers in understanding and exploring new phenomena so central to the progress of science ... from being an outcome of our thirst for knowledge, it has become an instrument for the scientist, which he shall take as given, which he shall use, which he shall teach as a mode of working, just as we teach our children to spell and add. . . .

This portrait was taken by the photographer Erik Petersen on Bohr's seventieth birthday.

In the summer of 1962 Niels Bohr fell ill. He was traveling with Margrethe to the social gathering held by Nobel prizewinners every year at Lindau, on Lake Constance. On the way they made a stop in Cologne, where Bohr had promised Max Delbrück to speak at the inauguration of the new genetics institute. By then Bohr was already tired. He had worked on the lecture in Copenhagen before he left, and he spent several long evenings continuing with it in Cologne. It was the lecture to which he himself attached such tremendous importance and which has been mentioned earlier under the title "Light and Life Anew." It must certainly have distressed him that he was not in form when he delivered the lecture. He became indisposed while they were driving on toward Lindau just afterwards. The travel plan had to be changed. They had driven down by car, but from Frankfurt Bohr flew home and was admitted to the National hospital. It was ascertained that he had had a minor stroke. However, it was quickly possible to discharge him, and he went to Tisvilde to recuperate showing no after-effects.

Soon Bohr was again fully occupied with "Light and Life Anew." As we already know, the lecture was to be edited into printed form, and Bohr was constantly thinking of new ideas.

In an address at the Academy of Sciences around Christmas of that

Bohr in intense discussion with Professor Per-Olav Löwdin, at the Institute in 1957.

year, the biologist Ole Maaløe told of his experiences with Bohr during the preparation of the lecture in Cologne. Maaløe began by quoting one of the year's Nobel prizewinners, who had expressed gratitude to Bohr in his speech in Stockholm, as so many others had done before him. The speaker on this occasion, however, was not a physicist but a biologist—James Watson, who had received the prize for one of the most momentous biological discoveries of recent times (the structure of the DNA molecule). In his speech, Watson wanted to underline the support and encouragement he had received from Bohr when, as a very young geneticist and against the advice of many older biologists, he had decided to try to attain a more detailed knowledge of the heredity biological structure of cells by purely physical means.

Maaløe revealed in his address that Bohr had not actually answered Delbrück's invitation right away. Instead, he had pondered over whether the topic which he was considering lecturing on was sufficiently prepared and well enough thought out:

> One of the trials to which Bohr subjected his own thoughts and ideas took the form of a series of conversations with younger biologists, fortunately including myself. Two things have later struck me as especially characteristic of these intense and enriching conversations: first to what a high degree it was urgent to Bohr to make completely clear that his ideas were extremely simple. It was clear the whole time that Bohr was plainly afraid that his

*Following his nomination as an honorary member, Bohr addressed the
Danish Students' Union in 1953.*

listeners—perhaps out of an easily understood respect for Bohr's immense knowledge—would get the impression that something complicated or difficult lay in his pronouncements. The second characteristic of these conversations was the great intensity and attention with which Bohr listened.

Today, so many years later, Maaløe recalls that during the conversations with Bohr he occasionally had the impression that Bohr was not hearing what was said at all. He would sit with his distant look—but at the next meeting it would become apparent not only that he had heard every word but that he also had further refined what had been said and incorporated a new element into his thoughts. Maaløe concluded his lecture: "After the Cologne trip and after Bohr had recuperated somewhat, I had a couple more conversations with him on the same subjects. Bohr's last remark went more or less like this: 'Yes, it is quite clear that some of the recent observations you have told me about may be difficult to fit in with my simple views: I shall go home now and think about it a little more.' "

"Light and Life Anew" remained an uncompleted manuscript, although he could not leave it alone despite his family's anxious efforts to restrain him. He also found time to receive a group of historians, led by Thomas S. Kuhn, who were collecting material for an archive of studies in quantum physics. It was a long and tiring process, which was not fully completed, but Bohr did manage to record five tapes. When the fifth tape was finished at Old Carlsberg on the morning of November 18, 1962, Bohr went upstairs to rest. Suddenly, just as he was about to get up again, all was over. Without forewarning a heart attack spared him from a long illness. A few minutes later the staff of the Institute knew that their lives had changed. And a few hours later the loss was already being felt wherever in the world some physicist sat and recalled the time spent together with him. Niels Bohr was seventy-seven years old when he died. On the board in the study was a hasty chalk drawing he had scribbled for a group of physicists the evening before: a symbol and Einstein's Box.

As a researcher, Bohr created the atomic theory. He mustered the greatest physicists of his age and by his incessant initiatives inspired them to build the cathedral of quantum mechanics, completing the edifice by introducing the principle of complementarity as a new concept in the human understanding of nature. He explained the system of the elements, predicted and interpreted the liberation of atomic energy, and contributed crucially to the understanding of electrodynamics, while at the same time influencing many aspects of Danish cultural life. His wonderfully warm human qualities continue to offer inspiration through books of memoirs currently appearing in many countries. And his words still stir the world of international politics.

Bohr has been compared to Newton, Galileo, and Faraday. But will

On the last evening of his life Bohr drew on the blackboard in the honorary residence a sketch of two interweaving planes to illustrate the ambiguity of language and underneath it a diagram of the "Einstein Box." Thus he left behind him a symbolic reminder of the beginning and ends of his thoughts on complementarity.

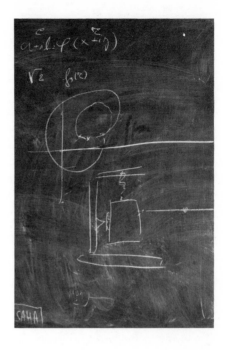

someone someday think of comparing a new-coming figure of a new epoch to Bohr? Geniuses can perhaps be ranked on an equal footing in terms of their contributions to science. But how can meaningful comparisons be made with the radiant human figure also presented by Niels Bohr. In his memorial address to The Royal Danish Academy of Arts and Sciences, Christian Møller said, "Geniuses belong to the whole world, and few have been such a true citizen of the world as Niels Bohr. But we know too that he was so deeply rooted in Danish culture and the Danish mode of thinking and feeling that if he had grown up in some other country, he would not have been—Niels Bohr."

The Institute on Blegdamsvej now bears his name. A university avenue is named after him. There is a memorial plaque on the facade of the house where he was born. His coat of arms hangs at Frederiksborg Castle, where there are busts of him, and a number of paintings show his portrait. He was laid to rest at the Assistens Cemetery in the grave plot of his father Christian Bohr, where at Christmas in 1984 Margrethe too was interred at the great age of ninety-four. The site is marked by J. F. Willumsen's sepulchral monument over Christian Bohr. But the matchless work of art that would adequately symbolize the harmony in the life and work of Niels Bohr, carved from granite by a great artist to reveal the essential meaning, as Bohr would have wished—this has not yet been made. It is in some glade under the tall pines of Tisvilde, close to Nature's heart, that the true memorial one day must rise.

Notes

In order to avoid the use of footnote numbers in the text itself, the notes are arranged so that the page number and lower case letter refer the reader to the appropriate paragraph of the relevant page. The first paragraph on each page is called a, the second b, and so forth.

Two works frequently cited in the notes have been identified by the following abbreviations:

His life; S. Rozental, ed. *Niels Bohr: His life and work as seen by his friends and colleagues*. New York 1967.

Mindebog; S. Rozental, ed. *Mindebog: Niels Bohr*. Copenhagen 1964.

13b
Kirstine Meyer's maiden name was Bjerrum; she was Niels Bjerrum's aunt.

13 caption
It is clear from the original photograph that the photograph of the group of people has been glued onto the large photograph. Constance Hannover presented the picture to the Bohr family.

14c
The source for everything except the Ole Chievitz quotation is Albert V. Jørgensen's commemorative articles in *Naturens Verden*, August 1963. In the same article he wrote that Bohr was like any other boy. As a special treasure he lent all of Cooper's Indian stories to one of his schoolfellows, and he did not hang back during the customary schoolboy fights.

18b
Mindebog, p. 295.

18c
Hendrik B. Casimir: *Haphazard Reality*. New York 1983, p. 70.

19c
The citation is from Vilhelm Slomann's feature article in the Danish newspaper *Politiken*, October 7, 1955.

20b
The citation is from Jens David Adler's summary of the memorial address for Harald Høffding given by Bohr at the Academy of Sciences in 1931. In *Mindebog*, p. 11.

24b
The lecture on Emil Christian Hansen was given on November 12, 1983 at the Carlsberg Research Center, on the one-hundredth anniversary of the first use of cultivated yeast in brewing at the Carlsberg Brewery.

32a
The title of Bohr's prize essay read: "Experimental investigation of oscillations of jets of liquid with a view to determination of the surface tension" (in Danish).

32b
The title of Bohr's paper for the master's degree read: "An account of the application of the electron theory to explain the physical properties of metals" (in Danish). The original paper is preserved at the Niels Bohr Institute, and it is amusing to see that even at that time Bohr invoked assistance with fair copying. It was his mother who wrote the fair copy by hand, while he himself took great pains to print the formulas clearly.

58d
Léon Rosenfeld's introduction to Bohr's book *On the Constitution of Atoms and Molecules* (in Danish), Copenhagen 1962. The citation is amplified in *Mindebog*, p. 52.

62a
The account of the lunch was given by Bohr on the tape which he made at Tisvilde in 1961.

70c
Christian Christiansen's letter of congratulations is in the Niels Bohr Archive.

82b
The conversation with Bohr is from *Mindebog*, p. 226.

87c
The account is taken from Casimir, *Haphazard Reality*, pp. 95–6.

89c and 90b
These accounts are taken from *Mindebog*, p. 219 and p. 223.

90d
From an article paying tribute to Niels Bohr written by Piet Hein which appeared in the newspaper *Politiken* on October 7, 1955.

93c
The information about the American physicists who felt they lagged behind is given in Peter Robertson, *The Early Years*, Copenhagen 1979, p. 84.

100c
Niels Bohr: Collected Works, vol. 4, Erik Rüdinger, ed., Amsterdam 1977, p. 27.

103c
Peter Robertson: *The Early Years: The Niels Bohr Institute 1921–1930*, Copenhagen 1979, p. 70.

105c
Werner Heisenberg: *Del og Helhed* (Part and Whole), Copenhagen 1971, p. 45ff.

107d
Casimir's account, see *Mindebog*, p. 106.

109b and e
The citations from letters are taken from *Sources in the History of Mathematics and Physical Sciences II*, Wolfgang Pauli, ed. by M. J. Klein and G. J. Toomer, Berlin 1979, pp. 193, 471, and 472.

110c
His Life, pp. 97–99.

111c
His Life, p. 100

111d
Niels Bohr: Collected Works, vol. 6, Jørgen Kalckar, ed., Amsterdam 1985.

112f
His Life, p. 103.

122d
His Life, p. 127.

130e
Casimir: *Haphazard Reality*, New York 1983, p. 98.

131c
The saying on truth was reproduced by Merete Bonnesen in *Politiken*, April 17, 1949.

133a
C. F. Weizsäcker: *Wahrnehmung der Neuzeit*, Munich 1983, p. 144.

133c
Casimir's story about Fredensbro is told in Casimir, *Haphazard Reality*, p. 93.

134 caption
The citation from Weizsäcker is from his book *Wahrnehmung der Neuzeit*, p. 135. When Bohr was discussing philosophy with him later on during the same visit, Bohr went to the board and wrote the word "Denken" (to think), after which he turned to Weizsäcker and said, "Now, I only want to say that I have written here something quite different from what I would have done if I had written any other word." (*Wahrnehmung*, p. 137).

146a
Citation from *Mindebog*, p. 20.

148c
His Life, p. 327.

150c
His Life, p. 318.

155d
His Life, p. 324.

161d
Sophus Claussen's poem *Atomernes Oprør* is from the *Heroica* collection, published in 1925.

162c
Karen Blixen wrote a long letter (January 13, 1955) to Bohr, in whose company she had just been at an evening function at Amalienborg, the royal residence. She is in process of collecting signatures against the use of dogs for scientific experiments, and she asks if she can add Bohr's name, concluding her letter:
"I have always been so terribly fond of animals, can hardly do without them, and perhaps feel a greater responsibility to them than to humans. In Africa I felt that I had a very distinguished circle of acquaintances—almost more so than at Amelienborg!—when I could ride in among elands and giraffes and in the evening hear the roaring of the lions."
Bohr answered with his usual care. He recalled how in his youth he had spent many hours in a physiology laboratory, where he received a strong impression of the seriousness with which his father and his fellow workers regarded this difficult question. He said that after receiving her letter he visited the zoophysiologist P. Brandt Rehberg in order to get a clearer idea of why dogs were still used in experiments, and he added:
"Each of us has often thought about how we are to defend the use we make of domestic animals as food, and it is difficult to see any justification other than that the lives of these animals hardly make any direct contribution to the development of those intellectual values for which the human race strives. I am also in agreement with

you, however, that dogs occupy a special position in this regard in that although they do not independently contribute to this development, their close relationship with humans causes them to share, as it were, in our general situation. Fortunately it is not a question of anyone's being obliged to expose any animal which has attached itself to us to treatment not in harmony with the position described; the question is how (in those cases where the best expert opinion is that the experiments, all things considered, should not be abandoned) the animals are to be selected and given considerate treatment. In these circumstances I do not feel that I can associate myself with your appeal, but I am sure that your warmhearted plea has contributed valuably to the elucidation of the question and will be helpful in finding a solution which takes full account of its many aspects."

162e
His Life, p. 321.

169b
Heisenberg has reported Bohr's answer to Einstein thus: "Well, it cannot be our task to dictate to God how he shall run the world." Cited from *Del og Helhed*, p. 87.

171d
The inspirer and verifier of the E.R.P. paradox was Alain Aspect, of the Université Paris-Sud.

172c
His Life, pp. 129 and 131.

173c
His Life, p. 226.

173d
Albert Einstein: Philosopher—Scientist, edited by Paul Arthur Schilpp,

volume 7 of the Library of Living Philosophers, Evanston, Illinois 1949.

174d
Niels Bohr: *Atomic Physics and Human Knowledge*, Ox Bow Press, USA 1987, p. 36.

175a
Niels Bohr: *Atomic Physics and Human Knowledge*, Ox Bow Press, USA 1987, p. 66.

175d
Albert Einstein: Philosopher—Scientist, Paul Arthur Schilpp, ed., Library of Living Philosophers, vol. 7, Evanston, Ill. 1949, pp. 45 and 47.

177c
Biographical Memoir, vol. 51, "Albert Einstein." By John A. Wheeler. National Academy of Sciences, Washington, DC 1980, pp. 520–521.

177b
Wheeler's account of Einstein's conversations in the gardens at Princeton was given during a conversation in Copenhagen in 1984.

177d
Einstein's remark was reported by Wheeler during the conversation in Copenhagen in 1984.

177e
Selected Papers of Léon Rosenfeld, Robert S. Cohen and John J. Stachel, eds., Dordrecht 1979, p. 520.

178b
Niels Bohr's speech, delivered at his twenty-fifth student class reunion on September 21, 1928, was printed on the occasion of the fiftieth class reunion in 1953.

185f
Bohr's remarks during the bicycle trip to Nærumgaard are from the article: "Niels Bohr's Contribution to Epis-

temology," from the *Selected Papers of Léon Rosenfeld*. Edited by R. S. Cohen and J. J. Stachel, Dordrecht, Holland 1979.

191c
J. Robert Oppenheimer: *Science and the Common Understanding*, Oxford 1954, pp. 88–90.

193e
From the last tape that Bohr recorded for Thomas S. Kuhn on November 17, 1962.

195d
A detailed account by Rosenfeld of the first Copenhagen Conference in 1929 is on p. 302 of *Selected Papers of Léon Rosenfeld*, London 1971.

195f
Selected Papers of Léon Rosenfeld. Robert S. Cohen and John J. Stachel, eds., Dordrecht 1979, p. 311.

196b
Selected Papers of Léon Rosenfeld, Robert S. Cohen and John J. Stachel, eds., Dordrecht 1979, p. 532.

196c
Selected Papers of Léon Rosenfeld, Robert S. Cohen and John J. Stachel, eds., Dordrecht 1979, p. 533.

202d
That Bohr disclosed the news of the Nobel Prize to Fermi is reported by Emilio Segrè in *From X-Rays to Quarks*, Berkeley 1980, p. 206.

203c
Hilde Levi: *George de Hevesy—Life and Work*, Copenhagen 1985, p. 71.

213d
His Life, p. 193.

214b
His Life, p. 194.

218a
Margaret Gowing: *Britain and Atomic Energy: 1939–45*, published by the United Kingdom Atomic Energy Authority, 1964.

218b
C. P. Snow: *The Physicists*, London 1981, p. 79.

220c
From Margaret Gowing: *Britain and Atomic Energy: 1939–45*, p. 262b.

223b
His Life, p. 204.

224a
Winston S. Churchill: *The Second World War*, vol. 5, Cassell & Co., 1951, p. 137.

224e
Gerald Campbell, who came to Bohr's rescue, was director of the British intelligence service in New York.

226b
Charles Moran: *Churchill—Taken from the Diaries of Lord Moran*. Boston 1966.

227e
Churchill, as above, p. 125.

227f
Churchill, as above, p. 125 and p. 16.

228c
Churchill, as above, p. 63.

228e
Churchill, as above, pp. 64–66.

229d
Churchill, as above, pp. 69, 147, and 150.

229f
Churchill, as above, p. 151.

229g
Winston S. Churchill: *The Second*

World War, vol. 5, Cassell & Co., pp. 623–624.

230c
Charles Moran: *Churchill—Taken from the Diaries of Lord Moran*, Boston 1966, p. 110.

230e
Margaret Gowing: "Niels Bohr and Nuclear Weapons" from the *Lesson of Quantum Theory*. Edited by Jorit de Boer, Erik Dal, and Ole Ulfbeck, Amsterdam 1986, p. 349.

231b
Winston S. Churchill: *The Second World War*, vol. 5, Cassell & Co., 1955, p. 940.

233b
Bohr's comments about using the bomb against Japan were first reported to the author of this book by Hans Hartvig Seedorff in 1953 and repeated by him as a clear recollection in 1983.

235b
Aage Bohr's comments to Jungk may be found in *Mindebog*, p. 186.

236a
Stefan Rozental's version of Heisenberg's visit is to be found in *Mindebog*, p. 166.

242c
The open letter is unabridged in *Mindebog*, p. 328, and in Niels Bohr's selected essays *The Description of Nature and Human Understanding* (in Danish). Edited by Jørgen Kalckar and Erik Rüdinger, Copenhagen 1985.

245a
Margaret Gowing's thoughts on the east-west conflict today were expressed in her lecture at the University of Copenhagen in 1984.

248b
The citation from H. H. Koch is from *Mindebog*, p. 302.

272a
Rutherford went so far in his thinking about the application of the complementarity approach to biology and ethnology that he discussed the possibility of obtaining experimental evidence of the origins of national traditions and prejudices by such unconventional methods as the exchange of newborn children between nations. Bohr reports this in his Rutherford lecture, which is reproduced in Bohr's collection of essays: *Atomic Physics and Human Understanding II* (in Danish), Copenhagen, 1964, p. 93.

Niels Bohr's Scientific Publications

Prize essay set by the Danish Academy of Sciences, submitted 1906, awarded the Academy's gold medal 1907. Printed under the title "Experimental investigation of surface tension in water droplets. Given as a lecture in Cambr. Phil. Soc. Summary, *Nature 88* (1907).

On the determination of the tension of a recently formed water-surface. *Proc. Roy. Soc. London, A 84*, 395 (1910).

Studies in the electron theory of metals (in Danish). Doctoral dissertation. Copenhagen (1911).

Note on the electron theory of thermoelectric phenomena. *Phil. Mag. 23*, 984 (1912).

On the theory of the decrease of velocity of moving electrified particles on passing through matter. *Phil. Mag. 25*, 10 (1913).

On the constitution of atoms and molecules. Part I. *Phil. Mag. 26*, 1 (1913). Part II. Systems containing only a single nucleus. *Phil. Mag. 26*, 476 (1913). Part III. Systems containing several nuclei. *Phil. Mag. 26*, 857 (1913).

The spectra of helium and hydrogen. *Nature 92*, 231 (1913).

On the hydrogen spectrum (in Danish). *Fysisk Tidsskrift 12*, 97 (1914).

Atomic models and x-ray spectra. *Nature 92*, 553 (1914).

On the effect of electric and magnetic fields on spectral lines. *Phil. Mag. 27*, 506 (1914).

On the quantum theory of line spectra. Part I (1917). On the general theory. Part II. On the hydrogen spectrum. *Kgl. Danske Videnskabernes Selskab*, Skrifter, Naturvidensk. og mathem. afd., 8. række, IV. 1 (1918).

Problems of the atom and the molecule. Paper presented at Natural and Medical Sciences Congress. Leiden 1919.

On the model of a triatomic hydrogen molecule. *Medd. Kgl. Vetenskapsakad.* Nobelinstitut, Stockholm 5, no. 28 (1919).

On the effect of the collision between atomic systems and free electrical particles (in Danish). Lecture given at the first Nordic Physicists meeting, 1920.

Über die Serienspectra der Elemente. *Zs. f. Phys.* 2, 423 (1920).

Atomic structure. *Nature 107,* 104 (1921).

Zur Frage der Polarisation der Strahlung in der Quantentheorie. *Zs. f. Phys.* 6, 1 (1921).

Atomic structure. *Nature 108,* 208 (1921).

Abhandlungen über Atombau aus den Jahren 1913–16. Braunschweig 1921.

On the series spectrum of hydrogen and the structure of the atom. *Phil. Mag.* 29, 332 (1915).

The spectra of hydrogen and helium. *Nature 95,* 6 (1915).

On the quantum theory of radiation and the structure of the atom. *Phil. Mag.* 30, 394 (1915).

On the decrease of velocity of swiftly moving electrified particles in passing through matter. *Phil. Mag. 30,* 581 (1915).

The structure of the atom and the physical and chemical properties of the elements (in Danish). *Fysisk Tidsskrift 19,* 153 (1921). Der Bau des Atome und die physikalischen und chemischen Eigenschaften der Elemente. *Zs. f. Phys. 9,* 1 (1922).

L'application de la theorie de quante aux problemes atomiques. Lecture given in Bohr's absence by P. Ehrenfest at 3rd Solvay Meeting, Brussels 1921.

Unsere heutige Kenntnis von Atom. Die Umschau (1921).

The difference between series spectra of isotopes. *Nature 109* (1922).

On the explanation of the periodic system (in Danish). Lecture at Second meeting of Nordic Physicists, Uppsala 1922.

On the quantum theory of line spectra, part III. On the spectra of elements of higher atomic number. Appendix to part III. *Vid. selsk. Nat.-math. afd.* IV (1922).

The effect of electric and magnetic fields on spectra lines. *Proc. Phys. Soc. London 35,* 275 (1922).

The Theory of Spectra and Atomic Constitution. Univ. Press, Cambridge 1922.

On the selection principle of the quantum theory. *Phil. Mag. 43,* 1112 (1922).

Drei Aufsätze über Spektren und Atombau. Braunschweig 1922.

Über die Quantentheorie der Linienspektren. Braunschweig 1923.

On the structure of atoms (in Danish). Nobel lecture. Lex prix Nobel. Stockholm 1921/22 and *Fysisk Tidsskrift 21,* 6 (1923). Über den Bau der Atome. *Die Naturwiss 11,* 606 (1923).

Röntgenspektren und periodisches System der Elemente. (With D. Coster). *Zs. f. Phys. 12,* 342 (1923).

The structure of the atom. *Nature 112,* 29 (1923).

Linienspektren und Atombau. *Ann. d. Phys. 71,* 228 (1923).

Les spectres et la structure de l'atome. Paris 1923.

Über die Anwendung der Quantentheorie auf den Atombau. I. Die Grundpostulate der Quantentheorie. *Zs. f. Phys. 13,* 117 (1923).

The correspondence principle. Discussion in Section A of British Association for the Advancement of Science, 1923. *Report of the Brit. Ass.*. London 1924.

The spectra of the lighter elements. *Nature 113* (1924).

The Theory of Spectra and Atomic Constitution, 2nd ed. Cambridge 1924.

On the application of the quantum theory to atomic structure. Part I. The Fundamental Postulates. *Proc. Cambr. Philos. Soc., 1*, 22 (1924) Suppl.

Über die Quantentheorie der Strahlung. (With H. A. Kramers and J. C. Slater). *Zs. f. Phys. 24*, 69 (1924).

The quantum theory of radiation. (With H. A. Kramers and J. C. Slater), *Phil. mag. 47*, 785 (1924).

Über den Bau der Atome. Berlin 1924.

Zur Polarisation des Fluoreszenzlichtes. *Die Naturwiss. 12*, 1115 (1924).

Über die Wirkung von Atomen bei Stössen. *Zs. f. Phys. 34*, 142 (1925).

Atomic theory and mechanics. *Nature 116*, 845 (1925).

Spinning electrons and the structure of spectra. *Nature 117*, 265 (1926).

Sir Ernest Rutherford. Supplement to *Nature 118*, 51 (1926).

Sir J. J. Thomson's seventieth birthday. *Nature 118*, 879 (1926).

Atom. *Enc. Brit. 13*, 1926.

The quantum postulate and the recent development of atomic theory. Atti del Congresso Internazionale de Fisici, Como 1927. Supplement to *Nature 121*, 78 (1928), and 580 (1928).

Sommerfeld und die Atomtheorie. *Die Naturwiss. 16*, 1036 (1928).

New problems in quantum theory. *Nature 121* (1928).

Wirkungsquantum und Naturbeschreibung. *Die Naturwiss. 17*, 483 (1929).

Atomic theory and the description of nature (in Danish). University of Copenhagen *Festschrift*, November 1929.

Atomic theory and the fundamental principles of the description of nature in Danish. *Fysisk Tidsskrift 27*, 103 (1929).

Philosophical aspect of atomic theory. Lect. Roy. Soc. Edinburgh 1930.

Chemistry and the quantum theory of atomic constitution. Faraday lecture. The Chem. Soc. 1930.

Die Atomtheorie und die Prinzipien der Naturbeschreibung. *Die Naturwiss. 18*, 73 (1930).

Atomtheorie und Naturbeschreibung. Springer, Berlin (1931).

Use of the concept of space and time in atomic theory. *Nature 127*, 43 (1931).

Maxwell and modern theoretical physics. *Nature 128*, 691 (1931).

On atomic stability, Lect. BAAS, Centenary Meeting, London 1931.

La théorie atomique et la description des phénomènes. Paris 1932.

Chemistry and the quantum theory of atomic constitution. *J. Chem. Soc.*, p. 349 (1932).

Atomic stability and conservation laws. Atti del Convegno di Fisica Nucleare della "Fondazione Alessandro Voltau," p. 5 (1932).

Light and life. 11th Congres Intern. De la lumiere. Copenhagen (1923). *Nature 131*, 421 and 457 (1933).

Zur Frage der Messbarkeit der elektromagnetischen Feldgrössen. (With L. Rosenfeld). *Kgl. Danske Videnskabernes Selskab, Mathem.-Fys. meddeleser 12*, No. 8 (1933).

Sur la méthode de correspondance dans la théorie de l'électron. *Septième Conseil de Physique*, Institut Intern. De Physique Solvay, Paris (1934).

Friedrich Paschen zum siebzigsten Geburtstag. *Die Naturwiss. 23*, 73 (1935).

Zeeman effect and theory of atomic constitution. *Zeeman Vorhandelingen*, p. 131 (1935).

Quantum mechanics and physical reality. *Nature 136*, 65 (1935).

Can quantum-mechanical description of physical reality be considered complete? *Phys. Rev. 48*, 696 (1935).

Neutron capture and nuclear constitution. *Nature 137*, 344 and 351 (1936).

Neutroneneinfang und Bau der Atomkerne. *Die Naturwiss. 24*, 241 (1936).

Conservation laws in quantum theory. *Nature 138*, 25 (1936).

The properties of atomic nuclei in Danish. *Fysisk Tidsskrift 34*, 186 (1936).

On the splitting of atomic nuclei (in Danish). Nordic Electrotechnician

meeting 1937. J. H. Schultz, Copenhagen, 1937.

Kausalität und Komplementarität. *Erkenntnis 6*, 293 (1937). Kausalitet og komplementaritet. *Naturens Verden 21*, 113 (1937).

On the transmutation of atomic nuclei by impact of material particles. I. General theoretical remarks. (With F. Kalckar). *Kgl. Danske Videnskabernes Selskab, Mathem.-Fys. meddelelser 14*, no. 10 (1937).

Transmutation of atomic nuclei. *Science 86*, 161 (1937).

Tribute to the late Lord Rutherford. Supplement to *Nature 140*, 1048 (1937).

Biology and Atomic Physics. Galvani Congress. Bologna 1937.

Wirkungsquantum und Atomkern. *Ann. d. Phys. 32*, 5 (1938). Virkningskvantum og atomkerne. *Fysisk Tidsskrift 36*, 69 (1938).

Analysis and synthesis in science. *Intern. Encyclopedia of Unified Science, vol. 1*, no. 1 (1938).

Nuclear photo-effect. *Nature 141*, 326 (1938).

Resonance in nuclear photo-effects. *Nature 141*, 1096 (1938).

Science and its international significance. Broadcast lect. 1938.

Structure of matter I. *Enc. Brit. 215* (1938).

Disintegration of heavy nucleus. *Nature 143* (1939).

Natural philosophy and human cultures. C. R. Congrès Intern. Sci. Antropol. et Ethnol., Copenhagen 1938. *Nature 143*, 268 (1939).

Physical epistemology and human culture (in Danish). *Tilskueren*, Jan. 1939.

Disintegration of heavy nuclei. *Nature 143*, 330 (1939).

Resonance in uranium and thorium disintegrations and the phenomenon of nuclear fission. *Phys. Rev. 55*, 418 (1939).

Nuclear reactions in the continuous energy region. (With R. Peierls and G. Placzek). *Nature 144*, 200 (1939).

The mechanism of nuclear fission. (With John A. Wheeler). *Phys. Rev. 56*, 426 (1939).

The fission of protactinium. (With John A. Wheeler). *Phys. Rev. 56*, 1065 (1939).

The causality problem in atomic physics. *New Theories in Physics*. Paris (1939).

Natural philosophy and human cultures. *Nature 143*, 268 (1939).

Scattering and stopping of fission fragments. *Phys. Rev. 58*, 654 (1940).

Velocity-range relation for fission fragments. (With J. K. Bøggild, K. J. Broström and T. Lauritsen). *Phys. Rev. 58*, 839 (1940).

Successive transformations in nuclear fission. *Phys. Rev. 58*, 864 (1940).

Velocity-range relation for fission fragments. *Phys. Rev. 59*, 270 (1941).

Recent investigations of transformations of atomic nuclei. *Fys. Tidsskrift 39*, 3 (1941).

Mechanism of deuteron-induced fission. *Phys. Rev. 59*, 1042 (1941). *Nature 148*, 229 (1941).

Newton's principles and modern atomic mechanics. Royal Society, *Newton Tercentary Celebrations*, July 1946, p. 56.

On the problem of measurement in atomic physics (in Danish).*Matem. Tidsskr. B*, 163 (1946).

Atomic physics and international co-operation. *Proc. Amer. Phil. Soc. 91*, 137 (1947).

Problems of elementary-particle physics. *Phys. Soc. Cambr. Conference Report*, p. 1. (1947).

On the notions of causality and complementarity. *Dialectica 2*, 312 (1948).

10th Anniversary of Rutherford's Death. Pamphlet 1947. Ed. *World Federation of Scientific Workers* 1948.

The penetration of atomic particles through matter. *Kgl. Dansk. Vid. Selsk. Mat.-fys. Medd. 18*, no. 8 (1948).

Some general comments on the present situation in atomic physics. Institut Solvay 8me Congres de la Physique. Univ. of Brussels (1948).

Causality and complementarity. Gifford Lect. Univ. of Edinburgh 1949. *Nature 164* (1949).

Discussion with Einstein on epistemological problems in atomic physics. *A. Einstein, Philosopher-Scientist*, p. 201, Evanston 1949.

Field and charge measurements in quantum electrodynamics. (With L. Rosenfeld). *Phys. Rev. 78*, 794 (1950).

On the notions of causality and complementarity. *Science 3*, 51 (1950).

Open letter to the United Nations. Sign. Copenhagen 1950. Broadcast 1950. Science 112. J. H. Schultz, Copenhagen 1950. Cambridge Univ. Press. *Nature 165* (1950).

Atomphysik und internationale Zusammenarbeit. *Universitas 6*, 547 (1951).

Medical research and natural philosophy. *Acta medica Scand. 142*, Suppl. 266, p. 967 (1952).

Physical science and the study of religions. Studie Orientalia Ioanni Pedersen septuagenario A.D. VII id. Nov. Anno MCMLIII, p. 385.

Greater international cooperation is needed for peace and survival. *Atomic energy in industry. 3rd Conference*. New York City, 1954.

Electron capture and loss by heavy ions penetrating through matter. (With J. Lindhard). *Dan. Mat. Fys. Medd. 28*, no. 7 (1954).

The physical basis for industrial application of nuclear energy (in Danish). *Tidsskr. f. Industri*, no. 7/8, p. 168 (1955).

Physical science and man's position. *Ingeniøren 64*, 810 (1955). (Geneva, U.N., August 1955). *Philosophy Today*, p. 65 (1957).

Rydberg's discovery of the spectral law. *Lunds Univ. Årsskr.*, N.F., avd. 2, 50, 15 (1955).

Albert Einstein: 1879–1955. *Scientific American, 192*, 31 (1955). Diskussionen mit Einstein uber erkenntnistheoretische Probleme in der Atomphysik. *Albert Einstein als Philosoph und Naturforscher*. W. Kohlhammer, Stuttgart 1955 (p. 115).

Mathematics and natural philosophy. *The Scientific Monthly 82*, 85 (1956).

Letter to the secretary general of the United Nations, Copenhagen 1956.

Autobiography of the honorary doctor (in Danish). *Acta Jut. 28*, Univ. of Aarhus 1956.

The atom and human knowledge: Survey of the activities of the Royal Danish Academy 1955-56 (in Danish). Copenhagen 1956.

On atoms and human knowledge. *Dædalus 87*, 164 (1958).

Atomic Physics and Human Knowledge. John Wiley and Sons, Inc., New York 1958.

Quantum physics and philosophy—Causality and complementarity. *Philosophy in the Mid-century, A Survey*, ed. R. Klibansky. Florence 1958, p. 308.

Über Erkenntnisfragen der Quantenphysik. *Max-Planck-Festschrift*, p. 169. Berlin 1958.

The Rutherford Memorial Lecture: Reminiscences of the founder of nuclear science and of some developments based on his works. *Phys. Soc. London* 1958.

R. J. Boscovic. In: *Actes du Symposium R. J. Boscovic, 1958*. Belgrade, Zagreb, Ljubljana 1958.

International Congress of Phramaceutical Sciences. The connection between the sciences. Copenhagen 1960. In: *Essays 58–62 on Atomic Physics and Human Knowledge*. Intern. Sc. Publ. New York 1963.

Quantum physics and biology. Symposia of the Society for Exp. Biology no. 14: Models and Analogues in Biology (1960).

Die Entstehung der Quantenmechanik, *Der sechzigste Geburtstag von Werner Heisenberg*, Verlag Fr. Vieweg & Son, Braunschweig, 1961.

The general significance of the discovery of the atomic nucleus. *Rutherford Jubilee*. Intern. Conf. Manchester 1961.

Recollections of Professor Takamine. Contribution to Japanese memorial volume to T. Takamine 1961.

Physical models and living organisms. *Light and Life*, ed. W. D. McElroy and Glass, the Johns Hopkins Press (1961).

Über die Einheit unseres Wissens. *Universitas 16*, 835 (1961).

Die Einheit menschlicher Erkenntnis. *Europa*, Monatszeitschrift für Politik, Wirtschaft und Kultur, August 1961.

Die Entstehung der Quantenmechanik. In: *Werner Heisenberg und die Physik unserer Zeit*. Verlag. Fried. Vieweg und Sohn, Braunschweig 1961.

The Rutherford Memorial Lecture: Reminiscences of the founder of nuclear science and of some developments based on his work. *Proc. Phys. Soc. 78*, 1083 (1961).

The Solvay meetings and the development of quantum physics. Institut international de physique. 1961.

Light and life revisited. Cologne 1962.

Atomphysik und menschliche Erkenntnis. Nobelpreisträgertagung, Lindau 1962.

With material assistance from the Carlsberg Foundation, the collected works of Niels Bohr are in course of publication under the title *Niels Bohr's Collected Works*. Léon Rosenfeld was editor-in-chief of the first three volumes, while Erik Rüdinger is editor-in-chief of the remaining three. Volume 6, edited by Jørgen Kalckar, was published in 1985. The work is planned for 11 volumes. The publishers are the North-Holland Publishing Company, Amsterdam, New York, Oxford.

Literature Consulted

Bohr, Niels: The structure of atoms and the chemical properties of the elements (in Danish). *Fysisk Tidsskrift 19*, 1921.

——. On the structure of atoms (in Danish). Lecture given in Stockholm 1929 after receiving the Nobel Prize. *Fysisk Tidsskrift*, special printing July. Copenhagen 1923.

——. Atomic theory and description of nature (in Danish). University of Copenhagen Festschrift, November 1929.

——. The atomic theory and the basic principles of the description of nature (in Danish). *Fysisk Tidsskrift 17*, 1929.

——. Light and life (in Danish). *Naturens Verden 17*, 1933.

——. Causality and complementarity. *Naturens Verden 21*, 1937.

——. Tribute to the late Lord Rutherford. Supplement to *Nature 140*, 1937.

——. Biology and atomic physics (in Danish). *Naturens Verden 22*, 1938.

——. The universities and research (in Danish). *Politiken* , 3 June 1941.

——. Danish Culture. *The Culture of Denmark to the Year 1940* (in Danish). Copenhagen 1941–43.

——. Speech at student class reunion 1903–1928. Printed on the occasion of 50–year student class reunion October 16, 1953. (Special printing.)

——. Albert Einstein: 1879–1955. *Scientific American 192*, 1955.

——. *Atoms and human understanding. Survey of the activities of The Royal Danish Academy of Sciences 1955–56* (in Danish). Copenhagen 1956.

——. *Atomic Theory and the Description of Nature* (in Danish). J. A. Schultz, Copenhagen 1958.

——. A memorial volume (in Danish). *Fysisk Tidsskrift 60*, 1962.

——. *Atomic Theory and Human Understanding II. Articles from the years 1958–62* (in Danish). J. A. Schultz, Copenhagen, 1964.

Casimir, Hendrik B. G.: *Haphazard Reality: Half a Century of Science*. Harper & Row, New York 1983.

Festschrift for Niels Bohr's 70th birthday. Ed. H. M. Hansen and K. G.

Hansen 1955. Published by the Academy of Sciences, special printing of Physics Magazine.

Gamow, George: *Thirty Years that Shook Physics, The Story of Quantum Theory, 1966.* Danish edition: *The History of the Quantum Theory,* Gyldendals, Copenhagen 1968.

Heisenberg, Werner: *Physik und Philosophie.* Ullstein Taschenbuchverlag, (Ullstein Bücher 249), Berlin 1959.

―――. *Der Teil und das Ganze: Gespräch erim Umkreis der Atomphysik.* R. Piper & Co. Verlag, Munich 1969. Danish edition: *Del og Helhed,* Thanning & Appel, Copenhagen 1971.

Memorial Book: Niels Bohr. His life and work related by a group of friends and colleagues (in Danish). S. Rozental, ed. Copenhagen 1964.

Moran, Charles: *Churchill—Taken from the Diaries of Lord Moran.* Houghton Mifflin Co., Boston 1966.

Møller, Chr., Rasmussen, Ebbe, and Kalckar, Jørgen: *Atoms and other small things* (in Danish). Rhodos, Copenhagen 1969.

Niels Bohr: His life and work as seen by his friends and colleagues. S. Rozental, ed. New York, 1967.

Oppenheimer, Robert: "Niels Henrik David Bohr, 1885–1962" in the *American Physical Society Year Book,* 1963.

―――. *Science and the Common Understanding,* 1953. Danish edition: *Naturvidenskab og Livsforståelse,* Gyldendals Uglebøger, Copenhagen 1963.

Rasmussen, Ebbe: *The structure of the atom. Quantum theory and natural knowledge* (in Danish).(I. F. Brandt and K. Linderstrøm-Lang: Videnskaben i dag). Schultz; Copenhagen 1944.

Robertson, Peter: *The Early Years: The Niels Bohr Institute, 1921–30.* Akademisk Forlag, Copenhagen 1979.

Rosenfeld, Léon: *Niels Bohr, An Essay Dedicated to him on the Occasion of his Sixtieth Birthday, October 7, 1945.* North-Holland Publishing Co., Amsterdam 1961.

―――. *Selected Papers of Léon Rosenfeld.* Edited by R. S. Cohen and J. J. Stachel, D. Reidel Publishing Co., Dordrecht, Holland 1979.

Segrè, Emilio: *From X-ray to Quarks.* University of California, Berkeley 1980.

Snow, C.P.: *The Physicists.* Introduction by William Cooper, Macmillan, London 1981.

Warburg, Erik: "On Bohr and Biology" (in Danish). In *Politiken,* August 11–13, 1963.

Weisskopf, Victor: *Physics in the Twentieth Century: Selected Essays.* Massachusetts Institute of Technology Press, Cambridge and London 1972.

Weizsäcker, Carl-Friedrich von: *Wahrnehmung der Neuzeit,* Carl Hanser Verlag, Munich 1983.

Additional References

Bergsøe, Paul: *Niels Bohr. Illustrated.* (in Danish) "Denmark" 1946, volume 6, no. 13–14, pp. 323–26.

Niels Bohr: A centenary volume. A. P. French and P. J. Kennedy, eds. Harvard Univ. 1985.

Bohr, Niels: *Atoms and nuclei* (in Danish). Selected articles from *Fysisk Tidsskrift* by Jørgen Kalckar and Erik Rüdinger, Rhodos, October 1985.

Bohr, Niels: *The Description of Nature and Human Understanding* (in Danish). Jørgen Kalckar and Eric Rüdinger, ed. Rhodos, October 1985.

Niels Bohr: 1885–October 7, 1955. A biography in pictures (in Danish). Henry Hellsen, ed. Berlingske 1955.

Folse, Henry J.: *The Framework of Complementarity. The Philosophy of Niels Bohr.* North-Holland Physics Publishing, 1985.

Forscher und Wissenschaftler von Hans Schwerte und Wilhelm Spegler. Oldenburg Stalling 1955, pp. 71–78, C. F. von Weizsäcker: Niels Bohr.

Frisch, Otto Robert: *What little I remember.* Cambridge University Press, 1979.

Heisenberg, Werner: *Schritte über Grenzen gesammelte Reden und Aufsätze.* München Piper Verlag, 1971, pp. 52–70. Erinnerungen an Niels Bohr aus den Jahren 1922–27.

Holst, Helge and H. A. Kramers: *Bohr's Atomic Theory—Popularly Explained* (in Danish). Gyldendal 1922, 2nd ed., 1929.

Holst, Poul: *Niels Bohr. The organizer of atomic physics* (in Danish). Gjellorup 1972, Monograph series.

Kosmos Physics Essays (in Danish). Swedish Physics Society 1936, pages 13–42. Torsten Gustaffson: Niels Bohr.

Michelsen, Børge: *Niels Bohr 1885–1962* (in Danish). Issued by the Carlsberg Breweries 1963.

Moore, Ruth: *Niels Bohr.* Knopf, 1966.

Müller, Poul and Jakob V. Pedersen: *Pioneers* (in Danish). Gyldendal vols 1–3.

Møller, Chr. and M. Pihl: *The basis of atomic physics* (in Danish). J. H. Schultz 1964.

Silverborg, Robert: *Niels Bohr, the man who mapped the atom.* P. A. Macre Smith 1965.

317

Skov, Sigvard: *Danish science of world renown* (in Danish). Historians group, Schultz 1944.

Great Danish personalities (in Danish). Berlingske 1949, vols. 1–2.

Weisskopf, Victor F.: *Knowledge and Wonder* (in Danish). Gyldendals 1964.

Wheeler, J. A.: *The presentation of The Atom for Peace Award to Niels Bohr*, National Academy of Sciences, Washington.

The Danish College of Heralds has published a biography of Niels Bohr written by the historian Tage Holst Karsted, while Stefan Rosental has described Niels Bohr's life and work in the *Danish Biographical Dictionary*.

Bohr's early work is described by H. M. Hansen in *Solomonsen's Lexicon* (in Danish) 1918.

Index

319